Private Equity 4.0

Private Equity 4.0

Reinventing Value Creation

Benoît Leleux,
Hans van Swaay
and Esmeralda Megally

WILEY

This edition first published 2015
© 2015 Benoît Leleux, Hans van Swaay & Esmeralda Megally

Registered office
John Wiley & Sons Ltd, The Atrium, Southern Gate, Chichester, West Sussex, PO19 8SQ,
United Kingdom

For details of our global editorial offices, for customer services and for information about
how to apply for permission to reuse the copyright material in this book please see our
website at www.wiley.com.

Wiley publishes in a variety of print and electronic formats and by print-on-demand. Some
material included with standard print versions of this book may not be included in e-books
or in print-on-demand. If this book refers to media such as a CD or DVD that is not included
in the version you purchased, you may download this material at http://booksupport.wiley
.com. For more information about Wiley products, visit www.wiley.com.

Library of Congress Cataloging-in-Publication Data is available

A catalogue record for this book is available from the British Library.

ISBN 978-1-118-93973-4 (hbk)   ISBN 978-1-118-93983-3 (ebk)
ISBN 978-1-118-93984-0 (ebk)   ISBN 978-1-118-93982-6 (ebk)

Cover Design: Wiley
Top Image: ©iStock.com/czardases;
Bottom Image: ©iStock.com/DNY59

All cartoons reproduced with permission by IMD and Lyrique

Set in 10/14 Sabon LT Std by Aptara India

Contents

List of case studies

About the authors

Dr Benoît Leleux

Dr Leleux is the Stephan Schmidheiny Professor of Entrepreneurship and Finance at IMD in Lausanne (Switzerland), where he was director of the MBA programme and director of Research and Development. He was previously Visiting Professor of Entrepreneurship at INSEAD (France) and Associate Professor and Zubillaga Chair in Finance and Entrepreneurship at Babson College (MA, USA). He obtained his Ph.D. at INSEAD, specializing in Corporate Finance and Venture Capital. He is recognized as a leading specialist in entrepreneurship, venture capital, private equity and corporate venturing, in particular in emerging markets. He also has a strong interest in family businesses and has been the director of the IMD-Lombard Odier Global Family Business Award since 2008. His latest books include *Investing Private Capital in Emerging and Frontier Market SMEs* (IFC, 2009) and *Nurturing Science-Based Start-ups: An International Case Perspective* (Springer Verlag, 2008). Dr Leleux earned an M.Sc. in Agricultural Engineering and an M.Ed. in Natural Sciences from the Catholic University of Louvain (Belgium) and an MBA from Virginia Tech (USA). His teaching cases have earned 17 European case writing awards and he has been running executive education programmes and consulting assignments for more than 50 leading global corporations and investment organizations. He is also involved with a number of private equity and venture capital funds as well as numerous start-up companies in various capacities.

Hans van Swaay

Hans van Swaay has a long track record in private equity as Partner of Lyrique, Head of Private Equity at Pictet & Cie, Managing Director of UBS Capital, Managing Director of Merifin and partner of Lowe Finance. His career has taken him through many cycles of the private equity industry. Today with Lyrique he is actively involved in private equity investments for private wealth, like family offices and private banks.

Hans has made direct investments in Switzerland, Germany, France, the United Kingdom and in the Netherlands. As an investor in funds he has been active in the

United States, Europe and Asia. As a direct investor he has on occasion assumed operational responsibilities in industrial situations as CEO in Germany and in Switzerland and he regularly publishes articles on private equity.

Prior to his private equity career Hans van Swaay worked with Shell in the United Kingdom in general and financial positions. He started his career in the construction industry with one of the Netherlands' major construction companies, HBG in the Middle East.

Hans van Swaay holds an MBA with honours from IMD (Switzerland), an M.Sc. in engineering geology from Leeds University (UK) and a B.Sc. in geology from Leiden University (the Netherlands).

Esmeralda Megally

Esmeralda Megally started working in the venture capital industry in 2007, when she joined Boston-based venture capital firm Commons Capital as manager to explore—with the Bill and Melinda Gates Foundation—a new business model in venture capital. At Commons Capital, she worked closely with venture-backed portfolio companies to develop and implement growth strategies and was in charge of identifying new investment opportunities globally.

She holds a B.S. and M.S. in Economics from the Université Libre de Bruxelles, Belgium, a Masters degree in Management of Technology from EPFL, Switzerland, and an MBA from the Massachusetts Institute of Technology's Sloan School of Management (MIT Sloan), US. She served as venture advisor to the NextLab at the MIT Next Billion Network and was part of the biotech committee of the MIT Technology Licensing Office, working alongside entrepreneurs, investors and large corporations to devise licensing strategies.

Esmeralda is a co-founder of Xsensio, a spinoff of the EPFL Nanolab in Switzerland which develops nanotechnology-based intelligent stamps. She is also a co-founder and board member of GCS, a Tanzania-based spinoff of the MIT D-Lab that was selected by Forbes' 30 under 30 and Bloomberg Businessweek America's Most Promising Social Entrepreneurs. Her innovations have been awarded the Harvard Catalyst Grant, the EPFL Innogrant, the MIT IDEAS International Technology Award, and the MIT IDEAS Graduate Student Award. Esmeralda is the co-author with Benoit Leleux and Michel Galeazzi of an IMD case study on the IPO of Tumi (EFMD Case Writing 2013 Award, Finance and Banking category).

Professional acknowledgments

The authors would like to acknowledge the contributions from Grant Murgatroyd and from Cyril Demaria. Grant contributed significantly and came up with the idea of the supporting cast which grew into a whole chapter of its own. He is now editor of *Alt Assets' Limited Partner Magazine*. Cyril these days is Executive Director at the Chief Investment Office at UBS. His insights were most helpful in formalizing the content of the book. The authors also acknowledge the help and support from the private equity research department at Preqin.

Nothing would have been possible without the invaluable contributions from many industry luminaries. Most of them donated their time generously to discuss the industry and its inner workings, opening doors for further engagement of key industry players. Their deep insights and phenomenal intellect made essential contributions to the authors' pursuit of the new paradigms of private equity. In particular, we would like to thank the following individuals, hoping not to have left too many contributors out:

Stephen Schwartzman - Blackstone, David Rubenstein - Carlyle Group, Conni Jonsson - EQT Partners AB, Dwight Poler - Bain Capital, Jon Moulton - Alchemy Partners, John Snow - Cerberus Capital Management, Peter Cornelius - AlpInvest, Rhoddy Swire - Pantheon Ventures, Martin Halusa - Apax Partners, Elly Livingstone - Pantheon Ventures, Stefan Fischer - TVM Capital, Angus Russell - Shire, Jeremy Coller - Coller Capital, John McFall - Labour MP, Tony Tamer - H.I.G., Chris Brown - Freshfields' international private equity group, Volker Heuer - Tognum, David Blitzer - Blackstone, Kenneth Mehlman - KKR, Piers Hooper - Equus, Jonathan Russell - EVCA, Tim Jones - Coller Capital, Erwin Roex - Coller Capital, Peter Bertone - Booz Allen Hamilton.

Professor Leleux would also want to thank hundreds of participants from private equity programs he delivered in the past around the world, at institutions such as IMD, INSEAD, Babson College, the Amsterdam Institute of Finance, The China Europe International Business School (CEIBS), the Shanghai Financial Authority, the European School for Management and Technology (ESMT), the Vlerick School of Management, the Moscow School of Management Skolkovo and Skoltech Institute of Science and Technology, the Ecole Polytechnique Fédérale de Lausanne (EPFL) and many others. Those participants were instrumental in furthering the intellectual curiosity to push further the investigations of some of the lesser known corners of the industry. Dr Leleux would like to acknowledge the generous support received over the years from the IMD Research and Development department. This book is built on almost 8 years of research, including a large number of original clinical studies on various private equity stakeholders, all supported by IMD financially and through research assistants. The Case Administration department was also instrumental in bringing those cases to fruition, providing editorial and registration support flawlessly over the period. Finally, the Information Centre regularly provided access to unique library resources to complete this book project. The book project was regularly delayed because its authors considered it essential to let the dust settle after the upheavals generated by the financial crisis in 2007 and the economic crisis that ensued. The patience and resilient support of IMD in this period is most appreciated and made a huge contribution to ensuring a longer-term perspective to this book.

Hans van Swaay wants to acknowledge the fact that the idea for this book was born when at Pictet & Cie, building its private equity business. Being part of Pictet helped access some of the greatest names in private equity and it was a treat to work with such a prestigious institution that understood the relevance of private equity to its business. Having done what private equity is all about, i.e. co-founding Lyrique, he has been able to test many of the ideas for this book with his partners at Lyrique and with his friends and partners at Providence Capital in the Netherlands. Lyrique took up the idea of the cartoons that were originally created for the book. Its tongue-in-cheek cartoon calendars, addressing private equity issues, have become a regular feature and are used by many private equity practitioners today. They would have been impossible without the help of highly professional cartoonists, Robert Thompson, Tim Harries and Matt Percival.

Personal acknowledgments

Benoit Leleux

Dr Leleux wants to thank Dina for her unflinching support during what can only be described as a roller-coaster emotional process, and Egor and Sophie for reminding him that there are indeed priorities in life. It would not have happened without them: they provided new meaning to the term "values creation".

Hans van Swaay

Hans van Swaay wants to acknowledge the patience and support of his wife Hazeline and their children, Harley and Quirine, as many evenings and weekends were spent on co-writing this book and not with them.

Esmeralda Megally

To my parents, with love and gratitude.

Foreword

Private Equity 4.0 is upon us, and with it hopefully enough experience to start drawing inferences about what works and what does not in private equity. Maturity is an expensive and time-consuming proposition sometimes; to paraphrase the infamous quote: good decisions are based mostly on experience, but experience is the cumulative result of many bad decisions... The financial and economic crises of 2007–2009 were very much the last nails in the long-rotting coffin of private equity "as it used to be". There is also a wonderful opportunity to take stock of the developments of the last 70 years in the industry and, with the dust slowly settling, to envision the future of this most original and resourceful industry. There is no doubt in our mind that private equity is here to stay. Its contributions to society and the economies of the world are too large to ignore. But yes, it did stray at times, taking advantage of temporary opportunities created by mismanagement and misguided economic policies. These arbitrage opportunities were low-hanging fruits; it is preposterous to blame private equity investors ex-post for having taken advantage of such blatant economic insanities. But these low-hanging opportunities have, for the most part, been arbitraged away (don't despair though on the creative ability of governments to create new ones...), forcing the private equity industry, against its better judgement, to start considering more sustainable business models, including the ultimate indignity of actually having to create value the hard way, i.e. earning it! Yes, this was said, of course, a bit "tongue in cheek", but the reality we will endeavour to describe in this book is not far removed from this somewhat crude caricature. Private equity post-crisis has indeed been going through its own revolution, one that we believe can finally be taken to maturity as an invaluable component of the world's economic system. New business models have emerged with fundamentally sounder groundings providing robust bases for sustainability.

The road to sustainability: from arbitrage to operational value creation

Private equity, in its original incarnation, was very much (ad)venture capital, born out of the industrial and technological advances brought about by World War II. Georges Doriot and his early fund, American Research and Development (ARD), wrote some of the fundamental rules of the game, most notably the fund and incentive structures. The model was picked up later on by buyout funds, which soon outgrew their venture capital brethren and came to dominate, size-wise, the industry. As such, private equity has often become synonymous with buyouts, even though technically buyouts are only a major segment of the private equity industry.

Since the creation of ARD in 1946, private equity adopted and capitalized on a series of business models, replacing them when new opportunities to create value emerged. **Private Equity 1.0** capitalized on the organizational inefficiencies of large diversified conglomerates, splitting them apart with the financial helping hand of the junk bond markets of the 1980s. The cycle came to a screeching end with the indictments of the junk bond kings and their patrons. The 1990s were around the corner, and with them a glorious period of GDP growth, multiple expansion and ultimately a technology bubble of epic dimensions, in which **Private Equity 2.0** bloomed under the guise of new technology and growth. The internet crash of April 2000 brought the club back to earth. As no good deed goes unpunished, central bankers came to the rescue of the faltering economies that followed the 2000–2001 correction, opening the floodgate of a liquidity surge private equity quickly took advantage of in its **3.0** iteration. As for all previous irrational exuberance episodes, the party had to come to an end when realities intruded on the collective hallucination, taking with it the cheap leverage dreams. The credit bubble was over: it was time to find a new model for value creation that would not be as dependent on financial engineering or the availability of cheap credit. Welcome to **Private Equity 4.0**, a model that spells the return to the sources of private equity: value creation through operational improvements and the enabling of growth, rather than on pure financial engineering. In other words, earning money the hard way...

In a sense, this is a most welcome development for the industry as the first real opportunity to make it sustainable. This is the age of maturity, the chance to capitalize on 50-odd years of deal making in a wide array of economic environments. Private equity has shown its mettle and its uncanny ability to re-create itself in the face of wildly changing circumstances. With some of the brightest minds involved, and backed by some of the smartest money available, private equity demonstrated the resilience expected of an industry whose impact goes far beyond the deals it actually engineers. Private equity for many has become the standard for corporate performance, the benchmark against which managers of all stripes are measured. Its simple existence and presence disciplines many economic actors to unleash upon themselves many of the measures private equity investors would have forced upon them. The total impact of private equity on economies is thus impossible to measure, but it is fair to assume that it is probably orders of magnitude larger than the deals it actually gets involved with or the value it generates in those transactions.

Instead of being thanked for the impact they had on whole economies, private equity players have been portrayed as barbarians, locusts, asset strippers and worse. How could such a small group of individuals reap such humongous profits if not by devious means? Were the convoluted tax structures used by the funds and their general partners not the proof of some malfeasance at play? Were the millions earned not unfairly taken away from employees and managers left in the cold? Private equity was the all-too-visible hand that proved markets were not anywhere close to efficient. Its very existence and survival proved that corporate governance systems were inappropriate at best, deeply flawed at worst. Unsurprisingly, this flew in the face of common wisdom. Private equity exposed the limitations of the system, and as such was a convenient scapegoat for its ills. And the privacy it likes to shroud itself in was further proof, if needed, of its Machiavellian intents.

Gaining perspective: The road ahead

With the perspective offered by three full cycles at least, it seemed appropriate to try to draw some pragmatic lessons for would-be investors and practitioners alike: What are the best strategies to invest in private equity? How best to select fund managers? What is the best time to commit money to funds? What are red flags in fund prospectuses? How is value really created in private equity transactions?

This book is anything but a blind endorsement of the industry. It is always incisive, and at times critical if not cynical. Some practices in the industry deserve to be criticized and attacked to the extent they hide or even harm the true contributions made. Like all industries it has its black sheep, and exposing those dubious practices only reinforces the credibility of the industry as a whole. The authors can best be described as "critical believers": they are convinced that private equity embodies and leverages some of the most effective tools of capitalism. But because of this, it also "packs a wallop", and as such its potential for misuse is great. Nobody ever said making money was easy... In this book, we offer insights into the industry deals and rules of engagement with a view to discovering the most effective ways to reap benefits from them. The recipes are not simple; but, like a good cooking book, the rewards can be most satisfying...

Introduction

Private equity at the crossroads

The economic crisis of 2008–2009 will stay in the annals of private equity as *Anni Horribili*, the years in which the bill was passed for all the prior misdeeds of an industry that had come to believe it could "walk on water". The downgrade to "villain" status was at the same time painful and immensely illuminating. This time, the very fundamental *modus operandi* of the industry was put under the limelight and seriously questioned. Was private equity really contributing to the strength of an economy? Were the various actors of the industry properly rewarded for their actions? Were the incentive structures properly aligning the various interests at play? Was it appropriate to let this important component of economic activity continue to operate with minimal levels of disclosure and regulation? Did it truly deserve the favourable tax treatment it had been able to engineer? And finally, was private equity truly delivering returns over the long term?

With private equity at a crossroads, the timing could not have been better to investigate its inner workings and provide some much needed direction for investors and industry watchers. The recent financial and economic crises have stopped private equity investments in their tracks, and forced a critical re-examination of the various business models and governance structures. Out of this extraordinary boom-to-bust cycle emerges a new understanding of the drivers of performance in the industry, laying the ground for stronger governance and incentive structures.

An historical perspective to gain insights for the future

If the attention focused on private equity is new, the principles behind it are not. For most of history, there has been a need to link capital from wealthy families or institutions with worthy enterprises or endeavours. Academic studies have traced adventurous relationships between investors and entrepreneurs as far back as King Hammurabi, who reigned over the Babylonian Empire from 1792 BC until 1750 BC.[1] A closer example of private equity activity is the financing of Christopher Columbus' adventures, who had, by the 1480s, developed a plan to travel to the Indies by sailing

---

[1] Gompers, P. A. and Lerner, J., "The Venture Capital Cycle", MIT Press; Cambridge, Mass, 1999.

west across the Atlantic Ocean. He tried to secure financing from King John II of Portugal and King Henry VII of England but it was Ferdinand II of Aragon and Isabella I of Castile who finally agreed to put resources into the venture, together with private investors. The agreement stipulated that Columbus would be made "Admiral of the Seas", and be given 10% of all revenues from the new lands.[2] Upon his return, Columbus never received what he was promised, Spain citing a breach in the contract.

The entrepreneurial nature of the adventure, Columbus' persistence to achieve his goal, the financing and reward structures and the sheer magnitude of profits (Spain's imperial power can largely be attributed to the venture), lie behind what many see as a beguiling comparison with today's private equity industry. In private equity speak, this first-time fund was raised with as much difficulty as new groups encounter today.

This book has been conceived as a timeless, unbiased investigation of the ways and means of the private equity industry. As authors, we clearly believe the private equity industry has a good story to tell; for many reasons, internal and external, it has not made the case powerfully so far. To a large extent, we see private equity as potentially the ultimate embodiment of effective capitalism, or what we sometimes colloquially refer to as "capitalism on steroids". The basic premises, i.e. detailed due diligence, efficient financial structuring, close and active support of management, alignment of interests throughout the entire value chain, and a rigorous focus on creating and realizing value are difficult to argue with. But the lack of transparency and the complexity of some business models have created suspicion and mistrust. Underneath the surface lie a number of myths and half-truths that in the end discredit the industry as a whole. To understand private equity as an asset class, it is thus essential to dive into its inner workings and hopefully make sense of those finer realities.

Keeping a perspective is always difficult when the storm has just passed and left few players unharmed. It is at this critical juncture of the industry's existence that this balanced perspective is most important, giving it a chance to re-establish itself for the future.

This book is grounded in interviews with some of the world's leading investors, case studies of successful and less successful deals, extensive research and the more than 50 years' combined experience of its authors, as academics, investors and practitioners. It seeks to explain how private equity actually functions, who the key players are, and examine the different segments of this rapidly maturing market. The objective is to develop a "How To" guide for potential investors and industry observers, providing a realistic "deep dive" into the inner workings of this most intriguing, often opaque and definitely deeply misunderstood industry, with guidelines about ways to invest and errors to avoid.

To discover the inner workings of private equity, we offer to take you down its most interesting alleyways, in search of its true *modus operandi* and value

---

[2] Demaria, C., "An Introduction to Private Equity", Wiley, 2010.

creation potential. Chapter 1 provides an assessment of where the industry stands today. Chapter 2 investigates the industry's dominant business models. Chapter 3 analyzes how financial and economic value are created in the industry. Chapter 4 details how value creation comes to be measured in the industry and examines the return characteristics and fund performances by industry segments. Chapter 5 gives an overview of the main characters in the industry, i.e. the successful firms in each of the industry segments and their "representative" deals, while Chapter 6 provides insights into what we refer to as the "supporting cast", i.e. the ecosystem of advisors, gatekeepers and professionals gravitating around private equity funds. Chapter 7 takes a fund investment perspective, trying to provide guidelines for the selection of funds to invest in. We conclude with Chapter 8, where we attempt to provide a map to the future of the industry, highlighting the issues at stake in an increasingly challenging environment and suggesting ways to improve the contribution of the industry. Throughout the chapters, case studies of successful deals are used as illustration.

Private equity: all about people

As often, headlines in the popular press tend to paint a rather biased picture of a situation or individual, and the more so the more secretive the target. Why bother with actual data when one can simply create them? Private equity in that sense has all the attributes to become the ultimate scapegoat for politicians and journalists alike: it caters to high net worth investors only (i.e. the privileged ones), involves a small number of professionals only (hence attacks on them do not disturb the voting base much…), keeps its practices suspiciously discreet, uses a colourful array of tax-optimized vehicles, enjoys a way-too-cozy relationship with the powers-that-be (from bankers to politicians), seems to lack all form of social or environmental responsibility credentials and, to make matters worse, seems to earn oversized salaries and bonuses not in line with the performance they generate. In other words, the ultimate form of leech: private equity lives off society's weaker elements without a trace of ethics or concerns for the very society that harbours it. In short, the ultimate abuse of capitalism…

But could this all be misplaced? Could this be the result of undue focus on some deviant behaviours within an otherwise perfectly healthy industry, or simply the upheavals of natural selection in a maturing industry? Are we throwing the baby out with the bath water? In this book, we make both a passionate plea for the contributions the industry makes to society and investors' portfolios, and mercilessly point out the weaknesses in its business models. In other words, while we can be described as "true believers" in private equity, we are certainly the most critical (and at times cynical…) observers of that very same industry. This critical sense is essential in analyzing the facts and developing a cohesive set of principles to make private equity work for you as an asset class. In other words, we have not sold our soul to private equity: as investors in our own right, we are attempting in this book to share some of the hard learned lessons about how to "do it right". As we will show you later, this is both one of the most exciting, creative and ultimately value generating segments of the world of finance and one of the most difficult to make sense of, or even to accommodate in a portfolio. Ultimately, it is one that relies more heavily than any other on people, managers at funds and at portfolio companies. People are the most difficult elements to assess and at times to motivate. But when properly supported and incentivized, they can be the most incredibly resourceful asset... Private equity is about people: incredibly sophisticated, passionate and focused people. And human nature remains one of the most elusive characters to capture...

The best capitalism has to offer? The conceptual groundings

In theory, private equity uniquely combines elements that could create one of the most sophisticated "economic animals" on earth, the ultimate embodiment of the powers of competitive markets, unfettered creativity and rapid adaptation. Of course, as Einstein once put it, "in theory there is no difference between theory and practice, but in practice there is". And the translation of these concepts and theories into practices has been a convoluted process at times polluted by raw opportunism. But what are the conceptual groundings of private equity? Why would we assume they would ever lead to superior performance?

Empowering and incentivizing: partnering for mutual success

What private equity masters more than any other investment form is the power of incentives to get the best out of people. Private equity deals are mostly about people: therefore, strong incentives have to be put in place to attract, retain and reward the best of them for performance. Not the incremental or marginal type of incentives found in many corporate environments, bonuses tied to vague corporate targets. Private equity builds into its relationships with key personnel the strongest forms of incentives, i.e. oversized and painstakingly handcrafted to match targets individuals have control over. This is probably the single most important driver of private equity deal performance, and one the industry rarely gets praise for. Granted, it tends to benefit a relatively small number of key executives (even though quite often a generous bonus pool is often created for other employees in the acquired firms). But private equity understood before any other industry the kind of ferocious talent war that was going on in the corporate world, and did something about it.

Competent people with the skills to really make a difference at a company level are rare, very rare, and they have multiple career opportunities. Why would they elect to get into the high pressure world of corporate value creation? Because you offer them what they aspire most to: freedom of action and oversized financial rewards. To be "in charge" and directly benefit handsomely from one's actions is the most emotionally rewarding situation, one in which most individuals would go to incredible lengths to ensure success. In a way, private equity investors understood before anybody else that you can only succeed **with** management teams, not against them. Hence their model is really one of "partnering for mutual success". This strong empowering and incentivization of managers is the foundation on which every other element of the private equity recipe is built. And this base is rock solid and will survive the taming of the wild leverage markets. Debt just comes in to leverage and complement the impact of the incentives: it was never the key driver of performance. Let there be no doubt that the horse that draws the cart is empowerment and strong performance incentives, and those are sustainable drivers of performance.

Focus, focus, focus

The second key building block in the private equity recipe is the obsessive focus on single transactions. Private equity is not about diversification within a portfolio: it is about building a collection of positions, each of which standing on its own and actively managed to create value. Asset managers for their part are mostly punting on assets, trying to assess them the best they can and then counting on the power of diversification to generate interesting results. For a private equity manager, diversification is a non-starter: they bet the house on each and every deal, and will dedicate the resources to make them shine. Yes, there will be losses, and when a deal has clearly reached a point of no return, private equity managers will turn into merciless cullers. They will not lose another dollar or another hour of their precious time trying to salvage what is clearly a "goner". This discipline of the deal is fundamental to the success of the recipe. By bringing to bear the full power of incentives and empowerment onto a single deal, they demonstrate that "dilution" (of incentives, perspective, focus, etc.) is the curse of the corporate world. Private equity portfolios are not portfolios by any stretch of the mind: they are collections of individual assets that are managed as such. And there lies another key to their success.

Strategy is cheap; operationalizing is key

The third key building block is the realization that value is created not out of some grand strategy but instead in the meticulous implementation of an internally consistent operational plan. Private equity managers often have backgrounds in strategy consulting, because being able to identify a strategy to leverage assets is a good starting point. But that's all it is: a starting point. To a large extent, a strategy is about as good as any other, or put in other words, having a strategy is definitely better than not having one. What matters in a strategy is not the strategy itself, i.e. the macro plan, but the internal consistency of its operational components. The strategy consultants that managed a successful move to private equity (many did not succeed…) are those who believed and enjoyed putting the plans into action. Consulting can be the most frustrating professional experience since you rarely get to implement, i.e. you do not really get to live the impact of the recommendations. Private equity puts its money where its strategy mouth is. For some of consulting brightest minds, the attraction of operationalizing the plans is just too much to resist, in particular when the incentive plan allows them to capture a big chunk of the value they have hatched.

Alignment brings cohesion

The fourth key building block is the alignment of incentives along the complete value chain. By alignment of incentives, we refer to a strong performance discipline that percolates through the system at all levels. General Partners are strongly incentivized to deliver performance to their Limited Partners, and the management teams in the deals are strongly incentivized to deliver performance to the GPs. Alignment is a tricky balance to achieve, one that is inherently unstable. For example, GPs typically collect income through two major channels: management fees and carried interest. The traditional fixed fee structure tends to create an incentive for GPs to raise ever larger funds and invest them, usually at the expense of their ability to find quality deals. The potential benefits of the carry quickly end up overwhelmed by the size and certainty of the management fee which, although never conceived of as an incentive per se, often turns into the dominant form of compensation for fund managers. Recalibrating these two constituents is a must to keep the LP and GP interests aligned.

Flexibility as strategic value

The fifth building block to be considered is the flexibility built into the private equity system. This is one of the most interesting areas to investigate because it is also one of the most misconstrued by the popular press, in an era more concerned with governance than with performance. The private equity industry has always been characterized by its extreme flexibility and creativity. Fund mandates are always loosely defined and give a lot of latitude to GPs to capture emerging opportunities. New funds are launched on a dime to capitalize on new markets and strategies. The speed at which this industry matures is a reflection of that flexibility as well, i.e. its ability to discover and capture the value in emerging niches. In a world where globalization has brought, not a standardization and reduction in volatility but very much the opposite, i.e. more risk and more rapid changes, the value of flexibility has increased dramatically, and private equity is perfectly positioned to respond to those changes.

Carrots and sticks: the value of discipline

So far we have focused on the "positive" externalities, i.e. arrangements that reward or incentivize superior performance and results. But a comprehensive and dynamic system should also include solid negative feedback loops, i.e. penalties for non-performance. These "disciplining devices" are as important as the incentives, but they would never deliver performance on their own. A number of tools are used to establish strong discipline. First, there is the use of limited lifetime vehicles for the funds. This forces GPs to periodically "return to cash" and show the real value of their hands, to use a poker analogy. Similarly, this show of hands gives them the ability, or not, to earn the right to manage the LPs' money for another round. In a world where investments don't have a natural horizon, forcing a shorter one is a way to indicate that value needs to be created on a shorter calendar. Second, the use of debt and leverage on deals is also a way to impose fixed costs and deadlines on the management teams. But let us not lose sight of the prize: leverage by and of itself does not create value.

Leverage… at all levels

It is not completely accidental that we mention financial leverage only at this point in the private equity recipe. Debt has been both a boon and a curse to the industry. In an early era, back in the early 1980s, the availability of high yield debt to support management buyouts created the ability to create value out of financial engineering, i.e. debt pyrotechnics. Since access to debt was relatively difficult, control over those markets created position rents for a limited number of clever financial institutions and their whiz kids to extract tremendous fee income. But the markets for private equity and sophisticated debt have matured, and with maturity money has become more of a commodity, available to most at competitive rates.

The value of leverage as differentiator and value creator has vastly diminished to the point of being essentially immaterial. Yes, debt still brings leverage and discipline, but both are useless if applied to bad deals. The real estate, banking and public debt crises of 2007–2009, and the subsequent full blown economic crisis, brought to the forefront an interesting philosophical question. The use of debt is effectively incentivized by governments in most countries by the tax deductibility of the associated interest expenses, sometimes with some cap. The very same governments realized during the crisis that individuals and companies indeed made use of that feature to lower their cost of capital, sometimes to the point of putting themselves in financial insolvency. The question is then the following: why did governments in the first place decide to favour the use of debt over that of equity?

Realistically, in a world where safety and sustainability are considered important, governments should be incentivizing the use of equity to finance companies, not debt. In other words, it is equity that should be tax-privileged, not debt. Again, as is unfortunately too often the case, it is the governments and their regulations that have brought upon themselves the very disaster they now want to disclaim… Debt's role in the private equity value creation formula is limited and a regulatory aberration. The deleveraging of private equity we are witnessing today is probably the best thing that ever happened to the industry, focusing people's minds on what it always was about, i.e. operational value creation through bottom line improvements.

The cash flow paradox

Another negative externality that cannot be escaped is the inherently difficult pattern of cash flows in the typical fund. For investors used to making "investments", the principal of commitment and progressive drawdowns in parallel to distributions is but an absurdity. It would seem to make so much more sense to just commit and allocate all capital upfront and collect at the end. But that would create a number of issues. First, because of the unpredictable timing of all key events (investments, recapitalizations, exits…), the capital allocated would likely remain unused in the fund for long periods of time. Second, and a direct consequence of the first, the reported **internal rates of return** (IRRs) on the investors' capital would necessarily be affected by this pattern. Third, it would eliminate the discipline of the periodic drawdowns.

Most funds include covenants that allow limited partners to stop contributions (also known as no-fault divorce clauses) if a majority of them lose faith in the investment abilities (or simply approaches and strategies) of the fund's GPs. This "option to stop contributions" in itself is valuable as an inter-fund intervention mechanism, allowing investors to potentially cut their losses. Finally, the inherent illiquidity of the positions makes it illusory to ever expect to smooth out the pattern. Even listed private equity vehicles have shown the limit of trading the claims, with often massive variations shown in their prices above and below the calculated net asset values. Private equity is illiquid and will remain so. As such, it can only be incorporated in an investment portfolio by investors who have the capacity to handle the complex cash flow pattern.

The buy-and-sell approach: capitalism on speed

Finally, it is important to stress the value of the buy-and-sell approach that is said to characterize private equity as investors. It is fundamentally different from the traditional buy-and-hold approach a-la-Warren Buffett. Buffett was once quoted as saying that his favourite holding period for an investment was "forever", and that is very much the way many investors still operate. And there is nothing wrong with that business model, except maybe its disconnection from a pressing deadline to meet. Private equity to a large extent is capitalism on speed: by providing tight investment horizons, it forces a quick realization of the value potential. Is this better than what could be achieved through a buy-and-hold approach? Probably not, but it achieves results faster. And in a world where uncertainties are increasing, not decreasing, having a tighter timeframe for value creation is probably ever more important.

Believers, sceptics and cynics

As will become obvious in the following chapters of this book, we can best be described as fundamental believers in the potential of private equity as value creator. At the same time, experience has taught us that every sophisticated system operates on the basis of a finally tuned arrangement, wherein minute changes can lead to catastrophic consequences. In other words, the difference between performance and failure is often linked to apparent details, especially when dealing with people skills. Private equity is no different: it is an asset class that requires extreme sophistication and dedication (not to mention, of course, caution) to extract its essence. It is both exciting and elusive, as demanding as it is rewarding. But equipped with a fair dose of scepticism and a realistic sense of criticism, it is possible to turn private equity into an indispensable asset class for many investors.

1

Private equity: from "alternative" to "mainstream" asset class?

Executive summary

Every day one reads about the latest private equity threat to a corporate icon. Some lament these threats, while others rejoice that at last an independent force has come in to shake up some lazy corporate assets. Private equity has been around for decades. However, in the years before the 2008 financial crisis, private equity funds gained the power to take on virtually any corporate target they chose. Some became household names—Kohlberg Kravis Roberts & Co. (KKR), Carlyle, and Blackstone from the US, Apax, Permira and CVC in Europe—just the most glamorous among the thousands of private equity funds in operation around the world. The trillion-dollar industry was bound to make some waves when it jumped into the corporate pool...

Whilst the basic principles of private equity have been around for a long time, the explosive growth of the industry is a relatively recent phenomenon. And with size comes a comprehensive "coming of age", including a broader geographic coverage. While the US remains by far the largest market, some Asian markets are gaining in popularity, with their share in global fundraising expected to reach 20% soon.

As deal size increased, the very large transactions caught the attention of the media, politicians and regulators. Inconsiderate compensations started to generate popular resentment and attempts at regulation in many countries. The tax treatment of the general partners' carries received a lot of attention, with their capital gains status questioned in face of the limited capital exposure by fund GPs. The use of tax-advantaged jurisdictions for the funds and special purpose vehicles for the deals fuelled the suspicion that private equity managers considered themselves somewhat exempt from greater social responsibilities, at a time when everyone was being asked to tighten their belt. A general move towards more transparency in all aspects of the financial world also put pressure on private equity to provide more disclosure.

All these signs in effect indicate an asset class that is slowly graduating to the mainstream and can no longer pretend to be "different".

Like many of man's greatest inventions, such as dynamite, private equity can make a great contribution to an investor's portfolio when the basic investment rules are properly applied, and can turn into a rather explosive nightmare if put to uncontrolled use. In other words, private equity can be at the same time the best and the worst the world of assets can offer...

"Private equity" earned part of its alternative credentials because of its cherished confidentiality and privacy. As one of the most exclusive clubs, where price of admission into the best partnerships runs easily in excess of $25 million, with few if any regulatory authorities to report to until very recently, the industry was keen to maintain an aura of secrecy that helped its cause and reputation. Data on performance, strategies and mechanisms of value creation were hard to find and equally hard to assess since most stemmed from self-reporting to industry trade groups. Academic studies abound but suffer from the same shortcomings, mainly the inability to access comprehensive, unbiased data about funds and investments, especially on their performance.

The press in general also had its gripes about the industry. It shunned institutionalized private equity, preferring to spotlight VC-backed entrepreneurs and their more visible value creation and life-changing innovations. But the sheer magnitude of the industry and its deep penetration in the economic activity of countries makes it impossible for private equity to be ignored.

Moving into mainstream

Private equity has always been classified as an "alternative" asset class, i.e. a loosely defined class of asset which includes all assets beyond the three primary classes—stocks, bonds and cash. In the world of finance, alternative assets may include special physical assets, such as natural resources or real estate; special methods of investing, such as hedge funds or private equity; and even in some cases geographic regions, such as emerging markets. Private equity usually covers investments in companies not quoted on a stock market, i.e. private companies, or sometimes divisions of larger groups, or even investments in listed companies with private capital using a creative combination of equity and debt. Freed from financial and corporate constraints, properly refinanced and equipped with a strongly incentivized and focused management team, these businesses would possibly shine and deliver strong performances. The private equity owners would then sell the company to a corporate rival or take it public, hopefully with great riches for all at the end.

Until a few decades ago, private equity was a small, dark corner of the financial markets that few people had heard of and even fewer cared about. But the recent growth of the industry—before the debt crisis hit in 2008—has been extraordinary, whether measured by the capital raised or the number of funds on the market, as seen below in **Exhibit 1.1.**

Exhibit 1.1 Annual private equity fundraising

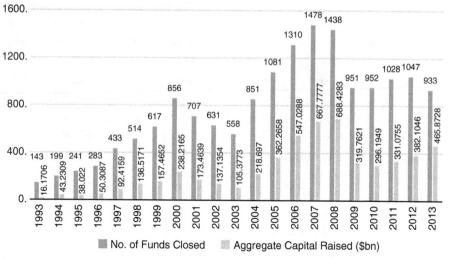

No. of Funds Closed ■ Aggregate Capital Raised ($bn)

Source: Preqin

This extraordinary growth, according to many observers, makes the label "alternative" not appropriate anymore. In its introduction to the *2007–08 Survey on Alternative Investments*, Russell Investments illustrated the new status:

> "As interest in alternative investments has grown, and as such investments have become more mainstream, the phrase 'alternative investments' itself is beginning to sound like a contradiction in terms. What were once considered fringe investments are now deemed essential components of many institutional investors' portfolios."[1]

Large institutional investors—such as insurance companies, university endowments, pension funds and sovereign funds—have for the most part adopted private equity as a significant component of their portfolio, playing a leading role in the almost $3.2 trillion current assets under management of the entire private equity industry as of June 2012.[2] For many, the move has been extremely beneficial: California Public Employees' Retirement System (CalPERS), one of the largest public pension funds, recently reported that, since its inception in 1990 to December 31, 2011, its private equity programme has generated $20.2 billion

---

[1] The 2007–2008 Russell Investments Survey on Alternative Investments.

[2] Global Private Equity Report, Preqin, 2013. Estimate as of June 2012. This estimate does not include committed capital that has yet to be called up by fund managers. It is calculated using the sum of the remaining value of portfolios of private equity funds that have reached a final close (excluding funds-of-funds, secondary funds, real estate funds and infrastructure funds).

5

CHAPTER 1 PRIVATE EQUITY: FROM "ALTERNATIVE" TO "MAINSTREAM" ASSET CLASS?

in profits.[3] Private equity is also a significant driver of returns for endowments, the most documented of which is probably the Yale Endowment Fund. In its 2013 report, the Yale Endowment Fund claimed its private equity investment programme has earned a 29.9% annualized return since inception in 1973.[4] The University's target allocation to private equity, at 31% of assets (June 2013 target), far exceeds the 9.5% actual allocation of the average educational institution, and is expected by the school to generate real returns of 10.5% with a risk of 26.8%.[5]

Private equity has clearly performed well for some investors but not for all, an issue that will be extensively covered in the coming chapters. One thing is clear though: private equity has slowly emerged as a mainstream asset class, one that is bound to affect many areas of the economy. For pension funds in particular, the strong pressure to meet liabilities despite an aging population, increased unemployment and disappointing financial markets has pushed many to increase their allocation to the asset class. And when one considers that the five largest investors in private equity among public pension funds in the US and in Canada together allocated more than $110 billion ($25 billion) to private equity in 2012, it is fair to say that a significant share of the general public is indirectly exposed to the asset class, whether it is aware of it or not![6,7]

Large sectors of the economy are also directly benefiting from the rise of private equity. The industry, with some 4,800 active private equity firms, employs approximately 89,000 people around the world[8], while the Private Equity Growth Capital Council (PEGCC), which acts as the US industry lobby group, estimates that the 15,680 US-based private equity-backed companies employ 8.1 million people in the US.[9] This is not counting the impact on the many service firms, such as consultants, auditors and law firms, that gravitate around the private equity industry.

As the industry graduates from alternative to mainstream, the marketplace is also maturing, developing more specific niches and adopting more complex and focused strategies. Historically, institutional money flowed to primary funds that in turn took equity share in companies. Over time, the industry has witnessed the

---

[3] www.calpers.ca.org.

[4] The Yale Endowment, 2013.

[5] Ibid.

[6] Global Private Equity Report, Preqin, 2013.

[7] These North American public pension funds are: California Public Employees' Retirement System (CalPERS), CPP Investment Board (Canada), California State Teachers' Retirement System (CalSTRS), Washington State Investment Board and Oregon State Treasury. These European public pension funds are ABP (Netherlands), Keva (Finland), West Midlands Pension Fund (UK), Strathclyde Pension Fund (UK) and AP-Fonden 6 (Sweden).

[8] Global Private Equity Report, Preqin, 2013. Some of these employees might also work for firms deemed inactive.

[9] PEGCC website: http://www.pegcc.org/education/pe-by-the-numbers/.

emergence of funds-of-funds and secondary funds structured either as primary funds or funds-of-funds themselves. Co-investments by investors alongside their primary fund directly into portfolio companies have become more widespread.[10] Funds are also becoming more specialized, with an increasingly large range of vehicles focused on specific investment stages such as turnarounds, on strategies such as buildups, on geographies such as Europe and on industries such as energy. This maturing of the industry, coupled with recent development in the credit industry as a whole, affects the way the industry functions and performs. These developments will be the subject of the following chapters.

A brief history

The birth of venture capital in the US is generally attributed to General Georges Doriot, a French-born military man who taught industrial management at Harvard Business School. Doriot founded the first modern venture capital firm, American Research & Development (ARD), in 1946 in the belief that when combined with professional management, R&D skills could provide economic growth and capital appreciation.[11] At the same time, wealthy families on the East Coast were also setting up their own "venture capital funds". The Rockefeller fund, which counts Eastern Airlines, one of the first commercial operators, as an early investment, was controlled by the Rockefeller family.

On the other side of the Atlantic, the conditions evolved very differently. Europe was in tatters after World War II and the "European Recovery Program" (which became known as the Marshall Plan) played a fundamental role in rebuilding Europe after the conflicts. The government and business leaders in the UK saw the need for an organization that would provide equity capital for small businesses to help rebuild a dynamic economy. In 1946, under the leadership of William Percy, Investors in Industry was established with £10 million of capital provided by banks.[12] For the next three decades, Investors in Industry (later renamed simply as 3i) was pretty much the UK private equity industry in itself. Progressively, commercial banks started to see the opportunity to invest capital from their balance sheets in opportunities that were generated through their corporate banking networks. For larger amounts of capital, merchant bankers continued to work hard marrying opportunities with their rich clients.

The leveraged buyout, in the sense that it is known today, emerged in the 1980s. In January 1982, a group of investors led by former US Treasury Secretary William Simon acquired card manufacturer Gibson Greetings for

---

[10] CFA Institute, Global Investment Performance Standards, Exposure Draft, 2010.

[11] Ante, S. E., "Creative Capital: George Doriot and the Birth of Venture Capital". Cambridge (MA): Harvard Business Press, 2008.

[12] 3i.com.

7

CHAPTER 1 PRIVATE EQUITY: FROM "ALTERNATIVE" TO "MAINSTREAM" ASSET CLASS?

$80 million, financing a substantial portion of the acquisition with debt. The business was floated 16 months later at a valuation in excess of $290 million. This marked the start of the first leveraged finance boom, which saw financiers such as Jerome Kohlberg and Henry Kravis, former bankers at Bear Stearns, buying up companies with tiny amounts of equity and huge amounts of debt, much of it raised through the issue of high-yield, or junk, bonds. The 1980s was characterized by the emergence of "easy money", facilitated by the creation of the high yield debt markets, the brainchild of financier Michael R. Milken, head of Drexel's high yield and convertible bonds department at Drexel Burnham Lambert.

However, the early 1990s were characterized by the disappearance of an active high yield bond market, prompting private equity players to change tactics. Large leveraged buyouts fell out of fashion. In came the industry consolidations through leveraged buildups or rollups. With the unravelling of junk bond financing and the recession of the early 1990s, private equity went into remission, though one would argue that during that time the industry enjoyed some of its best returns. Activity levels first plummeted, before gradually increasing during the late 1990s and entering a second period of stellar growth.

The 2000s benefited from a liquidity surge never seen before. According to research by financial data analysis firm Preqin, the amount raised by private equity firms worldwide increased from $92 billion in 1997 to $361 billion in 2005 and a staggering $664 billion in 2007.[13] This means that the compound growth rate exceeded 20% per annum over that period. Fuelled by the availability of leverage, buyout deals reached incredible levels during the period. Whereas the aggregate value of buyouts globally was only slightly more than $100 billion in 2000, it reached some $294 billion five years later, and $659 billion in 2007. During that period, first-time funds represented more than one in five funds raised in 2003 and 2004, and more than one in seven for the period 2006–2008.[14] The average private equity fund increased significantly in size, from $479 million in 2005 to $598 million in 2006, to $685 million in 2007 and to an astounding $770 million in 2008.[15] The growth was fuelled by the combination of easily available debt and solid industry returns, but also in part by the built-in incentives that encouraged fund managers to raise larger and larger funds (see Chapter 2: The Business System).

Funds were not the only entities growing in size: so did the deals. During the decade that led to the financial crisis, buyouts of $20, $30 and even $40 billion were engineered. Eight of the 10 largest buyouts ever done took place between 2005 and 2007, as **Exhibit 1.2** shows.

---

[13] Preqin, 2013.

[14] Global Private Equity Report 2010, Bain & Company.

[15] 2010 Global Private Equity Watch, Ernst & Young.

Exhibit 1.2 Largest private equity deals to date (billions)

Target	Acquirer	Date	Deal value – $ billions
TXU Corp	TXU Corp SPV	Feb 2007	
Equity Office Properties Trust	Blackstone Group LP	Nov 2006	
HCA Inc	Hercules Acquisition Corp	Jul 2006	
RJR Nabisco Inc	Kohlberg Kravis Roberts & Co	Oct 1988	
BAA PLC	Airport Dvlp & Invest Ltd	Mar 2006	
Harrah's Entertainment Inc	Investor Group	Oct 2006	
Kinder Morgan Inc	Knight Holdco LLC	May 2006	
Alltel Corp	Atlantis Holdings LLC	May 2007	
First Data Corp	Kohlberg Kravis Roberts & Co	Apr 2007	
Hilton Hotels Corp	Blackstone Group LP	Jul 2007	
Dell Inc.	**Michael Dell/Silver Lake**	**Feb 2013**	
Clear Channel Commun Inc	Investor Group	May 2007	
Archstone-Smith Trust	AB Acquisitions Ltd	May 2007	
Alliance Boots PLC	Koch Forest Products Inc	Nov 2005	
Georgia-Pacific Corp	AB Acquisitions LLC	Jan 2006	

```
         0   10   20   30   40   50
```

Source: Thomson Reuters

In this context, it was clear a financial crisis would deeply affect the private equity industry, and fundraising in particular. The sudden unavailability of debt on financial markets hampered deal making, and fundraising for new funds reached record lows. In 2008, fundraising still totalled $683 billion, but by 2009, that level plunged to $311 billion, and continued its downward spiral to $287 billion over the course of 2010, the lowest level since 2004, before slightly increasing to $312 billion and $327 billion in 2011 and 2012 respectively.[16] Significant write-downs and delayed exits of portfolio companies affected the performance of funds, many of which exhibited negative returns. By then, investors in private equity were holding back from making new commitments.

As in all prior crises, the industry did recover, adapting to survive and finding new ways to create value for investors.

An increasingly global industry

As the industry evolves and matures, the sources of funds for private equity and their destinations are becoming more diverse. According to estimates by Preqin, North American investors now only account for 56% of all capital currently invested in private equity, while the rest comes from Europe (31%) and to a lesser

---

[16] Global Private Equity Report, Preqin, 2013.

extent from investors based in Asia (7%) and elsewhere in 2012.[17] Similarly, private equity funds are deployed on a more global basis, with funds focused on North America accounting for only 55% of global commitments in 2011, the rest being deployed equally between funds focused on Europe and those focused on Asia and the rest of the world.[18]

There is also evidence that the industry is becoming not only more global but also more globalized. In a study published in 2008, Aizenman and Kendall found that the proportion of deals which are funded with some cross-border participation dramatically increased over time, to reach some 42% of the deals by 2007, before the recession hit.[19] The case study below (see **box** below), one of the many we showcase in the book, illustrates how private equity deals sometimes help reshape whole industries on a global scale. In this specific case, Carlyle transformed the forged ring industry through many cross-border investments.

9

CHAPTER 1 PRIVATE EQUITY: FROM "ALTERNATIVE" TO "MAINSTREAM" ASSET CLASS?

Case Study 1
Carlyle consolidates the forged ring industry

Carlyle, set up in 1987 with offices and operations in over 20 countries, is one of the largest private equity firms in the world. Its acquisition of forged ring manufacturers is a great story about consolidation of an industry that manufactures one of the most critical components used in aerospace, automotive, power generation and petrochemical industries. The forged ring industry was at the time fairly fragmented, putting it at a disadvantage when negotiating prices with raw material suppliers and its clients, mostly OEM manufacturers, powerful actors in the supply chain.

When Carlyle's Bud Watts and Cam Dyer looked at this picture they saw a huge opportunity. They could bring better management practices to these privately-owned companies which had traditionally been entrepreneurially-run and were for many still managed by their founders. The industry was crying out for consolidation but the players were averse to selling their company to each other. Carlyle—as an independent player—offered a respectable, and well-financed, third-party option to sell out.

When the founders of one such company, FMI, decided to retire and put the company up for sale, Carlyle jumped at the opportunity. A slump in the aerospace industry had caused valuations to tumble, driving the owners to exit the business. The company was well-managed, with low fixed costs and decent

[17] Global Private Equity Report, Preqin, 2013.
[18] Global Private Equity Report, Preqin, 2012.
[19] Aizenman, J. and Kendall, J., "The Internationalization of Venture Capital and Private Equity". NBER Working Paper No. 14344, Issued in September 2008.

margins. Carlyle acquired FMI at a reported price of $67.8 million. Right after the acquisition, the aerospace industry dived into a deeper recession. In 2002, another engineering company, UK-based Firth Rixson, which manufactured forged cast and rolled components in nickel, titanium and steel alloys, put itself up for sale too. Carlyle figured out that FMI and Firth Rixon together would create a formidable supplier for the aerospace industry. Carlyle's deep understanding of the aerospace industry gave it the means to engineer a successful merger. Initially, the two companies' product lines were overlapping, but over time each facility became a centre of excellence for different sizes, volumes and metallurgical properties, and production efficiency improved.

Soon another investment opportunity appeared on Carlyle's sensitive radar screen: Schlosser Forge. The company manufactured ultra wide rings, a product outside Firth Rixon's competencies. Schlosser Forge was based in California and its ultra wide rings were used in Boeing 777 and Airbus A380 latest generation airplanes. GE Aircraft Engines was its biggest customer, and because it depended on Schlosser Forge, GE was growing concerned with the company's owner getting old. Carlyle believed that Firth Rixon could easily absorb another acquisition, so Schlosser was acquired for $55 million in 2004. The build-up game plan involved squeezing annual savings through synergies totalling $5.1 million for a one-time upfront investment of $2.2 million.

The idea of consolidating the industry and becoming clear market leaders was an opportunity very difficult to resist for Carlyle. Building on the strength of its entities, the new Firth Rixson secured a five-year agreement with GE aviation to supply seamless ring forgings for the GEnx engine. After selling a 36% stake to Lehman Brothers in 2006, Carlyle completed the exit in a secondary sale to Oak Hill Capital Partners in November 2007, generating an aggregate transaction value of nearly $2 billion, 9.7 times the invested equity. During Carlyle's ownership of Firth Rixson, the company grew to operate 11 facilities across China, Europe and the United States and supplied products to every major aerospace engine manufacturer in the world.

Source: Case study written by the authors and included with permission from the Carlyle Group.

Private equity in North America

Regionally, North America is by far the world's largest and most mature private equity market. In 2007, private equity firms raised an astounding $353 billion, up from $96 billion in 1998, for a compound annual growth rate in excess of 15%. Fundraising had peaked earlier in 2000 at $181 billion, boosted by a significant influx of capital into high technology venture funds, right before the

11

CHAPTER 1 PRIVATE EQUITY: FROM "ALTERNATIVE" TO "MAINSTREAM" ASSET CLASS?

internet bubble exploded.[20] The 2008 financial crisis a few years later dramatically impacted fundraising in North America—merely dividing by two the amount raised between 2008 and 2009—except ironically for firms focused on distressed debt and turnaround investments. The situation slightly improved over 2011 and 2012, although the annual amount raised in the region has never exceeded $180 billion since 2008, when it peaked at $630 billion.[21]

The crisis has, however, led to an unprecedented amount of dry powder—capital which has not yet been invested. The majority of global dry powder is held by primarily North America-focused funds, which currently have over $500 billion available for new investments.[22] This dry powder, within the current economic woes in the US (as of August 2014), creates a bit of a paradox. On the one hand, it plays into the hands of private equity firms which have the capital—and the expertise—to step in and turn companies around, positioning them for exit in three-to-five years, when the economy will probably have turned around. On the other hand, the sheer size of the capital pool, and the urgency with which private equity partners are likely to want to put it to work, create upward pressure on deal valuations, in effect antagonizing the very value creation potential of these transactions.

But the industry is clearly getting back on track, after two years of low activity which prevented exits, and in particular private equity-backed IPOs, from happening. According to Dealogic, which tracks IPOs, the largest private equity-backed US IPOs on record have happened after the crisis: HCA, the largest US corporate operator of hospitals and health systems ($3.8 billion), pipeline and energy transportation firm Kinder Morgan ($3.3 billion) and media company Nielsen ($1.9 billion).[23] Moreover, the beginning of 2013 saw the biggest public-to-private transactions since the boom of 2006–2007: the $24.4 billion Silver Lake-backed privatization of Dell Inc. and the $28 billion Berkshire Hathaway and 3G Capital-backed buyout of H.J. Heinz Company.[24]

Private equity in Europe

Europe has also witnessed a huge increase in the scale of its private equity industry over the past decade. By the year 2000, fundraising by European private equity firms was standing at €48 billion, and investments at €35 billion, of which venture capital represented almost €20 billion.[25] When the internet bubble exploded, fundraising dropped to €28 billion in 2002, and venture capital investments fell

---

[20] Dow Jones LP Source.

[21] Global Private Equity Report, Preqin, 2013.

[22] Ibid.

[23] *Wall Street Journal*, "HCA: The Biggest PE-Backed IPO Evah, and Other Stats", March, 10, 2011.

[24] Preqin press release, February 20, 2013.

[25] EVCA Yearbook 2012.

below €10 billion. Private equity fundraising remained low until a steady influx of capital appeared in 2005, reaching a peak in 2006 at €112 billion.[26]

The financial crisis crushed the European private equity industry, as it did its US counterparts: in 2009, the total capital raised was only €18 billion and investments €24 billion. Venture capital then amounted to only 16% of all private equity investments. By 2011, the recovery of the industry was under way. In that year, €40 billion were raised and total exit values (at cost) went up. Values of IPO at cost were €3.9 billion for 2011 and €2.6 billion for 2007, and values for trade sales were €11.2 for 2011 and €7 billion for 2007.[27]

The disparity between European countries was always large: while GPs based in the UK and Ireland represented 43% of all European investments in 2011, those based in France and the Benelux accounted for only 27%, and those in the DACH region (Germany, Austria, Switzerland) for merely 11%. Southern Europe and the Nordic region each represented 8%, while the CEE accounts only for 3%.[28] Many European countries have been working hard to create a more private equity-friendly environment. In 2008, France actually replaced Ireland as having the most attractive fiscal and legal environment for private equity deals, highlighting a concerted effort by French policymakers to encourage private equity investment. The UK, which was ranked first in Europe until 2004, dropped out of the top three for the first time, mainly because of changes to the capital gains tax regime.

Private equity in Asia

The share of Asia in global private equity was less than 5% in 2003; it increased steadily in the following years to exceed 10% in 2005, 12% in 2006 and almost 14% in 2008. The amount of funds raised grew at a compound annual rate of close to 24% from 1998 to 2008, before the financial crisis hit the markets.[29] Aggregate capital raised for Asia-focused funds now stands at $47 billion in 2012.[30]

Because private equity was a relatively new creation in Asia Pacific compared to Europe and the US, it was generally perceived as lacking maturity, offering fewer buyout opportunities and limited exit options. However, the rapid economic growth the region was witnessing made it a tantalizing prospect for private equity investors. Whereas Japan, Australia and New Zealand (commonly referred to as JANZ) dominated the region in 2002, with 66% of Asian private equity fundraising, the trend sharply reversed in the ensuing years, with the rest of Asia (non-JANZ) attracting more than 90% of fundraising by Asia in 2012.[31]

---

[26] EVCA Yearbook 2012.

[27] Ibid.

[28] Ibid.

[29] PricewaterhouseCoopers: Global Private Equity Report 2008.

[30] Global Private Equity Report, Prequin, 2013.

[31] Emerging Markets Private Equity Association, Industry Statistics, 2012.

13

CHAPTER 1   PRIVATE EQUITY: FROM "ALTERNATIVE" TO "MAINSTREAM" ASSET CLASS?

Emerging private equity players

As of mid-2014, the world of private equity is also witnessing the emergence of new players. Many regions outside the US, Western Europe, Japan, Australia and New Zealand are becoming powerful players in private equity. Taken together, emerging markets accounted for about 20% of total funds raised in 2012 and 12% of funds invested, corresponding to $40 billion and $24 billion respectively.[32]

Of that group, non-JANZ Asia attracted the lion's share, about 60% of emerging markets' funds raised and invested in 2012. The CEE & CIS region attracted about 12% of the funds to emerging markets, while Latin America attracted about 10% (see **Exhibit 1.3**).[33] Overall, funds flowing to emerging markets remain strong, despite a recent notable decrease in funds flowing to China-, India- and Brazil-dedicated vehicles, offset by a recent increase in capital targeting pan-emerging funds and Asia-focused regional funds.[34]

> *"We expect to see an increase in private equity fundraising across the emerging markets as investors not only seek exposure to high-growth markets, but also increasingly develop a more nuanced and informed perspective on emerging market risk relative to developed markets,"* said Sarah Alexander, CEO of the Emerging Markets Private Equity Association (EMPEA).[35]

Exhibit 1.3 Private equity fundraising by region

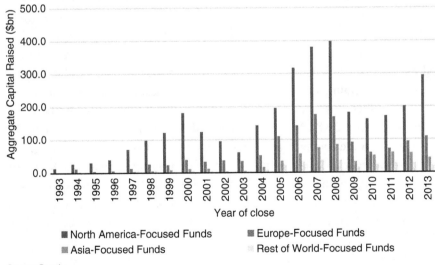

Source: Preqin

---

[32] Emerging Markets Private Equity Association, Industry Statistics, 2012.

[33] Ibid.

[34] Emerging Markets Private Equity Association, Press Release, February 5, 2013.

[35] Emerging Markets Private Equity Association, 2011.

Peter Cornelius, an economist at AlpInvest, one of the largest institutional investors in the world with over €40 billion under management, offered a cautious perspective:

> *"Economies in Asia and Latin America have gone through massive economic crises in 1998, and again in 2000–2002, which essentially wiped out returns. One could argue that those economies have become more robust, and significantly grown, but I think a number of challenges remain, in part related to coping with governance issues. Going forward, we are cautiously optimistic."*

David Rubenstein, head of the Carlyle Group, pointed to investors' behaviour during the crises:

> *"What you have seen in emerging markets this time is different. Western money did not pull out—people saw it as an opportunity to buy at lower prices. It is a sign of the maturation of people investing in these markets."*

Emerging markets have made substantial efforts to attract investors. The exit environment in **China**, for example, has greatly improved; Chinese stock exchanges, including the Hong Kong one, managed to raise three times the amount secured by initial public offerings across the US in 2010.[36] According to research conducted by Ergo for the EMPEA, Chinese private equity-backed companies increasingly choose to list on Chinese onshore markets rather than offshore ones because of larger exit multiples.[37] In terms of both private equity fundraising and investments, China manages to attract the largest share of total capital for emerging countries, around $10.8 billion in 2012 (see **Exhibit 1.4**).[38]

Governance, political risk and regulatory hurdles, however, temper some of the investors' enthusiasm. An example of the difficulties that could be faced came in November 2008, when TPG Capital was reported by the *Financial Times* to have come unstuck in China.[39] In 2007, TPG raised a $4.2 billion fund for investment in Asia, trumping the $4 billion fund raised by KKR for the region a few months earlier and, at the time, the largest fund ever raised for Asian investments. In February 2008, TPG took a 60% stake in troubled Japanese leasing firm Nissin Group. Part of the attraction was its subsidiary Nissin Leasing (China), the largest leasing company in China. The deal quickly went sour when TPG became embroiled in a dispute with local management. In

---

[36] *Financial Times*, "Chinese IPOs raise three times US", December 12, 2010.

[37] Ergo, "Exit Via IPO in China, An Examination of the Exit Environment", December 20, 2010.

[38] Emerging Markets Private Equity Association, Industry Statistics, 2012.

[39] *Financial Times*, "Tough lessons for TPG China deal", November 20, 2008.

Exhibit 1.4 Private equity fundraising by emerging markets

15

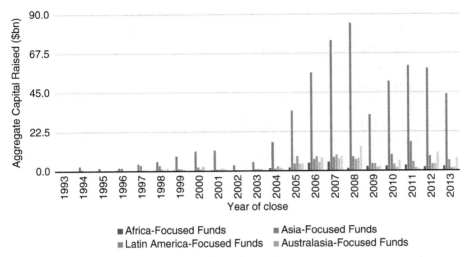

Source: Preqin

July 2008 TPG tried to remove management of the Chinese operation, naming Steven Schneider, former Asia Pacific head of General Electric, as the new regional head. When he went to the Shanghai office to deliver the bad news, he and his security guards were chased out of the building. TPG eventually managed to serve the severance notices, but remained embroiled in legal disputes with the former management.

The Chinese government has since encouraged the creation of domestic private equity funds. In parallel, Carlyle, Blackstone, TPG, Morgan Stanley and Goldman Sachs have all recently set up renminbi-denominated private equity funds to raise money directly from Chinese investors and access industries in which foreign investors are prohibited or subject to restrictions, such as media, telecoms, steel and transport.[40]

Case Study 2
Goldman Sachs' investment in Shenzhen Hepalink Pharmaceutical

A noteworthy private equity deal in China is Goldman Sachs' investment in 2007 in Shenzhen Hepalink Pharmaceutical, a small drug company developing Heparin, a blood thinner harvested from pigs' intestines. The company was founded

---

[40] *Financial Times*, "Wall St Banks to Launch Renminbi Funds", May 12, 2011.

in 1988 by a Chinese couple Li Li and his wife Li Tan. Goldman Sachs invested $4.9 million in 2007 to buy a 12.5% stake in the company that has now become the largest supplier of heparin in the world, and the only Chinese producer of finished heparin that is approved by the US Food and Drug Administration. On May 2010, Shenzhen Hepalink Pharmaceutical filed for an IPO on the Shenzhen Stock Exchange. The stock was priced at 73 times its 2009 earnings, making it the most expensive IPO valuation in China at around $8 billion.[41] Goldman Sachs saw a spectacular 20,000% unrealized return on the $4.9 million it invested in 2007, and the Chinese couple became China's wealthiest overnight.[42, 43]

With a business, legal and regulatory environment often seen as closest to the Anglo-Saxon model, **India** has also attracted a large share of emerging markets' private equity, with more than $2 billion invested in the country in 2012 alone, against $7.7 billion in 2008.[44] The country's private equity investments amounted to 0.14% of GDP in 2012, higher than China and Japan (both at 0.08%), but well behind the US and the UK (0.86% and 1.05% respectively).[45] INSEAD and LGT Capital Partners conducted a study of 335 Chinese and Indian private equity-backed companies who exited between 2001 and 2010, and for which there were entry and exit details. The study made interesting findings.[46] First, private equity-backed IPOs in India over the last 10 years managed to raise on average a much smaller amount than their Chinese counterparts ($79 million and $119 million respectively), whereas average trade sales were similar between both countries. Second, whereas IPOs were the dominant exit channel for Chinese companies with 63% of all exits, they represented only 33% of exits in India. M&A, by contrast, has been the prevailing channel for Indian companies with 67%. The authors put forward a number of reasons for this discrepancy, among which were the difficulty of obtaining controlling stakes in larger Chinese firms and the political and regulatory hurdles that could discourage private sales.

---

[41] Asian Venture Capital Journal, "Goldman Due 200x Return in China Pharma IPO", April 30, 2010.

[42] *Financial Times*, "IPO lifts couple to top of China's rich list", April 29, 2010.

[43] *Financial Times*, "Hepalink defies China market gloom on debut", May 6, 2010.

[44] Emerging Markets Private Equity Association, Industry Statistics, 2012.

[45] Ibid.

[46] INSEAD Global Private Equity Initiative (GPEI), Study on PE Exits in China and India, 2011.

Case Study 3
Warburg Pincus' investment in Bharti Tele-Ventures

One of India's most noticeable deals was Warburg Pincus' investment in Indian telecoms company Bharti Tele-Ventures from 1999 to 2001. At that time, the telecoms industry was facing major regulatory challenges and the company, founded in 1995 by entrepreneur Sunil Mittal, was acquiring regional licences at bargain prices. US private equity firm Warburg Pincus saw an attractive opportunity and invested around $290 million over the course of two years in return for a stake of around 20%. In 2002, Bharti Tele-Ventures went public on the Mumbai Stock Exchange to fund the expansion in its cellular, fixed-line, and national long-distance network.[47] Preparing an exit, Warburg Pincus sold its shares in tranches: first 3.35% for $204 million in August 2004, then a 6% stake for $553 million in March 2005 and finally the remaining 5.65% sold to UK-based Vodafone for $766 million. All in all, the private equity investor generated a 450% return on its original investment, with cumulative proceeds exceeding $1.83 billion.[48]

Brazil is slowly emerging as a powerhouse in private capital. The Coller Capital survey conducted with the Emerging Markets Private Equity Association in 2011 found that Brazil had displaced China as the most attractive emerging market for investors.[49] Private equity investment in Brazil had been, however, severely affected by the crisis but rebounded strongly in 2010 when investments more than quadrupled over a year.[50] Several reasons have been put forward by *The Economist*, among which the maturing of the country's capital markets, the recent change in regulation to allow pension funds to place money more freely with alternative-investment firms and most importantly declining interest rates.[51] Global players like JP Morgan and Blackstone acquired local private equity companies, and Apax Partners recently closed the biggest private equity deal Brazil has ever seen by acquiring a majority stake in **Tivit**, a public Brazilian

---

[47] Fang, L. and Leeds, R., Warburg Pincus and Bharti Tele-Ventures, The Global Economic Impact of Private Equity Report 2008.

[48] Ibid.

[49] Emerging Markets Private Equity Association and Coller Capital, Emerging Markets Private Equity Survey, 2011.

[50] Emerging Markets Private Equity Association.

[51] *The Economist*, "The Buys from Brazil", February 17, 2011.

integrated IT application systems and BPO solutions company valued at about $1 billion.[52, 53] Brazilian investors are also becoming active global players involved in high-profile international deals, such as the recent acquisition of US fast food giant Burger King for $3.25 billion by 3G Capital, a US investment group backed by Brazilian investors.[54]

A peculiarity of the Brazilian private equity industry was its lack of reliance on debt financing for its deals. Contrary to the US or Europe, where high leverage was used to increase returns, deals in Brazil often relied entirely on equity.[55] Debt in fact remained very expensive there—although less expensive than a few years ago—and access to capital was difficult for many companies. If those hurdles were removed, Brazil would greatly improve its standing in the private equity industry.

An industry in the limelight

As the scale of the industry grew, and its influence over large sectors of the economy expanded, so did its profile and the level of public scrutiny vested on it. An early indication of this came on November 25, 2004, when *The Economist* ran a leader under the headline: "The new kings of capitalism".[56] The magazine wrote:

> *"To study firms such as Blackstone is as good a way as any to find out what is going on at the sharp end of capitalism today. Hedge funds may be sexier, at least for now, but it is surely Mr. [Stephen] Schwarzman and his peers in the private equity industry who control the really smart money and wield the lasting influence."*

Few followed *The Economist*'s advice, until the level of scrutiny was taken to a new level as the market peaked in 2007. As private equity firms swooped on household names, such as Alliance Boots (bought for £11 billion by KKR) or Hilton Hotels (bought for $26 billion by Blackstone), it seemed that no company was too big to be bought by these buccaneering raiders.

Despite the dramatic growth in funds under management until 2007, the scale of the industry was still dwarfed by public markets. In 2006, the value of companies taken private (public companies bought and delisted, usually with private equity backing) hit a record $150 billion but, even with this peak of activity, the total value of capital raised on world markets outstripped the amounts taken private by more than $100 billion, according to data from Thomson Financial.[57]

---

[52] *Financial Times*, "Apax takes lead stake in Brazil's Tivit", May 10, 2010.

[53] *Financial Times*, "Buy-out groups rush back to Brazil", June 28, 2011.

[54] *Financial Times*, "Burger King approves 3G Capital's bid", September 2, 2010.

[55] Knowledge@Wharton, "Private Equity in Brazil: Entering a New Era", January 26, 2011.

[56] *The Economist*, November 25, 2004.

[57] *Financial Times*, January 1, 2007.

19

CHAPTER 1 PRIVATE EQUITY: FROM "ALTERNATIVE" TO "MAINSTREAM" ASSET CLASS?

The sudden surge of attention from the press did not fit well with a fiercely private industry. Furthermore, the mainstream media largely took the view that privacy was proof of something to hide. Journalists quickly zoomed in on the outsized bonuses of celebrated private equity executives and the managers of their companies, as well as the level of tax they did—or more pertinently did not—pay. Nick Ferguson, chairman of private equity firm SVG Capital (and former chairman of Schroder Ventures Europe, now Permira, Europe's largest private equity firm), kicked up a storm in January 2007 when he told the *Financial Times*:

> *"Any common-sense person would say that a highly paid private equity executive paying less tax than a cleaning lady or other low-paid workers... can't be right."*[58]

Media attention also focused on the activities of the largest funds—also referred to as mega funds—whilst largely ignoring the activities of the vast majority of private equity firms, who continued to buy and support small and medium-sized enterprises (SMEs), an area of activity that has long been supported by governments and policymakers all over the world. There was definitely more glamour in the large deals than in the smaller ones.

The easy money of the 1980s, facilitated by the creation of the high yield debt markets, generated the first very public "bubble" in private equity, culminating in the infamous RJR Nabisco deal by private equity firm Kohlberg Kravis Roberts (KKR) (see **case study** box below). The era came to personify greed and the pursuit of personal wealth at the expense of employees and other stakeholders. Value creation happened through a combination of asset stripping and massive use of high-yield debt, then known as junk bonds.

Case Study 4
Barbarians at the Gate: KKR's buyout of RJR Nabisco

RJR Nabisco, an American conglomerate formed in 1985 by the merger of Nabisco Brands and R.J. Reynolds Tobacco Company, was purchased in 1988 by Kohlberg Kravis Roberts & Co. in what was then the largest leveraged buyout ever. The RJR Nabisco leveraged buyout was, at the time, widely considered to be the pre-eminent example of corporate and executive greed. Bryan Burrough and John Helyar published "Barbarians at the Gate: The Fall of RJR Nabisco", a successful book about the events. The battle for control played out to gasping audiences between October and November 1988. It all started relatively innocuously when

---

[58] *Financial Times*, January 4, 2007.

RJR management and Shearson Lehman Hutton, a reputed investment banker, announced that they would take RJR Nabisco private at $75 per share. That move effectively put the company "in play" and generated offers and counter-offers from anyone that was anybody in the world of private equity, including Morgan Stanley, Goldman Sachs and Salomon Brothers. RJR Nabisco proved to be not only the largest buyout to that date, at $25 billion ($31.1 billion, including assumed debt), but also a high water mark and sign of the end of the 1980s buyout boom. The buyout of RJR Nabisco was completed in April 1989 and KKR spent the next few years repaying RJR's enormous debt load through a series of asset sales and restructuring transactions. The shutdown of the high yield bond market, following the collapse of Drexel Burnham Lambert in February 1990, was the last nail in the coffin of the financial engineering era for buyouts.

The Carlyle Group, ranked by Private Equity International as the largest private equity firm in the world with more than $97.7 billion under management in 2007, attracted a particularly heavy dose of criticism. Founded in 1987 and still led by David Rubenstein, the Washington-based private equity firm was routinely described by the media as "secretive"—an accusation it deserved no more than any of its peers. The firm's coterie of advisors, which at various times included luminaries such as former US President George Bush and former UK Prime Minister John Major, raised eyebrows, with some observers arguing that there was something patently wrong with this all-too-obvious link between business and politicians, even if they were former politicians.

Blackstone was also on the receiving end of harsh treatment, particularly over the wealth made by its principals and the firm itself. Stephen Schwarzman, the firm's founder, was ranked by *Forbes* as the 41st richest person in America in 2007 (falling to #171 in 2010…), and perhaps appropriately his Park Avenue apartment was once owned by John D. Rockefeller, the first US dollar billionaire who was named "The Richest Man in History" by *Fortune* magazine, and allegedly contributed at one point some 1/65th of US GDP.[59]

Headquartered in Fort Worth, TPG Capital (formerly Texas Pacific Group) was founded in 1992 by David Bonderman, James Coulter and William S. Price. It rapidly grew to become one of the largest, most successful and often original private equity firms, making its name with the turnaround of Continental Airlines and a series of high-profile investments, including Ducati (see Chapter 2), Neiman Marcus, Burger King, J. Crew, Lenovo, MGM and a swathe of other household names. Tales of extraordinary wealth abounded, with reports even suggesting that

[59] *Fortune*, CNNmoney.com, February 2007.

21

CHAPTER 1 PRIVATE EQUITY: FROM "ALTERNATIVE" TO "MAINSTREAM" ASSET CLASS?

The Rolling Stones were paid $7 million to play at Mr Bonderman's 60th birthday party in Las Vegas in 2004.[60]

But it was Blackstone's initial public offering (IPO) and associated Securities & Exchange Commission (SEC) filings that lifted the lid on the money being made by the world's premier private equity funds. Blackstone floated in June 2007 in one of the New York Stock Exchange's most talked about IPOs, raising $4.1 billion and valuing the investment company at around $38 billion. The firm detailed fund management fees of $852 million and advisory fees of $257 million in 2006[61], while media reports picked up on other "perks" received by management, including more than $1.5 million paid to Mr Schwarzman in 2006 for the use of a private jet that he owned and maintained.[62] Mr Schwarzman pocketed $677 million from the listing, but retained a 23% stake in the firm, worth around $10 billion at the time of the filing.

These numbers were honey to the ears of politicians eager to find a popular cause to fight for in the eyes of potential voters. In April 2005, Franz Müntefering, chairman of the Social Democratic Party of Germany, gave a wide-ranging speech criticizing the market economy and accusing private equity firms of being "locusts", a comment quickly picked up around the world.[63] Mr Müntefering was not alone in voicing scepticism about the role and possible lack of contribution of the industry to the economy. A common grievance was the alleged destruction of local jobs, through aggressive restructurings and massive delocalization to lower costs, even though a recent study by the World Economic Forum had reached mixed results on this front, concluding that the evidence supported *"neither the apocalyptic claims of extensive job destruction nor arguments that private equity funds create large amounts of domestic employment".*[64]

Less popular were studies looking at the positive role private equity could play in the economy, especially when compared to public equity. Anecdotal evidence was more widespread, such as the comments attributed to Ian Smith, the former CEO of Taylor Woodrow, a FTSE 100 UK house-builder. Mr Wilson, in a prior life, was also the CEO of hospital group General Healthcare between 2003 and 2006, when it was owned by European private equity firm BC Partners. The firm was sold in 2006 for £2.35 billion to a consortium led by South African hospital group Netcare. This gave him the ability to compare the private and the public equity markets.

---

[60] The Forbes 400, 2007.

[61] Securities & Exchange Commission, Form S1, Filed: March 22, 2007.

[62] Reuters, March 22, 2007.

[63] *Time*, May 15, 2005.

[64] World Economic Forum, "The Global Economic Impact of Private Equity Report 2010."

"The attention on private equity is, at best, misplaced, and, at worst, a bandwagon that irresponsible politicians and union leaders are trying to exploit. The bigger problems are in the public company world, where shareholders are for the most not very good and take up a lot of management's time with diverse and inconsistent demands. I contrast this with the private equity world where investors are extremely well informed about the business, have a singleness of purpose and have their interests aligned with management."

But politicians did not see it that way. After private equity buyers bought or targeted such famous names as Boot's, the AA, Marks & Spencer and J Sainsbury in the UK, scrutiny was inevitable. In March 2007, the House of Commons Treasury Select Committee launched an enquiry into the role of private equity in the UK: *"The scale and significance of the industry is now huge,"* John McFall, the combative Labour MP who chaired the committee, said at the publication of an inconclusive interim report in July 2007. *"It is absolutely critical that we ensure transparency and accountability"* Treasury Committee, Tenth Report: Private Equity (HC 567-I), July 30, 2007.

Increased transparency and accountability became the centre of discussions in 2009 and 2010, when the AIFM Directive and the Volker Rule were fiercely debated in Europe and the US. The industry organized itself to rebut attacks. The Private Equity Growth Capital Council, the buyout industry's lobbying group, was established in 2007 in the US to "develop, analyze and distribute information about the private equity and growth capital investment industry and its contributions to the national and global economy". EVCA plays the same role in Europe.

Mitt Romney's run for President in the US 2012 presidential campaign did nothing to reduce attacks. On the contrary, scrutiny has increased considerably, shedding light on the few disastrous deals the industry has produced and their consequences on employment. With hindsight, it can be justly argued that the worst excesses of the subprime crisis cannot be laid at the door of private equity firms, where the opportunity to make serious money only comes over the long term. Private equity is often criticized for a relative short-term perspective, with a typical investment horizon of three to five years, though many in the industry argue this is longer than in the public company environment, with its demands for quarterly reporting and focus on earnings targets.

Jonathan Russell, chairman of EVCA in 2008–2009 and head of buyouts at 3i, the London-listed private equity firm, said:

"Today, private equity is seen by some as the monster under the bed. The next few years will be crucial in determining the future of the industry and the environment in which we operate. Private equity must stand up and show that it is a force for good in the economy."

2

Private equity as a business system

"We like focus."

Executive summary

Private equity is a complex asset class, with intrinsic characteristics which make it appropriate only for savvy investors. With its low liquidity, long investment horizon and peculiar cash flow pattern, it requires professional management and a keen awareness of the risks and processes involved.

Performance in the asset class is to a large extent the consequence of a strong alignment of interests between the managers (general partners) at the private equity firm, the management teams at the portfolio companies and the investors (limited partners) in the funds. A large share of the compensation of both general partners and top managers is strongly linked to performance, i.e. a strong IRR at exit or various operational targets. Incentives in private equity are generally stronger, more focused, performance-driven and internally consistent than those available to managers in other firms or public institutions. These strong incentives, and the means to deliver on value creating strategies, unleash performance at all levels.

The growth of the industry, particularly in terms of fund sizes, has, however, adversely affected this alignment of interests, especially between the general partners and the limited partners. Larger fund sizes and fixed management fee structures have led to an imbalance between performance- and size-driven rewards, leading to a blind pursuit of growth and size for the sake of size. Management fees were meant to cover the actual operating expenses of the funds, not provide incentives *per se* for fund managers. Re-balancing incentives towards delivered performance is proving a challenge for the industry.

The specific investment characteristics of private equity make it more or less adequate for various types of investors. It is thus natural that allocations to private equity vary widely across investor types and regions. Allocations typically range from 5 to 10% of investable assets, with special categories of investors, such as university endowments, pushing the allocation sometimes to above 30%.

Another proof of a maturing industry is the development of a large secondary market that is starting to provide some form of liquidity for the fund commitments—albeit at a cost. The discounts offered are narrowing, indicating the market is becoming more efficient.

To gain a proper understanding of the private equity industry, one needs to consider it as a complex business system with layers of key players. In this chapter, we will first analyze the relationship between investors in funds and (private equity) fund managers. Then we will look at the dynamics between private equity firms and their portfolio companies.

Setting the stage

As Richard Lambert, director-general of the CBI[1] in the UK, and former editor of the *Financial Times*, put it: *"Private equity is a highly efficient form of corporate ownership."* It creates and captures value in responses to temporary imbalances and arbitrage opportunities. Information asymmetries and other distortions, when identified, are immediately exploited by an industry which is flexible and can act quickly.

The raison d'être of private equity funds

Private equity funds pool capital from investors in search of entrepreneurial and smaller opportunities. Stock markets enable investment in larger and relatively transparent companies by clicking a mouse, whereas private equity funds enable investors to access transactions, which are privately negotiated by the fund managers.[2]

Private equity and venture capital funds hold large stakes in companies, if not outright majorities (in most buyouts). They are, therefore, nearly always activist investors and insiders. The industry can and must create value, not only by buying low and selling high, but by being a responsible owner and actively supporting management to make companies better.

Private equity funds usually have a finite lifetime, after which they must be liquidated and all proceeds must be returned (after fees) to investors. The legal structure is more often than not a so-called Limited Partnership (LP) managed by a General Partner (GP). The fund investors are referred to as "Limited Partners" (LPs) with limited liability and a passive role, whilst the "GP" has a very free hand in selecting and managing the investments (see **Exhibit 2.1**). The partnership is managed according to the terms of a Limited Partnership Agreement, covered extensively in Chapter 7.

Limited Partnerships are generally created for a period of about 10 years, with a 4–5 year investment period during which new investments may be made. In practice it often takes more than 10 years to completely liquidate a fund and sell the last remaining investment. A GP will first go through a "fundraising" period, to sell the new fund to LPs. Once a minimum amount of capital is raised, the GP may hold a first close to be able to start making investments and to start drawing management

---

[1] Confederation of British Industry.

[2] Some transactions involve converting a publicly-listed company into a privately-owned one to avoid the burdens of being listed or simply because the stock market underpriced the company in question.

Exhibit 2.1 Typical structure of a private equity partnership

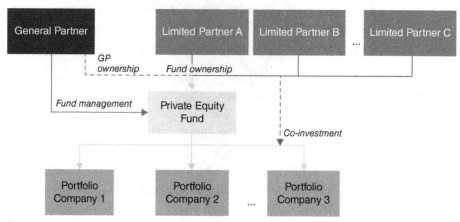

Source: Prequin

fees. Fundraising will continue until the "final" close. Investors coming in later will pay a small monetary penalty for that delay in entering the fund capital; at the same time, they may also benefit from investments made after the first close which have already grown in value. In favourable times, reputed GPs are able to raise a fund in only a few months; in inclement times, or for fund managers with less stellar track records, it can take up to a couple of years to arrive at a "final close".

After a close, a number of years will be spent generating a "deal flow": identifying opportunities, vetting them through due diligence and effecting the transactions. A typical buyout fund will make 10 to 15 investments and a venture fund more. This investment period lasts usually between four and six years. Following each investment, the investors will strive to make their companies better by working hard with management. Top management of investee companies will be given very specific goals, as well as supersized incentives to meet those ambitious performance targets. Part of the incentive package usually involves upfront investments in the deals as well as performance- and exit-based bonuses. When the time is ripe, the GP, with help again from the company management, will help engineer and execute an exit for the portfolio company. At the end of the fund life, all investments should be exited, and the fund will eventually be liquidated (see **Exhibit 2.2**).

Successful private equity investments can make both company managers and investors very wealthy. This did not go unnoticed by governments and private equity professionals alike. While governments tried to capture as much as possible of the wealth created, private equity players devised more and more sophisticated

Exhibit 2.2 Phases in the life of a private equity fund

Source: Prequin

(read complex and convoluted) structures to reduce their tax exposure. Practically speaking, governments often drove the entire industry out of their countries (offshore), while private equity investors spent fortunes on advisors and fiscally optimized structures for profits that may actually never come.

"Now that you've got this far, I'm
interested in your carry."

In Europe, that usually means capitalizing on antiquated English Limited Partnership laws dating back to the 19th century, with only limited adaptations to the modern world. Many European funds organize themselves as Jersey or Guernsey Limited Partnerships. In the US, Delaware is a very popular destination.

To complicate matters further, the various compensation and reward elements of the fund managers often incur very different tax exposures. While the management fees have a clear "income" tax potential, the treatment of carries (the percentage of the capital gains created that is retained by the fund's general partners) has generated extensive debate in many countries. Historically, there was a general understanding that these would normally be treated as "capital gains" (subject to much reduced tax rates, if not zero) since they indeed represented a form of wealth creation above and beyond the capital put at risk. The question that started to be asked after the financial crisis of 2007 was whether the "capital at risk" was actually the fund managers' or that of their investors. In most instances, since general partners often commit very small percentages of the money in a fund, it was indeed highly questionable whether a capital gains reduced tax rate was appropriate for carries, considering the beneficiaries never actually put much capital at risk. We will cover at length the theme of performance-based and other fees in this book.

Private equity's market segments

Private equity has developed a wide array of specialized funds with various investment strategies. For example, it has developed a large spectrum of investment strategies along the typical life cycle of businesses, i.e. the infamous S growth curve (see **Exhibit 2.3**).

Exhibit 2.3 Company life-cycle private equity investment strategies

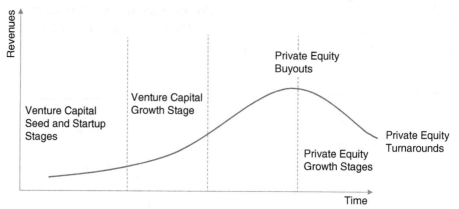

Source: Prequin

At the left end of the spectrum, referred to collectively as "early stage" activities, are venture capital investments, from seed investments into fledgling ideas (a great idea with immense potential but with no prototype yet and an incomplete business plan) to startup rounds (when the proof of concept and prototype is available and the business plan is very much complete) to various rounds of growth capital (also referred to sometimes as "expansion capital"). (Fast) growing companies need money to grow and most of the investment ends up in the company, whereas in buyouts the money tends to end up in selling shareholders' pockets. The shift from venture capital to private equity is a progressive one, often associated with access to external debt financing. With real assets, some profitability and a track record, companies become "bankable", while still requiring fresh equity injections to cover the cash deficits. This becomes the territory of "growth/expansion" private equity. Maturity, a period associated with a natural slowdown in growth, is actually a peak in terms of financial stability, with great asset bases, superb cash flows and little requirements for capital investments. Firms at that stage are usually ripe for "management buyouts", where new owners and stronger incentives for management teams can create renewed opportunities for growth, or even turn around companies heading south. Case studies across the chapters illustrate in detail the rich variety in the industry.

In the US, the term private equity is used to cover both the industry as a whole as well as its late stage segments (growth, buyouts and turnarounds). In Europe, and in particular in the UK, the term "venture capital" has often been used loosely to cover the industry as a whole, though in the US it is taken to mean primarily the early stage investments in high growth companies, usually in sectors driven by rapid technological change, such as telecommunications and life sciences. For the rest of this book, we will try to use the term private equity to refer to the overall industry, and the terms venture capital and buyout to refer to the largest sub-segments within the private equity industry.

Not transparent, illiquid... and yet attractive; such is the puzzle of this asset class. For industry executives, the reasons behind private equity's success are easy to see. Hugh MacArthur, partner and head of the private equity practice at Bain & Co., told Harvard Business Publishing[3]:

> *"The results speak for themselves: the top 25% of US private equity funds raised between 1969 and 2006 have earned IRRs of 36% per annum on average, through good times and bad. That's close to 10 percentage points higher than the equivalent S&P 500 top quartile".*

Although the financial crisis tempered that optimism, it is quite stunning that investors poured more than $320 billion in 2012 into a private equity industry that has almost $3.2 trillion assets under management, despite the deep macroeconomic uncertainty.[4] It is especially remarkable when considering that many new (smaller) funds were raised by new GPs instead of existing ones. If anything, the industry has shown amazing resilience in the face of adversity...

Judging by the non-negligible allocations of sophisticated investors to private equity, the asset class must indeed be showing performances that more than make up for its limitations, such as illiquidity, volatility and lack of transparency. In Chapter 4, we investigate in detail the track record of the industry, and look at the impact of fund size, deal size, past performance and timing on performance. Private equity has established itself as a potent and effective economic force and is, without doubt, set to play a major role in reshaping companies and economies over the coming decades, as it has done throughout its history.

The private equity industry defines transactions by the purpose for which the investment is required, with sub-categories to refine the typology. The British Private Equity and Venture Capital Association (BVCA, the industry body and public policy advocate for the private equity and venture capital industry in the UK) recognizes the following categories by stage of investment[5]:

VENTURE CAPITAL Venture capital as a category tends to cover early-stage investments, often with a technological component and high potential for growth.

---

[3] Gadiesh, O. and MacArthur, H., "Lessons from private equity any company can use", Harvard Business Publishing, March 7, 2008.

[4] Global Private Equity Report, Prequin, 2013.

[5] Classification comes from BVCA Private Equity and Venture Capital Report on Investment Activity 2009.

The term "venture" is indeed meant to cover the more adventurous side of private equity. These high-risk/high potential return investments target startups before their true revenue potential has been validated. Venture capital, as a class, is further subdivided into more specialized segments.

Seed capital allows a business concept to be developed, perhaps involving the production of a business plan, prototypes and additional research, prior to bringing a product to market and commencing large-scale manufacturing. Seed investments are usually small, often less than $250,000, and are conducted by highly specialized venture capitalists that will make early bets on promising companies or ideas.

Start-up capital is used to develop a company's products or services and fund initial marketing. With a prototype or proof-of-concept at hand and a decent business plan, the entrepreneurial venture is ready for funding. Although start-ups are typically small companies, some technology developments do require significant amounts of capital that could run in the millions of dollars.

Venture growth capital, by contrast, serves to scale up commercial manufacturing and sales in companies that have completed the product development stage, but have not yet generated profits. These companies usually still face a large amount of commercial uncertainty.

The industry is keen to promote its support of start-up and early-stage companies, principally because these investments are usually in high growth sectors that are seen as the engines of economic development and job creation in the future, such as technology, telecommunications, life sciences and, more recently, clean and green technologies. It is these market segments that have helped private equity firms achieve cross-party political support in most countries and get fairly generous tax treatments, particularly of capital gains, a policy that has attracted much political wrath in the past. However, the small size of such investments means that they account for just a small share of the total.

EXPANSION CAPITAL Expansion capital is used to grow and expand an established company. The financing could be used to finance increased production capacity, product development, marketing or to provide additional working capital. It is also known as "development" or "growth" capital, and the limit between what constitutes "venture growth" and "expansion" capital is sometimes hazy and subject to interpretation. Generally speaking, growth capital would be put under "venture" if it still involves a relatively large amount of product and market risk and under "expansion" if the product or service has demonstrated its pull and the company is mature enough.

Part of the attraction may be related to the fact that growth capital deals tend to require less money than buyouts. Historically, growth capital has largely been shunned by private equity funds because of the extensive work it requires in systems development, heavy recruitment of management team members, investments in production and distribution systems, build up of advertising, etc... Buyouts, on the other hand, require much less active involvement. But with growing competitive pressures on buyout deals, growth capital is regaining some attractiveness...

BUYOUTS At the high end of the spectrum, buyouts provide capital to mature companies with stable revenues and some further growth or increased efficiency potential. Buyout funds hold the majority of the industry's current assets under management.

The buyout category is also subdivided into more specialized segments. Management buyouts (MBO), for example, enable the incumbent management teams to acquire or purchase a significant shareholding in the company or business unit they manage. MBOs range from the acquisition of relatively small, formerly family-owned businesses, to multi-billion divisions of large corporate entities. A related transaction, referred to as a management buy-in (MBI), enables a group of external managers to buy into a firm. At times, the situation involves a mix of insiders and outsiders, where the company management acquires the business they manage with the assistance of some incoming management. These transactions are often labelled buy-in management buyouts (BIMBO). An increasing number of deals are also described as institutional buyouts (IBOs), where the transaction is led by a private equity firm, who then works with the existing management team and/or brings in new management. The management team is incentivized to take an equity stake in the acquired business.

The widely-used term leveraged buyout (LBO) is somewhat non-descript since almost all buyouts involve leverage, i.e. the acquisitions are part-financed by debt. In general though, the term applies to transactions that involve large amounts of debt relative to equity. The International Monetary Fund (IMF) thus defines an LBO as *"the purchase of a controlling interest in a company largely through the use of borrowed funds"*.[6]

TURNAROUND CAPITAL Finally, turnaround capital is financing made available to existing businesses which are experiencing difficulties and declining revenues, with a view to re-establishing prosperity. These are properly thought of as specialties within private equity, involving a small cadre of specialized operators.

---

[6] The International Monetary Fund, Global Financial Stability Report, April 2011.

Case Study 5
The founding of Tribeca Capital Partners and the OndadeMar investment

Luc Gerard, born to Belgian-Congolese parents, spent most of his youth in Congo, before moving to Belgium for his studies. He then joined Caterpillar, before being offered an M&A job at Philip Morris in 1996. In this role, he was responsible for many deals in different European countries, before taking over the management of retail channels for Latin America. When his stint in Uruguay came to an end, Luc invested his savings with others bidding for duty free shops at Buenos Aires' International Airport, but the venture did not take off and Luc returned to Philip Morris, where he was sent to Colombia.

Under his stewardship, Philip Morris acquired Coltabaco, Colombia's largest independent tobacco company, gaining a 48% market share in the process. At that time Colombia—the fifth largest economy in Latin America and the third largest population—still carried a negative image linked to drug cartels, violence and anarchy: foreign investors and international companies stayed away. So, when Philip Morris made the investment, the largest foreign investment in the country ever, the public media took notice and Luc came into the limelight. The deal marked the return of Colombia to investment grade status, making it one of the hottest Latin America countries to invest in. Exports increased dramatically, tourism saw a huge upswing and investors followed suit. Small regional players started to expand regionally and enter other industries, soon becoming conglomerates. This created huge opportunities for private equity deals as large companies were actively looking to hive off their non-core businesses.

The change in the business environment convinced Luc of the huge opportunities in the country. He started toying with the idea of running an entrepreneurial venture in Colombia. But why stop at one? Why not set up a private equity fund in Colombia? There were very few funds active in the market and Luc soon conducted intensive market research to shortlist potential target companies. The list of local brands that needed help to scale up and become global players quickly grew, confirming Luc's initial hunch.

With a partner with more than 20 years' experience in investment banking, Luc decided to set up Tribeca Capital Partners, a growth capital fund with local investors and for local investments. He was confident he could find the right companies to invest in. But the first marching order was to establish a track record, a pre-condition for investors to consider committing funds.

He soon realized that the traditional American and European private equity recipes would not work. Finding distressed assets and turning them around was utterly difficult in the country: layoffs, though not illegal, could instigate fierce community reactions while refinancing loans was very expensive and time consuming. Luc decided to focus on companies that were doing well: market leaders with strong brand equities, positive cash flows, scalable business models and the ability to go global. He would work with companies to help strengthen human capital, improve efficiency and expand geographically to international markets, starting first with Latin America before going global. He envisioned that the game plan would be best deployed in the healthcare, luxury goods and energy industries.

One of the first companies that caught his attention and met the rigorous investment criteria was OndadeMar. The company designed, manufactured and distributed luxury swimwear in a limited number of markets, mostly the southern part of the US. Its founders, Pily Queipo and Alvaro Arango, had built a strong franchise around the brand, positioning it neatly into the luxury segment at upscale US outlets like Saks Fifth Avenue and Neiman Marcus.

Pily Queipo was the maverick designer behind the brand. After a first career designing for others, she decided in the late 1990s to focus on designing swimwear, initially for friends and acquaintances. Her designs stood out for their vivaciousness, quality and colourful Italian fabric. She brought talent and passion in equal measure to the brand. Alvaro, the serial entrepreneur and former colleague, suggested that they start a brand and grow the business together. OndadeMar was formally established in Colombia in 1999, with designs done in their garage. The founders scaled up the business and soon big upscale retailers like Saks Fifth Avenue and Neiman Marcus in the US were falling over themselves to carry the collections. But while the company's products were broadly applauded, the company was plagued by serious working capital problems. Orders from big retailers were flowing in, but the company did not have the cash to build a healthy inventory of textiles. The best fabrics needed long lead times and the partners were always trying to find a balance between their financial exposure and meeting customers' needs without breakdowns. While Pily was happy to design and bring the creative energy to the brand, Arango was constantly grappling with their financial situation. With their very different personalities and divergent views on where to take the company, the partners ended up in constant argument. While the brand continued to grow beyond their wildest expectations, the two could not see eye to eye anymore. The situation came to a head when Pily decided to move to the US: the physical distance between the two strained relations even further. Both of them were now barely talking to each other.

When Luc started to look at the company, he was struck by how underdeveloped and yet vibrant the fashion industry was in Colombia. Many local Latin American brands, led by maverick designers, were unable to bring financial discipline to scale up. Tribeca was searching for exactly that: brands that would be able to break out of the mould and capitalize on a strong regional ethos to make a name in international markets. These "Made in Latin America" brands would hopefully generate good margins using quality, cheap local skills.

OndadeMar faced many challenges though. Competition came from different angles. Nike and Speedo had entered the sports segment, while Chanel and Gucci were already very present in the luxury segment. Apparel retailers such as WalMart and Target had also launched their own line of swimwear. OndadeMar's selling proposition was built around a potent combination: it sold fashionable, hand-made swimwear with a distinctive Latin touch. Its designs were sensual but wearable. The strong local touch, with vibrant colours and images portrayed on beautiful Colombian girls, helped make the brand stand out in its industry. Sales in 2006 were expected to reach $4 million and margins remained low by industry standards.

The company presented huge potential for improvement, mainly in working capital and the disrupted supply chain. With an aggressive growth plan, Luc thought sales could reach $60 million and profitability surpass $11 million by 2013. For Tribeca, the main task after the acquisition would be to bring about some serious organizational changes with a focus on expanding the sales team to cope with an aggressive growth strategy. Quality control and the purchasing process would have to be revamped as well. A leading retail store designer would be hired to develop an original store model that would capitalize on the Colombian inspiration of the OndadeMar brand. New flagship stores would be opened in the country in places such as Medellin. The brand would be rebuilt to improve recognition and increase sales volumes and margins. Sales offices would be set up in key locations in the US, Europe and other Latin American countries. Tribeca also planned to diversify into lingerie, clothing and accessories, while swimwear would remain the heart of the company. OndadeMar would be the first company under the umbrella of Tribeca Fashion, one of the three pillars of the soon-to-be-created fund. More companies would hopefully be added to the portfolio to leverage the international sales offices, and share marketing costs.

The deal was not easy to engineer, especially considering that Tribeca was still being established as a growth capital fund. A regulatory framework for the industry had to be developed with the Colombian authorities, and OndadeMar became part of a collection of pre-fund deals. Ultimately, and on the back of the success of the OndadeMar acquisition, Luc finally closed its first fund (PEF I) in late 2006, the largest such vehicle ever raised in the country. The game plan for OndadeMar included improving the working capital situation, rebuilding the supply chain entirely, turning from a distributor-based distribution to a direct retail channel to capture a larger part of the value and bringing in the expertise needed to support fast international growth. Flagship stores were opened in Miami and Dubai. Sales tripled in the first two years, while profits soared.

Source: Case study written by the authors and included with permission from Tribeca Capital Partners.

The fuel behind private equity: investors

Who would want to invest in an asset class promising the following exciting characteristics: (a) illiquidity over a long period of time, (b) a very limited level of regulation resulting in little protection for investors, (c) significant transaction costs and multiple layers of fees, both fixed and performance-based, (d) unpredictable cash flows, both to and from the fund, (e) high entry tickets, (f) limited transparency, making portfolio diversification difficult to effect, (g) returns potentially generated in non-cash items, (h) a great degree of difficulty to benchmark performance due to the diversity of strategies followed, and finally (i) non-standard performance evaluation tools, leading to questionable reported returns?

To justify the investments, superior returns would have to be expected. But beyond that, the asset class is clearly not for the faint-hearted and requires deep pockets. A simple calculation will illustrate the quagmire facing potential LPs. Minimum commitments in private equity funds often run in excess of $5 million per fund. To obtain a certain degree of diversification in a private equity portfolio requires taking some 15–25 such positions, well distributed among asset managers, geographies, strategies and vintages. In other words, a properly diversified portfolio requires the ability to commit at least $100 million to the asset class over a 10–12 year period, with limited needs for intermediate cash flows. Given the characteristics mentioned above, few investors can justify committing more than 5–10% of their total investable wealth to it. Assuming an allocation of say 10%, this requires a total fortune of at least $1 billion to invest...

This explains why investors in the asset class are generally institutional investors, able to mobilize substantial amounts of money to single funds, ranging from around $1 million for all but the smallest to hundreds of millions of dollars for the largest, sophisticated ones with teams of experienced investment professionals, and most of all a very, very patient approach...

Exhibit 2.4 Composition of LP universe by investor type as of December 31, 2013 (number of LPs)

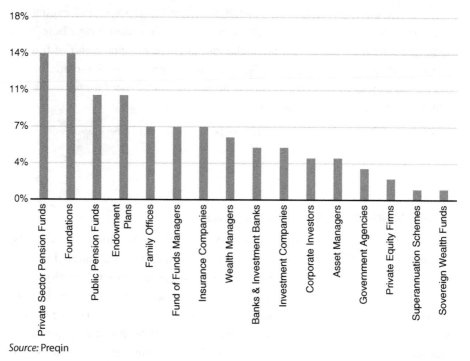

Source: Preqin

In the end, few investors qualify. According to private equity research organization Preqin, 23% of all LPs in 2012 were large pension funds, divided in half between public pension funds and private pension funds. Foundations and endowments represented together another 26%, and fund-of-funds managers another 8%. The rest was divided up between a large number of smaller groups, among which were banks and investment banks (6%), insurance companies (7%) and family offices (5%) (see **Exhibit 2.4**).[7]

Looking at the breakdown of capital invested by investor type, the picture evolves somewhat. Public pension funds contributed a staggering 29% of all capital invested in 2012. Private sector pension funds (14%), foundations (9%) and insurance companies (8%) also contributed significant shares of capital, while banks and investment banks, endowment plans and sovereign wealth funds each represented between 6% and 9%, while family offices accounted for another 5% (see **Exhibit 2.5**).[8]

---

[7] Global Private Equity Report, Preqin, 2013.

[8] Ibid.

Exhibit 2.5 Breakdown of aggregate capital currently invested in private equity by investor type as of December 31, 2013 (excluding funds-of-funds and asset managers)

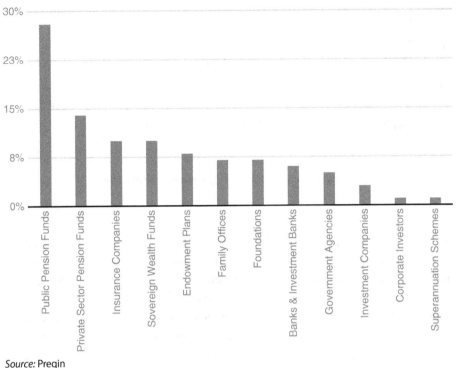

Source: Preqin

Portfolio allocations by investors

Treating all investors as a single class is not appropriate: they differ significantly in terms of risk appetites and the ability to cope with the illiquidity inherent to private equity. Regulatory issues may also force restrictions on their ability to commit money to private equity funds, in particular liquidity requirements. The very confidential character of the industry also makes it difficult to estimate the precise allocation choices of the different investor categories. According to Preqin data, investors such as endowments and foundations have an average target allocation to private equity of around 12%, while superannuation schemes, private and public pension funds all have an average target allocation between 6% and 8% (see **Exhibit 2.6**). Preqin also estimates that family offices have an average target allocation of almost 30% and a current allocation of almost 25%.[9]

Variations in the allocations within each investor type are very high. This is particularly evident in data provided by a 2007 EVCA-sponsored study of leading

---

[9] Global Private Equity Report, Preqin, 2013.

Exhibit 2.6 Average private equity allocations by investor type as of December 31, 2013 (as a % of AUM)

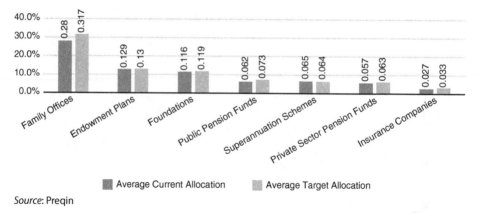

Source: Preqin

family offices in Europe[10], which showed that some family offices were allocating up to 30% of their wealth to private equity, while others allocated only a very small share (or no share at all) to the asset class. **Exhibit 2.7** summarizes the asset allocation distribution of these European family offices.

Many of the most successful investors in private equity have substantially larger commitments to the asset class. CalPERS, the giant Californian Public Employees Retirement System pension fund, has an allocation of 13% to private equity, which translated into $32 billion in December 2012.[11] The Yale Endowment—widely regarded as one of the most sophisticated investors—dramatically increased its private equity weighting from 14.9% in 2003 to 18.7% in 2007 and 26% in 2009, and

Exhibit 2.7 Strategic allocations of leading European family offices

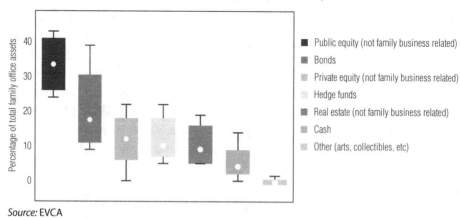

Source: EVCA

---

[10] Europe's Family Offices, Private Equity and Venture Capital, An EVCA Special Paper, November 2007.

[11] CalPERS, Facts at a Glance, February 2013, www.calpers.ca.gov.

finally to an astounding 31% in 2013.[12, 13] In its 2013 Endowment report, Yale said that private equity offers "extremely attractive long-term risk-adjusted returns".[14] The approach paid off for Yale: as mentioned earlier, since inception in 1973, private equity investments have generated 29.9% annualized return to the University.[15]

Regional differences exist. In the US, the most mature private equity market, average commitments stabilized at around 6–8% of total assets under management before the financial crisis. In 2001, North American investors had a mean strategic allocation to private equity of 7.5%, a figure that stayed fairly constant in the biannual survey Russell Investments has been conducting throughout the decade (recording mean allocations of 7.5% in 2003, 7.0% in 2005 and 6.5% in 2007) until the financial crisis hit the markets and the allocation fell to 4.3% in 2009. By contrast, European investors have been slow to hop on the private equity bandwagon, only recently trying to catch up with their US counterparts. Over the past decade, European allocations to private equity have risen from 3.6% in 2001 to 4% in 2003, 4.5% in 2005, 4.6% in 2007, but fell in 2009, as did their North American counterparts.[16]

---

[12] Yale press release, September 24, 2010.

[13] The Yale Endowment 2013.

[14] Ibid.

[15] Ibid.

[16] Russell Investments.

Accurate and up-to-date data are hard to find, although we know from the Russell Investments' 2012 Global Survey on Alternative Investing (which was completed by 146 institutional investors, representing 144 organizations with a total of $1.1 trillion in assets)[17] that 64% of respondents now hold private equity in their portfolio, achieving a combined allocation of 5.1%. The survey also revealed that 78% said that they were currently at or below target and 82% expected to either keep their current allocation to private equity constant or increase it in the coming one to three years.[18]

As discussed extensively in the book, private equity exhibits unique characteristics when it comes to the pattern of cash flows—both inflows and outflows—between the LPs and the GP. When allocating part of their portfolio to the asset class, LPs need to bear in mind that the timing of these cash flows remains unpredictable for the most part. As Doug Miller, founder of UK-based private equity placement agent International Private Equity Limited, explained:

> *"The optimal allocation depends almost entirely on the investor's objectives and the structure of his liabilities. Private equity is a very long-term game and an investor needs to match the earnings potential with the nature of his liabilities. Hence, private equity is a most appropriate asset for pension funds, endowments and sovereign wealth funds who are looking for returns that stretch for decades."*

This partly explains why the current largest contributors to the industry are pension funds (CalPERS with $32.3 billion in private equity, CPP Investment Board with $33.4 billion and CalSTRS with $22 billion) and sovereign wealth funds (Kuwait Investment Authority with $30 billion and Abu Dhabi Investment Authority with an estimated 50.1 billion).[19]

The (apparent) madness of private equity fees

The industry prides itself on the strong alignment of interests between the three key protagonists in the value creation game, namely the fund investors (LPs), fund managers (GPs) and target company managers. By alignment of interest, one usually implies that 1) everyone is strongly incentivized to generate value and that 2) no single group makes money while the others don't. The dizzying array of fees have made the validation of that promise a bit complicated, so we venture to re-visit the various compensation components and "stress test" their alignment potential.

---

[17] Of the 146 institutional investors who responded to the Russell Investments' 2012 Global Survey on Alternative Investing, 45% are in the US, 14% in Europe and the UK, 16% in Asia including Japan, 14% from Australia and New Zealand and 11% from Canada.

[18] Russell Investments' 2012 Global Survey on Alternative Investing.

[19] Global Private Equity Report, Preqin, 2013.

Fund managers or GPs generally make money in three ways: 1) a management fee, usually paid each quarter in advance; 2) a carried interest, calculated in general as a percentage of the value created and 3) relatively controversial fees received for services provided to portfolio companies.

Management fee

The management fee is meant to cover the operational expenses of a management team, such as salaries, office overheads, travel, external due diligence costs, etc. It is usually paid by LPs as a percentage of committed capital and typically varies between 1.5% and 3% depending on the size of the fund and the specific fund focus, with 2% being most common. Turnaround and expansion capital funds, as well as venture capital funds, typically charge more than buyout funds because they are smaller and tend to incur higher costs to deliver on their strategies. Over the life of the fund, and in particular after the end of the investment period, management fees tend to go down. **Exhibit 2.8** illustrates the distribution of management fees among private equity buyout funds.

Carried interest

The carried interest is the share of the capital gains of the fund paid to the GP after a certain "hurdle" rate of return has been attained for the limited partners. Once that hurdle has been attained, carried interest is usually paid on the entirety of the gain, not just the gain above the hurdle, unlike hedge funds. Gains are only considered realized when an investment is exited, usually via a trade sale, IPO, refinancing or secondary buyout, not while the company is still in the portfolio.

Exhibit 2.8 Distribution of management fees among private equity buyout funds (all funds Raising & Vintage 2012/2013 funds closed)

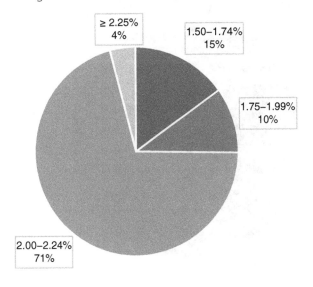

≥ 2.25%
4%

1.50–1.74%
15%

1.75–1.99%
10%

2.00–2.24%
71%

Source: Preqin

Compensation structures can vary from fund to fund, with a carry typically around 20%—sometimes 30% for the top-tier US venture capital firms—while the hurdle rate is generally based on long-term public equity returns and on interest rates, and usually ranges from 5% to 8%. **Exhibit 2.9** shows the distribution of hurdle rates amongst European private equity funds.

"This is easy thanks to a low interest diet."

Exhibit 2.9 Distribution of hurdle rates among private equity funds (all funds Raising & Vintage 2012/2013 funds closed)

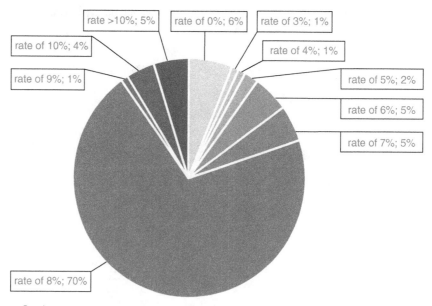

rate >10%; 5%
rate of 0%; 6%
rate of 3%; 1%
rate of 10%; 4%
rate of 4%; 1%
rate of 9%; 1%
rate of 5%; 2%
rate of 6%; 5%
rate of 7%; 5%
rate of 8%; 70%

Source: Preqin

There are two main philosophies regarding the "waterfall", the term used to refer to the prioritizing of returns among the LPs and the GP. In the US, carry is often paid on a "deals realized to date" basis, while in Europe, the predominant model is that of the "return all contributions first". At the end of a fund's life, both forms will usually converge to the same performance payout to the GPs but the distribution through time will defer quite significantly. In general, "plums", i.e. great deals, tend to mature faster in a portfolio than the not-so-great investments. In other words, quite often the pattern of realizations for a fund tends to be "front-loaded". Under a "deals realized to date" carry distribution basis, there is thus a material danger that carries get distributed to GPs that would later prove to be undeserved. To cover for that eventuality, so-called claw-back provisions are included that will claw back unjustified fees from GPs.

Exhibit 2.10 Management fees, carries and hurdles rates in US buyout and VC funds

	VC	Buyout
Panel A: Fee Terms		
# of fluids with initial fee level		
greater than 2%	40	11
equal to 2%	44	59
less than 2%	9	74
% of funds changing fee basis after investment period	42.6%	84.0%
% of funds changing fee level after investment period	55.3%	45.1%
% of funds changing both basis and level	16.0%	38.9%
Panel B: Carry Terms		
# of funds with carry level		
greater than 20%	4	0
equal to 20%	89	144
less than 20%	1	0
% of funds requiring return of fees before carry	93.6%	83.3%
% of funds with hurdle return	44.7%	92.4%
# of funds with hurdle level		
greater than 8%	5	18
equal to 8%	28	104
less than 8%	7	11

Source: Metrick, A. and Yasuda, A., "The Economics of Private Equity Funds", *Review of Financial Studies*, Vol. 23, 2009, pp. 2303–2341

In a landmark study, Metrick and Yasuda (2009)[20] analyse the fees in the private equity industry, for 238 venture capital funds and 144 buyout funds, between 1993 and 2006.

The median buyout fund in their sample has $600 million in committed capital, five partners and thirteen professionals, although the variance is not insignificant. **Exhibit 2.10** shows the management fees typically chosen by buyout funds (Panel A): the most common level is 2%, although most funds give concessions to LPs after the investment period is over, by switching to invested capital basis (84% of buyout funds), by lowering the fee level (45% of buyout funds), or by doing both (39% of buyout funds).

In the sample they use, all buyout funds use a carry of 20% (Panel B), and a large majority use a hurdle rate (92.4%), typically amounting to 8%.

General partner interest

To provide a stronger alignment of interest, GPs might be asked to have "skin in the game" and become a significant investor in their own funds. Investments by GPs typically vary between 1% and 5% of the total capital raised, and sometimes much more. For example, Bain Capital, one of the most successful private equity firms, and one that belongs to the exclusive club of GPs with 30% carry, ensures that its GPs are also the largest LPs in its own funds. This "double dipping", as significant LPs and 30%-carry GPs, undoubtedly increases the performance incentives of GPs, and signals to the LP base a commitment to high performance.

STRESS-TESTING THE ALIGNMENT OF INTERESTS: WHEN SUCCESS BREEDS... PROBLEMS The rationale for the combination of fixed and performance-based compensation was strong and seemed to work well under normal conditions. The management fee was meant to cover the fixed costs of operating a fund, while the carried interest and GP interest offered strong incentives to perform.

However, the increase in average fund sizes, combined with the decrease in fund performances observed in the last few years, have dealt a potentially serious blow to the alignment of interests. In practice, the fixed management fee has become a more significant component of compensation, if not the only one. Even at the bottom of the fee range, a 1% management fee on a $10 billion fund generates a princely $100 million a year. Given the fact that a GP in this size bracket will be managing a series of funds concurrently, perhaps as many as four, the sums involved are extremely generous, regardless of performance. The original fee structure was created for venture capital funds of $100–200 million.

---

[20] Metrick, A. and Yasuda, A., "The Economics of Private Equity Funds", *Review of Financial Studies*, Vol. 23, 2009, pp. 2303–2341.

Exhibit 2.11 When fund sizes wreak havoc in incentive structures: revenue estimates for a sample of 144 buyout funds

	Mean	Median
Carry per $100	$5.41	$5.35
Variable revenue per $100	$7.54	$7.46
Management fees per $100	$10.35	$10.34
Fixed revenue per $100	$12.22	$11.78
Total revenue per $100	$19.76	$19.36

Source: Metrick, A. and Yasuda, A., "The Economics of Private Equity Funds", *Review of Financial Studies*, Vol. 23, 2009, pp. 2303–2341

Buyout funds, however, have proven to be much more scalable and have grown enormously in size. Management fees have fallen somewhat in percentage terms on the largest funds, but they have not fallen very far in comparison to the fund sizes.

In a landmark study, Andrew Metrick and Ayako Yasuda[21] put their finger on the real scale of the problem. Using both empirical evidence from actual funds and simulations, they highlighted that for a standardized revenue generated from investment of $100, on average $7.54 would accrue to GPs in the form of variable revenue (mostly in the form of carried interest + monitoring and exit transaction fees charged to the portfolio companies) and $12.22 would take the form of fixed revenues over the life of the fund (in the form of management fees + entry transactions fees charged to portfolio companies), for a mean total revenue to the GP of about $19.76 per $100 of value created (see **Exhibit 2.11**).

In percentage terms, and based on the current arrangements in terms of management fees and carries, roughly 38% of the GP revenues would accrue in the form of performance-related components and 62% in the form of mostly fixed components: definitely not a sustainable mix between fixed and variable components. And while management fees increase with size, relative internal costs decrease significantly (see **Exhibit 2.12**).

Another potential perverse effect of that incentive structure is the encouragement it provides to firms to complete larger and larger deals. If a company is bought for $10 million and sold for $30 million, the capital gain would be $20 million, or 200%, and the carried interest would be $4 million (20% of $20 million), ignoring all other fee deductions. When transactions are larger, the absolute amount of carry increases even when returns, in percentage or

---

[21] Metrick, A. and Yasuda, A., "The Economics of Private Equity Funds", *Review of Financial Studies*, Vol. 23, 2009, pp. 2303–2341.

Exhibit 2.12 Average number of employees by firm assets under management as of December 31, 2013

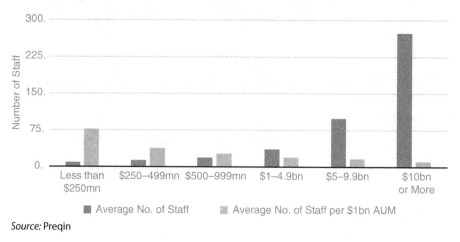

Source: Preqin

multiple terms, are lower. For example, if a company is bought for $1 billion and sold for $1.5 billion, then the capital gain is $500 million, or 50%. Assuming the same hurdle, the GP would receive 20% of $500 million—or a whopping $100 million. According to a study by management consulting firm McKinsey, 40% of the equity capital that private equity firms invested from 2004 to 2007 financed 55 megadeals, representing only 2% of all private equity deals.[22]

In 2002, David Swensen, chief investment officer of the Yale Endowment, told EVCA's International Investor Conference that the firm was considering cutting its target allotment for private equity from 25% to 16–17% (although Yale subsequently increased its allocation considerably). The bursting of the technology bubble certainly played a part in the reduction, but Swensen singled out fee structures for a special mention:

> *"Carry should work as an incentive to getting good returns, and profit incentives should only kick in when those good returns come in. There should be a recognition that there is an opportunity cost in investors providing capital to GPs. The industry is moving further away from this. As funds get larger, management fees rather than carried interest are becoming the main source of income for GPs. Instead of going out and doing the best possible job of finding the best investments, the temptation is to collect safe deals."*

---

[22] Kehoe, C. and Palter, R., "The future of private equity", *McKinsey Perspectives on Corporate Finance and Strategy*, Spring 2009, Number 31.

The industry as a whole has acknowledged the fact that the very structure of the largest funds is failing to properly align the interests of fund managers and investors. Jon Moulton, founder of private equity firm Alchemy Partners, put it in very simple words:

> *"The alignment-of-interest difficulties are that fees are relatively high, which can mean that the manager does pretty bloody well even if the investor really does not. I am genuinely surprised at the lack of diversity in funding structures. Why has nobody ever appeared in the market place with the equivalent of a discount mutual fund?"*

MONITORING, TRANSACTION AND ADVISORY FEES: WHERE REASON FAILED...
Over time, other fees have crept into the private equity system, including monitoring, transactions and advisory fees for portfolio companies. These fees became the focus of much attention, with few people supporting the idea of transaction fees—other than the GP receiving them, of course. Rhoddy Swire, founder of Pantheon Ventures, one of the longest-established fund-of-funds managers, did not mince his words:

> *"Transactions fees are what you pay the management fee for. Worse are the funds that are charging the underlying company M&A fees as well. That is just unacceptable in my opinion."*

Even though it must be said that quite often these revenues generated by the GPs in the normal course of business are often deducted from the LP management fees, there is indeed something fundamentally unsavoury with the "double billing" implicit in those arrangements. Large investors—notably pension funds—regularly make headlines when choosing to circumvent traditional private equity funds to make their own direct investments in companies, generally out of frustration with the high level of fees paid to GPs and the amount of time spent by GPs fundraising for their next fund.[23, 24]

These transactions fees grew in usage during the 1990s and 2000s, reflecting the shifting balance of power in the GP–LP relationship in favour of the GP as LPs desperately tried to access funds. The financial crisis of 2007–2008 and its consequent substantial losses on their 2005–2007 vintage funds seems to have started a natural rebalancing of power towards LPs, and transaction fees could find themselves consigned to the dustbin of history.

Commitments versus investments

A second characteristic inherent to private equity funds is that they will only invest their total commitments over a period of years, i.e. fund managers do not call LPs' commitments upfront but instead draw them down progressively as they identify investment opportunities. This improves the reported cash-on-cash rates of return, since those rates are calculated on the money effectively at work at any point in time, not on the investors' commitments.

This can frustrate investors wanting to optimize their cash management. It also generated an acrimonious debate as to whether returns should be measured on invested or on committed capital. The higher an investor's relative allocation to private equity the more critical this becomes with commitments that can be called on short notice (15–90 days) at any point during the investment period. The effect of this widely accepted industry practice is to push the difficulties of cash flow management to investors, while the private equity funds measure only the returns on the invested money.

Sophisticated investors have developed strategies to manage this uncalled capital, estimating more or less accurately when the capital is likely to be called, temporarily placing at least some of that money into higher-yielding, liquid investments. However, when private equity represents a large proportion of the portfolio, or 100% as is the case for funds-of-funds, the issue becomes much more critical. (Listed) funds-of-funds have responded with over-commitment strategies to increase the returns on the capital entrusted to them, committing more capital

---

[23] *Business Week*, "The Pension Fund Beating Private Equity", February 2010.

[24] *Financial Times*, "Sceptical Investors Taking the More Direct Route", July 2010.

to funds than they really have, in the expectation that 1) not all commitments will be called and 2) that early distributions will offset future capital calls. In normal times this strategy proved quite effective, but it turned disastrous when exits dried up, leaving the funds-of-funds unable to meet their commitments. A number of listed funds, including some managed by SVG Capital and Pantheon Ventures, ran into problems in 2008–2009 for this reason.

Distributions in cash, please!

One of private equity's great disciplines is the obligation to give money back to investors upon the realization of exits. Private equity performance is measured on IRRs and on multiples; giving cash back fast thus helps IRRs enormously. The combination of calling the cash only when needed and paying out realizations as fast as possible, of course, optimizes the reported return on capital employed. Distributions are made when investments are sold to strategic/trade buyers or financial investors, listed or refinanced. When debt is easy and cheap, re-financing LBOs can also be attractive to return (part of) an investment to investors. There is always much talk about IPOs, as these happen when stock markets and investor sentiment are at a high. Clearly, investors have a preference for cash distributions, as opposed to distribution in shares (also known as distribution in kind).

A trade sale is often the simplest to effect, with proceeds returned straight to investors. Part of the proceeds may be held back because of guarantees to the buyer, but a significant part will go directly into investors' pockets. However, if an exit takes the form of shares, like in an IPO or in a trade sale paid for in shares, things can become more complicated. A large fund-of-fund manager once remarked at a conference "… and don't you dare distribute us shares!" Most funds reserve the right to choose their distribution policy. These flexible distribution policies enable fund managers to count (for IRR calculation purposes) these distributions of shares at their estimated values at the distribution date, even though there may be elements preventing an actual realization, such as low liquidity or absence of a market for the shares (in the case of the restricted shares common in venture capital). There are many reasons for GPs to consider distributing securities back to the LPs instead of cash—and, of course, just as many reasons why LPs do not appreciate the practice! Let us review the arguments succinctly in the context of an investee company introduced via an initial public offering (IPO) to an American stock exchange[25]:

[25] Leleux, B., "Note on distribution strategies of venture capital firms", IMD technical note GM-1120, 2002.

SEC restrictions: Even after the lock-up agreement (the period when an existing shareholder is not allowed to sell shares after an IPO, usually six months) expires, the private equity firm usually cannot sell most of its stock. This is because it is considered an insider, and the SEC restricts insider sales. Private equity firms typically hold large portions of a firm's equity, so liquidations can take a long time. If stock is distributed directly to the LPs, the latter will not be subject to the SEC restrictions: they are usually not considered insiders because they do not play an active role in the management of the firms and have only a small stake in the company. Therefore, LPs are able to sell their shares immediately, whereas the private equity fund cannot.

Price effects: The sale of a large block of shares at or immediately after an IPO may have a negative effect on price, due to the downward pressure caused by the stock sale and due to the implications of an insider selling a significant position. The decrease in stock price could affect not only the selling shareholders but also the remaining shareholders and the private equity fund's reputation. This is another reason why funds prefer not to sell the shares.

Effects on reported returns: Private equity funds are very concerned by the IRR figures they generate, as these returns impact their ability to raise money in the future. If stock is distributed instead of cash, it can provide a fund with the ability to claim higher "stated returns". In fact, the sale is booked at the closing price on the date of share distribution, without the potentially depressing impact of actually selling the shares. Thus, a stock distribution often creates a higher stated return even though the investor's eventual selling price and actual return may be lower.

Compensation issues: By not selling shares and instead distributing them directly to investors, the stock price is likely to remain higher, indirectly increasing the return on invested capital. This tends to accelerate the repayment of invested capital, allowing the GP to reach sooner the point where he shares in the profits of the fund through the carried interest.[26]

Investors generally don't appreciate stock distributions. Many argue that a private equity fund chooses a stock distribution for its own benefit, not for the benefit of the LPs. Clearly, increased compensation and higher sale prices received by the funds when distributing securities support this claim. Stock distributions are at times seen as detrimental by LPs: first, they cause a substantial administrative burden in record keeping and tax calculations; second, these distributions come with little notice and insufficient information on the portfolio company itself.

---

[26] Gompers, P. and Lerner, J., "Venture Capital Distributions: Short-Run and Long-Run Reactions", Working Paper. Harvard Business School, May 1997: 4–7.

Furthermore, the GP avoids giving any advice as to whether the stock should be held or sold, for fear of being identified as an investment advisor. Typically, LPs have three ways in which they can deal with these distributions. The first is to liquidate shares immediately upon receipt. The second is to let internal analysts review the company and then make a sell or hold decision. And the third is to send the stock to an independent financial intermediary or stock distribution manager who makes decisions on whether to sell or hold.[27]

Due diligence, leverage, focus and... incentives

GPs are picky shoppers. It is not unusual to sift through a hundred potential investments just to make one. Investments are only made after detailed due diligence, excruciatingly detailed contracts and intensive governance. Private equity firms try to identify under-performing companies, i.e. assets they believe they can manage more effectively. Such under-performers can be, for example, corporate orphans, i.e. small parts of larger groups which do not fit well and hence do not receive sufficient attention and resources to thrive. Or they can be family owned businesses, where the entrepreneur has no obvious succession and has skimped on investment and new initiatives. Buyout funds often look for mature businesses in relatively unexciting niche markets, where things are not likely to change much or too fast.

How the private equity fund actually creates, delivers and captures value will be discussed in detail in Chapter 3, but we review below the main value drivers:

- Superior information, through extensive due diligence and excellent relationships with management;
- Active ownership as a very significant (often majority) shareholder;
- Financial leverage to amplify returns;
- Strong alignment of interests between the GP and portfolio companies' management.

Later in the chapter, we will take a detailed look at a private equity transaction— the $325 million acquisition of Italian motorcycle manufacturer Ducati in 1996, taking the story from the company's origins through multiple owners to near collapse, rescue, turnaround through an IPO and on to a successful exit. It is a story that combines many of the issues that arise during the life of a private equity transaction (although seldom all in one transaction) and shows how value is created and sustainable businesses are built.

---

[27] Lerner, J., "A Note on Distributions of Venture Investments", Harvard Business School, January 10, 1995: 3–4.

Superior information

Private equity firms conduct extensive due diligence on the companies they invest in. They have access to high level financial and other corporate information and will insist on spending as much time with management as possible. This level of due diligence is considerably higher than usually conducted by corporate or public investors.

Active ownership

Private equity brings focus. Focus in turn brings attention and support, and a dedicated push towards performance. Management will set very specific goals and will be handsomely rewarded if these goals are met or exceeded. Private equity investors treat each investment as "special"; they start with a clear plan to improve a company so that it will be worth significantly more five years later. The firm becomes the focal unit of attention. Compared to publicly listed companies private equity brings a long-term view to the scene. This longer time horizon is welcomed by many companies and by their management, allowing more aggressive transformations albeit at the cost of early cash flows. Similarly, aggressive short-term plans are often drawn up, sometimes referred to as "100-day plans"—extensive to do lists for the period immediately after the transaction.

With increasing competition and a generally tougher economic environment, private equity is working its companies harder. Larger firms have specialized operating teams and even smaller groups now routinely seek specialist help to make their investments better operators.

The industry usually prefers sectors and companies, which do not need a very heavy asset base. It will also try to reduce working capital needs and may generally focus on that part of the assets that generates the highest return. Real estate may be sold off and leased back, to focus on investments and activities yielding the highest returns.

Supporters of private equity argue that this direct form of active ownership leads to better management practices within portfolio firms and higher productivity growth. A study of 4,000 manufacturing firms in the US, Europe and Asia by Nicholas Bloom *et al.* found that private equity-owned firms had better management practices than any other form of corporate ownership.[28] A study by Anuradha Gurung and Josh Lerner of US manufacturing firms demonstrated that private equity-owned firms' productivity was two percentage points higher than non-private equity-owned companies, with more than 70% of the improvement being attributable to better management of existing facilities.[29]

---

[28] Bloom, N., *et al.*, "Do private equity-owned firms have better management practices?", The Global Economic Impact of Private Equity Report 2009.

[29] Gurung, A. and Lerner, J., "Private equity, jobs and productivity", The Global Impact of Private Equity Report 2009.

Financial leverage

Private equity's leveraged buyouts rely aggressively on leverage, because they can borrow money. The underlying companies tend to be profitable and stable. Leverage (borrowing money) will typically amplify returns... and precipitate losses. Because debt is an essential piece of the private equity structure, GPs go to great lengths to nurture relationships with bankers, providing them with generous sourcing fees and a stream of business. In return, banks offer preferential treatment with terms unavailable to many listed companies, and what can be seen as a volume discount.[30] It is thus very often the quality of the relationship with bankers that differentiates one private equity fund from another, with recent studies suggesting that buyouts sponsored by the most reputable private equity groups allegedly benefit from better loan terms, such as lower spreads and longer maturities (see Chapter 3 for a discussion).[31]

More controversially, lenders have often been accused of willingly forfeiting some standard protective covenants (conditions) by providing loans with significant holidays on principal repayments, or loans that are covenant light, or even loans where "payment in kind" provisions provide for interest to capitalize and then convert to equity. This has especially been the case during boom years, when leverage reached very high levels because of intense competition between lenders flushed with money.

Alignment of interests

Private equity injects management talent and offers supersized performance incentives. Well-structured incentives closely align the objectives of the portfolio company management and those of the GP. Managers in private equity-backed companies are typically paid a relatively low wage and have few perks. They are also encouraged to invest their own money, a meaningful amount, which would be painful to lose. If management is successful, it will take home may times their original investment and become seriously wealthy.

Overall, the private equity model has—again—much to commend it, particularly for companies that are undergoing periods of change, whether internally or because of changing market dynamics. In a widely quoted 1989 paper, "The eclipse of the public corporation", Michael Jensen argued that the LBO could become the dominant form of corporate ownership because of its emphasis on corporate

---

[30] Nicholls, L.B., "Private Equity: Pirates or Saviors?", The Conference Board, Executive Action Series No. 249, September 2007.

[31] Demiroglu, C. and James, C.M., "The role of private equity group reputation in LBO financing", *Journal of Financial Economics*, Vol. 96, no. 2, May 2010.

governance, concentrated ownership by active owners, strong managerial incentives and efficient capital structure—a model far superior to the public corporation model, with its dispersed shareholders and weak governance.[32] Jensen's prediction may have been a little premature and extreme, but no one can refute the claim that incentives in private equity-backed companies are better aligned with performance than in public companies, where the CEO compensation tends to be more closely correlated with company size and less with shareholder return, where generous severance packages exist, and where the compensation of non-executive directors is usually a flat fee irrespective of performance.

Mitigating possible conflicts of interest

If things go well private equity is a well-oiled machine channelling capital from LPs to interesting companies and entrepreneurs. To do this, and maximize value creation, the system relies on a sophisticated set of incentives described above that seek to align interests between all its stakeholders.

Conflicts of interest may occur, however, at different stages of the LP–GP relationship (see **Exhibit 2.13**):

Fund size: As we have seen above, a GP benefits from increases in fund size, so as to pocket a larger management fee. This poses a significant conflict of interest because the chosen fund size might not be optimal given availability of good investment opportunities. Furthermore, as we noted earlier, GPs might not put in the same level of effort when the fund is very large and management fees are lavish. GPs, aware of this, will usually put in a so-called "Hard Cap" at which they limit the fund size.

Investments by the GP: We have seen earlier that GPs are encouraged to become LPs themselves, and invest in the fund they do manage, and even co-invest alongside the fund, further aligning incentives. However, conflicts of interest might arise if the GP is allowed to cherry pick which investments he makes, and as a result alter his investment decisions for the fund he manages. Investors avoid this situation by stipulating in advance the conditions under which co-investments are made: generally, pro rata participation in all deals *pari passu* with fund investors, while co-investments on a deal-by-deal basis are typically not allowed.[33]

---

[32] Jensen, M., "The eclipse of the public corporation", *Harvard Business Review*, 1989 (revised 1997).

[33] See IOSCO, "Private Equity Conflicts of Interest", Technical Committee of the International Organization of Securities Commissions, November 2009.

Overlapping funds: Managers are generally not allowed to raise or to invest in a new fund with an overlapping strategy until the current fund has invested a predetermined amount of its committed capital (typically between 75% and 90%).[34] Beyond that threshold, however, two similar funds can be managed concurrently by the same manager, paving the way for possible conflicts of interest. If a follow-on investment is made in a company held in the portfolio of the first fund, can the new fund participate—even if it means that one investor group gains more than the other?[35] The situation becomes even more complex if the follow-on investment is used to rescue an investment held in the preceding fund.

Risk level: The compensation structure, and in particular carried interest, ensures that incentives are well aligned since the manager typically receives around 20% of the upside. However, the GP might be incentivized to take on excess risk, as it is also a free option.

Risk-taking is affected by the way the carried interest is structured. One might expect to see more risk-taking activities in a *deal-by-deal* carry system, where the carried interest is payable if the rate of return for an individual deal exceeds the hurdle rate or preferred return. Good deals are rewarded, while bad deals are not penalized. By contrast, in a *fund-as-a-whole* scheme, overall performance with any previous loss is taken into account.[36]

Exhibit 2.13   Relative importance of value drivers

	LP	GP
Size of investments	0	+++
Ability to buy low	++	++
Multiple expansion	++	++
De-leveraging	+	+
Operational improvement	+++	+++

[34] Ibid.

[35] Mueller, K., "Investing in Private Equity Partnerships: The Role of Monitoring and Reporting", Gabler, 2008.

[36] Ibid.

Illiquidity… and new ways to cope with it

Private equity is a long-term asset, and investors who choose to invest in a fund are expected to remain LPs for the full duration of the fund and honour all commitments. But 10 years is a long time...

Secondaries market

A secondary market has emerged to provide investors with some form of liquidity. Reasons for exiting early are varied: liquidity needs, fund underperformance, portfolio rebalancing, re-focus on core assets and more recently compliance with government regulations such as the Volcker Rule and Basel III all contribute to increasing supply.[37] The development of the secondary market could be one of the most important structural changes in the industry, although there are still today significant challenges that limit the attractiveness of this new market among LPs:

- Offers to buy commitments are usually available for significant portfolios, not smaller, single-fund commitments. Some large, diversified portfolios can remain difficult to exit at once.

---

[37] "Preqin Special Report: Secondary Market Outlook", Preqin, March 2011.

- The interim valuation of the fund is very difficult to estimate because neither the fund nor its investments are actively traded. Investors who wish to sell their stake heavily rely on the GP to ascribe a value to its investments.
- The cost of the provision of liquidity can be high, often private equity fund positions are traded at 20% discounts or more. Pricing depends very much, like anywhere else, on supply and demand. In situations with much demand and little supply premiums rather than discounts are even paid.
- And finally, the GP retains the ultimate right to accept the transfer of the commitments.

The secondary market is, however, becoming more sophisticated. Increased competition and the emergence of a cadre of intermediaries are redefining how the market functions. It is, for example, becoming much more common for LPs' portfolios to be broken up into more manageable parcels and sold to the most appropriate bidder. Moreover, one might assume that demand on the secondary market does not only come from cash-constrained LPs but also from LPs wishing to diversify their portfolios by vintage years or by fund type and geography, from LPs wishing to gain access to a previously oversubscribed top-tier fund or from LPs simply looking opportunistically for good deals.[38]

Like the primary market, the secondary market is driven by supply and demand factors, which shift in time during market cycles. During the boom years of 2006–2007, many LPs were able to sell positions to secondary investors at a premium. When the market turned, sellers were forced to accept very heavy discounts to liquidate their positions, selling at a price of less than 40% of net asset value in the first half of 2009, according to Cogent Partners, a secondary market advisor.[39] **Exhibit 2.14** depicts the evolution of secondary pricing and transaction volume. One year later, that price has gone up, to almost 90% of net asset value, and 95% by mid-2011—levels last seen before the financial crisis.[40] In October 2010, the *Financial Times* reported that three of Europe's biggest investors in the buyout and venture capital secondary market were raising almost $12 billion to launch secondary funds, anticipating that banks and financial institutions would be willing to sell a significant share of commitments made during the 2005–2007 boom, now that discounts had fallen.[41]

---

[38] Global Private Equity Report, Preqin, 2013.

[39] *Financial Times*, "Investors seek $12bn to grab private equity assets", October 7, 2010.

[40] *Financial Times*, "Private equity secondaries", May 26, 2011.

[41] *Financial Times*, "Investors seek $12bn to grab private equity assets", October 7, 2010.

Exhibit 2.14 Private equity secondary market: pricings and global transaction volume

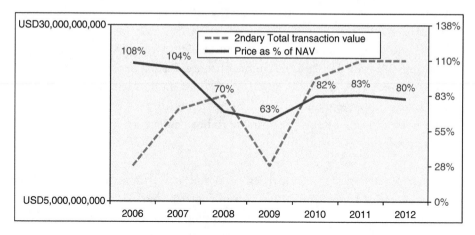

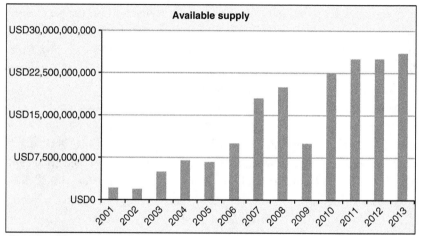

Sources: Graphs created by authors on the basis of data derived from Cogent Partners and Capital Dynamics

The strong growth of the secondary market means that private equity has become more liquid. There may, of course, be a substantial financial penalty for doing so, particularly if the vendor is a forced seller, but this is not dissimilar to other asset classes, including public equities, when an investor is forced to accept a discount when having to sell a large block of shares in a particular stock.

Publicly listed private equity vehicles

Investors wishing to keep their investment fully liquid or smaller investors wishing to get exposure to the private equity asset class but unable to access traditional private equity limited partnerships are still able to invest in the industry through publicly-traded vehicles on the stock exchange. These can take the form of listed funds that are traded daily, with a net asset value that typically follows trends similar to those of unlisted private equity partnerships.[42] The financial crisis severely affected those vehicles that were traded at heavy discounts to net asset values throughout 2008 and the beginning of 2009, although discounts have since been largely reduced. Investments in listed funds-of-funds do, however, offer investors significant advantages: liquidity since the funds are traded daily, accessibility since the minimum entry ticket is one share and diversification across vintage years and regions. They are, however, fairly expensive.

An alternative to purchasing shares in a listed fund is to purchase shares in a listed private equity firm. By being a shareholder in the management company, instead of in just one fund, this allows an investor to get a share of the management fees and carried interest earned by the investment team of the private equity firm. As mentioned in Chapter 1, the IPO of Blackstone in 2007, the first in the private equity industry, attracted significant scrutiny to an otherwise discreet industry, allowing the public to witness for the first time the amount of money that partners were pocketing. We will cover some of these public firms in Chapter 5.

Case Study 6
Texas Pacific Group (TPG) and Ducati

If a private equity deal ever attracted the popular press's attention, and had all the hallmarks of a *Comedia dell'arte*, then the 1996 acquisition of Italian motorcycle manufacturer Ducati by Texas Pacific Group (TPG), the Fort Worth-based global private equity firm, would be that deal.

As a story, it had it all: a product that had won more acclaim in motorcycle racing than any other; a world-leading brand and reputation equivalent only to that of Ferrari in automobiles; a complex ownership structure and "colourful" Italian family shareholders; a history of poor management; muddled and incomplete financial information; and the financial rectitude of the Pisa tower. The story also featured one of the most successful private equity firms, straight out of Texas, with a reputation earned in the US on major deals such as Continental Airlines. The clash of cultures, both at the negotiating table and on the shop floor, was bound to spark a pyrotechnical masterwork. Ducati, which belonged to the cash-flow constrained Cagiva Group, was facing massive waiting lists and deteriorating product reliability. Ducati was producing the most exceptional racing machines… yet it was in dire need of a comprehensive turnaround, from product to assembly, distribution, marketing and sales.

---

[42] Preqin Research Report, September 2010.

In the beginning

A bit of history is crucial to understand how the company came to be in the situation it found itself in 1996. In 1926, Antonio Cavalieri Ducati and his three sons, Adriano, Bruno and Marcello, with support from other local investors, founded Società Radio Brevetti Ducati, a radio and electrical components business, just outside Bologna in northern Italy. The business prospered and grew to become the second-largest manufacturing company in Italy, with offices and branches in London, Paris, New York, Sydney and Caracas, and more than 7,000 employees worldwide. In fact, during the 1930s, it was really Mr Siemens and Mr Ducati who ruled the world of consumer electrics. When the Second World War broke, Ducati supplied materials to the Italian army, a business it paid for dearly as the Bologna factory was leveled to the ground in 1944 by a bombing offensive of the Allied forces.[43]

After the war, the Italian government took over Ducati via the state holding company tasked with rebuilding the economy. In 1946, the company made its first foray into motorcycles, bolting a 48cc, four-stroke engine known as Il Cucciolo ("the puppy") onto a bicycle. It was fast, cheap and economical and within a year it had a 50% share of the motor scooter market in Italy. It developed increasingly fast bikes throughout the 1960s and 1970s, building up a racing pedigree and a tremendous reputation on the racetracks.

In 1983, the state holding company sold its shareholding to the Cagiva Group, a diversified Italian conglomerate controlled by Claudio and Gianfranco Castiglioni, two brothers who shared an enthusiasm for motorbikes. Cagiva also manufactured small motorcycles, and the new entity married Ducati's expertise in engine design with Cagiva's superior frame technology. But the early 1990s proved difficult for Ducati. Cagiva was a typical Italian, family-owned conglomerate, with interests ranging from motorcycles to metal stamping and hotels. Like most of its peers, it was structured in a most complex manner to minimize tax liabilities making it virtually impossible for anyone to get a clear picture of the health of the group or its real profitability.

Excessive leverage and poor financial controls placed a great strain on Ducati, with many in the industry believing that Ducati was being used primarily to subsidize loss-making operations elsewhere in the group. Ducati relied on Cagiva for product design, information systems, human resources, advertising and distribution. As a result of financial problems at its parent, Ducati's operations began to falter. Quality deteriorated, warranty costs increased and problems paying suppliers led to considerable delays in delivery. Waiting times for new

---

[43] www.ducati.com/heritage.

machines soared to more than a year. Problems came to a head in the mid-1990s, when Ducati's performance—by almost any metric—nosedived. From 1995 to 1996, motorbike sales fell 32.7%, earnings before interest, taxes, depreciation and amortization (EBITDA) dropped 58%, and market share fell from 4.5% to around 3%.[44]

The motorcycle market

As with the car industry, the 1970s saw Japanese manufacturers master the mass production of cheap, reliable motorcycles, with the likes of Honda, Suzuki, Yamaha and Kawasaki capturing market share from the established European manufacturers such as BSA, Enfield, Norton, Agusta, Laverda, Moto Guzzi and Triumph. By 1995, the big four Japanese manufacturers were all producing motorcycles in each of the large categories, as well as smaller transport-orientated machines, with market shares between 70% and 88%. Among the "old world" manufacturers, Ducati was the clear leader. And despite the emerging quality issues, Ducati customers were extremely loyal, and paying a price premium over other brands. The typical customer was between 25 and 35, with at least 30% owning more than one machine. In Italy, 64% of customers said they would purchase another Ducati.

A fine mess

Ducati was closely tied into the labyrinthine structure of its parent company, the Cagiva Group, which was in control of its finance and administrative functions, in addition to its product design, information systems, human resources, advertising and distribution. Despite capturing market share and improving profitability, Ducati saw its accounts payable stand at €20.7 million and debt at €93.8 million by the end of 1995. By then many suppliers were refusing to deliver, and the shortage of components slowed production which soon fell from 140 bikes a day to only ten. Ducati had more than 6,000 outstanding orders and customers had to wait for more than a year to receive their order, compared to only six months at Harley Davidson.

Marketing would have been described as poor, if there had been any. Ducati had no marketing department and sold its motorcycles through Cagiva Trading and its network of non-exclusive dealerships, which were not particularly incentivized to sell Ducatis. And whilst Cagiva Trading was charging 70% of its costs to Ducati (€10.5 million), only 54% were actually attributable to Ducati, an example of the murky transfer pricing within the group. Production was

[44] Rebuilding a passion brand: the turnaround of Ducati, IMD, November 2004.

inefficient and the company was still using a block order system, with parts being ordered every four months, in stark contrast to the just-in-time processes adopted by the Japanese.

Riding to the rescue[45]

In the spring of 1995, the Castiglioni brothers approached Dante Razzano, head of Deutsche Morgan Grenfell (DMG) in Italy, to secure a bridge loan. Familiar with private equity, Dante noticed characteristics that could appeal to Texas Pacific Group, a large private equity player now known as TPG Capital. And indeed, TPG quickly saw a brand with development potential. TPG had been founded in 1992 by David Bonderman and Jim Coulter, buyouts veterans and Bill Price, a VP at GE Capital. TPG Group's past investments had included Burger King, J. Crew and Bally and the firm had gained a reputation for spending a lot of time courting deals they wanted. TPG's team was led by Abel Halpern, who teamed up with Federico Minoli to explore the Ducati opportunity. Minoli was a marketing specialist who started his career in brand management at P&G in 1974, then moved to International Playtex, followed by McKinsey & Company and Bain & Company before joining Benetton as CEO of the US subsidiary. The TPG strategy was to install Minoli as CEO and bring on other senior executives to run the company.

It is often said of buyout firms that they walk into a room backwards to see the exit. If the turnaround proved successful, Ducati could be a candidate for an IPO, an exit that could generate a higher return than a sale to a rival. But the Italian stock market was a tricky destination, lacking the depth and liquidity of US markets, and their corporate governance rules.

Negotiations soon started, but the parties had to keep a low profile: the Castiglioni brothers did not want to be seen selling a controlling stake, especially not to Americans. So the transaction was structured to give the impression they were only selling 49% of the business. TPG purchased 49% of the equity, and another 2% would be registered in the name of an independent fiduciary company. Cagiva would retain the remaining 49% plus an option to repurchase the 2% in the event of an IPO. TPG would gain control of the board and in a gesture of goodwill, the eldest brother, Claudio, stayed on as chairman, though his executive powers were limited. Perceptions also play an important role in transactions, particularly when family shareholders are concerned. In the case of Ducati, it was important to come up with a large headline number for the transaction, to give the Castiglionis bragging rights at the country club. Subject

---

[45] Ducati & Texas Pacific Group—A "wild ride" leveraged buyout, Harvard Business School, March 2004.

to due diligence, the purchase price was set to be in the 400–500 million Italian lira bracket. Part of this was paid to Cagiva, but another part went directly to Ducati to compensate for past under-funding. TPG was also concerned about possible bankruptcy of the seller, and the possible "look-back" features of Italian law. To control that unknown, the deal was structured as an asset sale.

The transaction was relatively conservatively structured, with a debt-to-equity ratio of 2:1, compared to the 3:1 benchmark for US buyouts at the time. Razzano at DMG wanted in on the deal, and TPG syndicated 20% of its equity to the firm. Debt finance proved tricky, however: the lack of financial transparency, concerns over working capital levels and the credit risk of the Cagiva Group made banks nervous. Eventually, DMG stepped up to lead the syndication and a 280 million lira senior debt facility with a coupon of 11.25% was arranged. In the summer of 1996, after a tense and fraught negotiation that saw the Italian side returning many times to issues the Americans thought had been closed, a deal was signed for TPG to acquire a stake of the struggling manufacturer for $325 million.

The turnaround plan

With TPG in control of Ducati, the branding and marketing specialist Minoli was installed as CEO. Top of the priority list was a repositioning of the company. The plan was to turn Ducati from a "metal mechanics" company into an entertainment company built around the brand and the passion of its customers. Rationalizing the factory or investing in R&D would come later.

Minoli's first task was to recruit a new management team. David Gross, an international corporate lawyer specializing in M&A, joined the firm to head strategy development. A long time ago, Gross had been a journalist covering popular culture and business for Time and the New York Times magazine, an experience well suited to the repositioning of Ducati as a consumer brand. Pierre Terreblanche, a South African native, was recruited from a design agency that had previously worked with Ducati to head design and engineering. Christiano Silei, a former colleague of Minoli's from Bain who had also worked on the due diligence for the acquisition, came on board to be responsible for product development. The organizational structure was revamped: Ducati wrested full control of finance and administration from the Cagiva Group, and created a sales and distribution division.

"It was difficult to build a new culture in the beginning," recalls Minoli. "I tried to find common ground between my American and Italian staff and then I realized that the passion for Ducati was the glue. The turnaround would only be successful if everyone wanted to be part of it."

He instigated a series of changes, from taking prime parking spots at the factory away from management and giving the spaces to employees who owned Ducati bikes, to sending all employees on motorcycle training courses and offering them weekend use of bikes and discounts on purchases. Ducati extended its market focus, from mainly performance and function, to comfort and lifestyle, segments dominated by the Japanese manufacturers and Harley Davidson. The product range was pushed into the sport touring segment, and the women segment, and into clothing, apparel and accessories through new partnerships.

Every initiative was designed to create a community around the brand and make employees and customers feel a part of the firm. A Ducati museum was built on the main floor of the corporate headquarters to house an enviable collection of famous Ducatis. The poorly performing distribution network was revamped. The dealership structure was changed to place greater emphasis on exclusivity and brand image, sales assistance and after-sales service, resulting in a dramatic increase in the number of units sold by each dealer and in a reduction in the number of dealerships. Wholly-owned subsidiaries filled with more than 250 motorcycle enthusiastic new recruits were set up to manage dealers in the different key countries. A series of flagship stores were opened, and an online sales channel was launched to sell motorcycles over the internet.

Improvements to production processes began with the introduction of the "Kaizen" system in 1997, a Japanese approach to manufacturing whereby improvements are achieved through a series of small, incremental steps—with the involvement and collaboration of workers and no significant investment—and the introduction of just-in-time methods. These led to a 12% increase in machine reliability and a 23% reduction in hourly costs.[46]

The second phase of the turnaround plan began in 1999 with "Operation Turnaround", aimed at more than tripling production volumes over five years without increasing factory floor space or taking on more employees. Non-core activities were outsourced and the supplier base reduced from 380 to just 175. The changes dramatically improved manufacturing efficiency, with production costs down 25%, throughput time shortened by 50% and build quality before delivery increased by 70%, over the next three years.

Phase three of the turnaround involved investing in engine design, resulting in a reduction of product development time from 36 months in 1995 to 15 months in 2003.

---

[46] http://www.oracle.com/us/corporate/press/017273_EN.

The outcome

In July 1998, TPG, DMG, Development Capital Italy and other co-investors bought the Castiglioni's 49% stake, assuming full control of the company. In 1999, Ducati went public on the Italian and New York stock exchanges, raising $285 million. TPG and other investors sold a 65% share, netting a six-fold return on their investment.[47] In March 2006, TPG and DMG achieved a final exit, selling their remaining 30% share to InvestIndustrial Holding, an Italian investment firm. Minoli stepped down as chairman and CEO in May 2007.

The success of the IPO reflected the turnaround of the venerable manufacturer's fortunes. During its period of private equity ownership, Ducati's performance on the race track was spectacular—winning 13 of the 14 World Superbike Championship titles. Global market share increased from 3% in 1996 to 5.6% in 2003, with the number of motorcycles sold increasing at compound annual growth rate of 17.8%.

Financial performance was equally impressive. Net sales increased at an annualized rate of 20.4%, from €105.8 million in 1996 to €388.2 million in 2003. EBITDA went up from €11.8 million to €45.2 million over the same period, a compound annual growth rate of 21.1%.

The successful investment and turnaround of Ducati is a textbook example of what can be achieved under the active ownership and guidance of a private equity firm. Contrary to popular perception, it also shows a relatively long-term approach to the investment. Far from being stripped of its assets (there were effectively none to strip), Ducati saw—under TPG's ownership—increased investment in sales and marketing, branding, advertising, racing, research and development and improvements in production efficiency. TPG turned around an ailing, yet promising company by creating value in its brand, manufacturing and distribution and by improving employee morale.

Source: Case study written by the authors and included with permission from TPG.

---

[47] *Business Week*, October 22, 2001.

3

Value creation in private equity

Executive summary

Private equity firms are choosy shoppers, aggressive value builders and often discreet sellers. So how do they engineer value creation in deals? Is private equity contributing to public wealth or simply transferring money across different owner groups? Are they barons or villains, as the popular press often likes to depict them?

In this chapter, we take a micro perspective and try to understand how private equity firms engineer value creation in their target companies. Principally, they operate jointly four key value levers. First and foremost, private equity investors seek to improve the bottom line, i.e. they create solid operational value. They bring focus to the target firm, a long-term investment approach, a creative asset usage review and clear priorities and goals. Strong incentive schemes are activated, including a strong participation in the equity by the company management team, complemented by very strong performance-linked bonuses to attract and reward talent and operational expertise. Second, private equity investors endeavour to change the growth profile of the target company. By creating higher growth expectations for the firm, they seek to earn a higher valuation multiple from the market. Third, even if the intrinsic growth profile of the firm cannot be affected, by timing purchases to occur during low periods in the economic cycle and sales in higher periods, investors hope to benefit from the general industry sentiment, also reflected in higher multiples in general. This approach is sometimes referred to as "surfing the cycle". Finally, bank debt is used aggressively both as a tax-privileged source of financing, as leverage on the equity investments but also as a disciplining device, through the heavy supervision brought by the banks, through the covenants on the debt. To illustrate how value creation works in practice, we look at some of the best deals the industry has produced.

On average, private equity firms hold LBO investments for four to six years, though holding periods have been getting longer. Private equity funds are clearly "buy-to-sell" investors, not "buy-to-hold"; this discipline helps focus all parties on the creation of shareholder value during the relatively short holding period.

In Chapter 2, we explored the private equity industry's inner workings, and tried to understand how it achieved a better alignment of interests between LPs, GPs and portfolio companies. Such alignment between stakeholders creates the best environment for sustainable value creation. In this chapter, we look at private equity firms through the prism of the GPs to understand how value is effectively created in portfolio companies.

The art of private equity

It has often been argued that private equity flourishes on market inefficiencies, and hence is more akin to an arbitrage play. A lack of information, weak competition for deals, difficult access to management talent or distribution channels, illiquidity and inefficient capital markets all collude to create conditions that can be exploited by successful fund managers. The prevailing logic is that these conditions allow private equity investors to pick assets on the cheap and on borrowed money, give them a quick polish and then sell them on to a new buyer, usually a strategic trade investor, at a higher multiple.

The industry has not always produced successful deals, of course. Many deals failed, and the list of reasons for failure is long. One of the leading drivers of failure is the lack of experience of GPs. First-time funds tend to underperform, as shown by Kaplan and Schoar (2005).[1] This happens for many different reasons: inadequate due diligence skills that often lead to the overpayment for a company or the discovery—post-deal—of negative surprises; sudden changes in the market conditions; lack of experience in adding value or limited scope to do so; limited number of hands-on management experts in a fund's network; difficulties in engineering successful exits. Failure also occurs when the company acquired needs to be heavily restructured. Restructurings are expensive, time consuming and unpredictable, and often fail to deliver to satisfaction. In effect, it has been said that the private equity model is generally more appropriate for companies that need small operational and strategic changes, than for major shake-ups. Finally, as in many investment classes, timing does play a key role in the ultimate return. Investments done during boom times, when too much capital is chasing too few deals, tend to generate lower returns. But few managers have the discipline to abstain from investing during periods of exuberant enthusiasm because of pressure from LPs to put their money at work.

Realistically, the corporate world is operating relatively efficiently today. The number of firms that can actually benefit from "dramatic" improvements

---

[1] Kaplan, S. N. and Schoar, A., "Private Equity Performance: Returns, Persistence, & Capital Flows", *Journal of Finance*, Vol. 60, no. 4, 2005.

in operational performance is growing smaller by the day. So, when a private equity firm insists that it invests only in "world-leading companies with world-class management", one has to wonder how it intends to dramatically improve their performance...

Behind the generic recipes, and the public relation rhetoric, it is interesting to look at a number of successful private equity investments to understand how these value creation elements played out. Like a well-oiled orchestra, private equity investors know how to capture the best sound out of the instruments available, not hesitating at times to deviate from the partition to get the most out of the situation. Like a good jazz ensemble, the solo pieces come in to highlight the underlying, never changing theme...

We suggest that the theme is intense value creation and unlocking the value hidden in many assets. The case studies below—Argos Soditic and the Kermel management buyout, Tumi and the Doughty Hanson Value Enhancement Group and Blackstone and the Celanese acquisition—all represent situations in which the private equity investors brought in not only financial investment but also deep expertise. The examples cover a number of areas, from growth capital in emerging markets, to consolidation and management buyouts in established industries and markets. We also document the entrepreneurial beginnings of funds by discussing the creation of Tribe Capital Partners and Chrysalis Capital.

Case Study 7
Argos Soditic and the Kermel management buyout

Venkatesh "Ven" Tulluri, a mechanical engineer from the University of Massachusetts, was a Strategy Director for Rhodia's Technical Fibers Division back in 2001. In his position, he provided strategic advice to half a dozen companies. One of them was Kermel, a small outfit in Colmar, in the middle of Alsace (France) occupying a small but profitable niche producing fire-resistant fibers used mostly in protective work-wear.

Rhodia, for its part, was a huge French specialty chemicals company reputed for its R&D and manufacturing competences. Formally part of Rhone Poulenc, it was the world leader in the production of Polyamides, the product commercially known as Nylon. However, in early 2002 Rhodia faced crushing financial problems and looked to spin off Kermel, which accounted for less that 1% of its revenues but did not fit well with Rhodia's long term strategy.

Ven, faced with limited promotion opportunities within the fast retrenching group, started to contemplate alternative opportunities for his career, including the possibility of going entrepreneurial. Kermel actually caught his attention. Its market niche was small but quite exciting, and Ven thought the company would actually do well as a stand-alone, with a strong technology, an experienced management team and good potential for growth in the niche. He realized he could not effect a transaction of this type and size alone: it would require the involvement of a private equity specialist. With no prior experience as a general manager, no personal fortune to finance the deal and no expertise in buyout transactions, he felt the odds were somehow stacked against him. But with some good advice, maybe he could structure a deal that would simply "make sense", i.e. that would be credible and acceptable to investors and sellers alike.

With these concerns in mind he set about to find an investor for his planned MBO. His enthusiasm waned when he received negative feedback from one private investor group after another. While they mostly liked Kermel, they all felt it was way too small to warrant an MBO. With 2001 sales of around €14 million and earnings before interest and taxes (EBIT) around €1.7 million, it was difficult to envision a valuation in excess of €25 million, which would put the deal below the small cap category.

Finally Argos Soditic, a Swiss private equity firm focusing on European small to medium sized deals, agreed to meet Ven and examine the opportunity. Unbeknownst to him Argos, like many other private equity operators in France, had been circling Rhodia for spin-off opportunities, so far to no avail. Ven managed to convince Argos Soditic of the seriousness of his intentions and together with Kermel's management team he convinced Argos to submit a non-binding offer.

For years, Kermel had not received much attention and resources from its mother company; it was just too insignificant to justify investments, which in the end would not impact Rhodia's bottom line. So Kermel lived on, deprived of the resources to aggressively compete and pursue the promising technical fibers applications market. For the investors, the value triggers in the buyout were clear: it would involve the provision of sufficient resources to target more aggressively existing markets for fire-resistant fibers in work-wear and to develop the emerging and promising new applications markets. In parallel, it made sense to also boost R&D and marketing expenditures to ensure the sustainability of these new markets.

Argos Soditic sealed the deal in August 2002. With a selling company under tremendous pressure to divest assets as quickly as possible, the purchase price was at the lower end of the investment bankers' estimates. Ven and the management team were able to turn around the company rapidly, with EBIT jumping from €1.7 million in 2001 to €3.7 million in 2002 and €4.8 million by 2003. This allowed the company to rapidly refinance the shareholders' loans.

2004 was challenging, with the EBIT increasing but still below target and technical applications taking time to catch hold in the market. Despite these developments all parties involved with the deal were extremely satisfied. By 2006, Argos Soditic engineered a leveraged recapitalization, only to execute a full exit through a secondary buyout in April 2007. The investment proved a phenomenal success, generating an IRR for its equity investors well in excess of 80% per annum. The management, still committed to the growth potential of the firm, stayed on, reinvesting a substantial portion of their performance incentives to increase their ownership in the firm to about 25%. For Ven, this was the best of all worlds. Not only was he running a company he truly loved, but he also owned a nice share of it and had been generously rewarded for his, and the management team, interventions to create value.

Source: Case study written by the authors and included with permission from Argos Soditic.

Sourcing deals

To a large extent, private equity firms exist because other forms of owners do not seem to extract the full value potential of a collection of assets, or are not able to implement the rather simple value improvement mechanisms detailed above. It is, therefore, interesting to look at the sources of deals as an early indication of what can be done to improve value.

In its 2010 Buyout Report, EVCA offers an overview of sources of European buyout deals, by amounts invested and by number of companies. Among the main sources of buyout transactions, one finds family and private owners, corporations and private equity firms.[2] In the first category, one often finds founders of high potential companies who seek a new, professional pair of hands to grow the company and expand internationally, as well as aging owners who face challenging generational change. In the latter category, one finds businesses that are sometimes described as "corporate orphans", because they have often been starved of investment and have received little attention from their parent company. Managers within these companies may have ambitious plans or see opportunities to develop the business, but have not been given the go-ahead or the means to capture those opportunities. A buyout can potentially free the business from these constraints, finally enabling the management team to pursue their entrepreneurial ambitions.

Private equity firms represent another important source of deals. Those secondary buyouts—which could disparagingly be referred to as "second-hand

---

[2] 2010 EVCA Buyout Report (October).

"So that's how he does it."

buyouts", where portfolio companies are traded twice or even three times or more between private equity firms—are a growing trend in the industry, because of supply and demand imbalance (too much money chasing too few deals) and the natural maturating of the industry (there are simply more private equity-owned companies in the market).

Secondary buyouts have always attracted a fair bit of scepticism as to how and where value can still be created. As a fund-of-funds manager put it in a recent *Financial Times* article[3]:

> *"I support secondary buyouts that take a company from a clear milestone into a new phase of growth, which may be better pursued by a new owner. But few companies can grow strongly enough to produce private equity-style returns several times in succession."*

If one private equity firm has owned the business and exhausted the standard private equity toolkit of cost-cutting, focus on profitable operations and management incentives, what is left for the new owner? Also, and a very practical consideration, how does one even incentivize the management team now that it is rich with the rewards of the first buyout? The rationale that one private equity firm may guide a company through one stage of its development (such as from a high-growth early-stage company through to a more professionally-managed and institutional business), before another private equity firm steps in and takes the firm to the "next level" (perhaps by expanding overseas or into new markets) is rightfully questionable, if not in its motives but at least in its true value potential…

---

[3] *Financial Times,* "Investors fret over 'pass-the-parcel' deals", November 29, 2010.

IT WON'T WIN THE RACE, BUT IT'S BEEN TESTED BY THREE PREVIOUS EQUITY HOUSES

The other main sources of buyout deals in the EVCA 2010 Buyout Report were:

- capital markets, with public-to-private (PTP) transactions involving an offer for part or all of the share capital of a listed target company;
- institutional owners, where the seller is a financial institution;
- receivership, where the sale is triggered by reorganization procedures to avoid liquidation;
- privatizations of previously state-owned enterprises.[4]

These numbers warrant two comments. First, PTP transactions, where a private equity firm acquires and then de-lists a public company, have attracted much media attention because they often concern high-profile companies (such as the 2013 buyout of Dell by Michael Dell, the Founder, Chairman and CEO and Silver Lake), and because they are the focus of much academic research. They account, however, for just a small share of all buyouts. These transactions are most commonly pursued because management and shareholders feel that the

---

[4] 2010 EVCA Buyout Report (October).

market does not properly value the company in question, thereby restricting the ability to raise funds for growth or acquisitions, while imposing onerous reporting and compliance duties and costs.

Second, the perception that private equity firms have been draining the public markets of firms is also disputed. According to the 2008 WEF survey[5], PTP transactions accounted for 6.7% of all transactions between 1970 and 2007, while the proportion of leveraged buyouts exited via an IPO was 11%, showing a net positive flow of corporate assets into public markets over the long term.

Case Study 8
Chrysalis Capital's entry into India

Venture capital firm Chrysalis Capital was set up by two Harvard graduates, who decided to enter India in 1999 to fill the gap between seed fund investors and established private equity firms in India. Ashish Dhawan and Raj Kondur, both born and raised in India, met at Harvard Business School and, like many Indian students there, shared a yearning to return to India someday. They hit it off quickly and started playing with several ideas for starting a business together. They had many brainstorming sessions and conducted market research on their frequent visits home, and met with industrialists, IT firms and foreign investors. By the end of their MBA they were convinced that the future of IT in India looked very bright and they began to seriously think of setting up a venture capital fund there.

While they toyed with various ideas, nothing concrete happened. Post MBA, Ashish accepted a position with Goldman Sachs' Risk Arbitrage Group and Raj Kondur joined Morgan Stanley's M&A Group. They found their work interesting but India continued to exert a strong pull and they kept thinking of the idea. Finally in October 1998, the duo decided to set up a USD 50 million fund backed by IRR, MDC and Microsoft in India, which would invest in technology and software services companies. In 1999 they left their job, moved to India and started scouting for potential investments. Goldman Sachs supported Dhawan's plan with several senior partners while the CEO invested his personal funds. Microsoft was also a key participant in the fund. Although the partners were looking at a $50 million fund, they closed it at $65 million with Stanford's endowment, 10 technology CEOs and Rajat Gupta, CEO of McKinsey, as investors.

Baazee, which had been founded by two Harvard MBAs and was modelled on eBay, was one of the first investments by Chrysalis Capital. Baazee created an online marketplace where buyers and sellers could buy and sell goods directly

---

[5] The Global Economic Impact of Private Equity Report 2008, World Economic Forum.

without the middleman. Kondur and Dhawan invested $550,000 for a 26.8% stake in Baazee's first round in January 2000 at a post-money valuation of $2 million and helped set up the company since they knew the two founders well. Baazee's acquisition by the highly profitable and global company eBay allowed the latter to get into the nascent Indian online auction market through an existing company, thereby eliminating all costs associated with developing either a local portal or the market as a whole.

Another Chrysalis investment was in Spectramind, a web-enabled Services Company that provides customer relationship management and outsourcing services to multinational firms in all geographies. Dhawan and Kondur convinced Raman Roy, regarded as the leading expert on IT-enabled services in India, to join the team. Roy had previously been the CEO of the outsourcing service centres at both GE Capital and American Express. Spectramind was launched in March 2000 and Chrysalis invested a total of $6.1 million in two rounds for an 83% stake.

Chrysalis Capital today manages $2.5 billion across five funds with investments in Suzlon, the fifth largest energy company in the world, Mphasis, a leading IT services/BPO firm, and Axix Bank, one of the most prominent private banks in India.

Creating value in private equity

Before heading down the specifics of value creation, it seems important to understand the key drivers of value. To do this, the easiest way is to use the classic earnings multiple valuation formula found in corporate finance textbooks. A firm's value is driven by its ability to deliver earnings and cash flows in the future and by its risk profile. The higher the future expected earnings, and the lower the risk embedded in those future earnings streams, the higher the valuation of the company. If V_0 is the present valuation of the firm and $EBIT_0$ its current Earnings before Interest and Taxes, then, according to the formula:

$$V_0 = EBIT_0 \cdot Multiple_0$$

where the multiple is obtained by looking at the multiples applied by the market to 1) "comparable" companies listed in the market or 2) comparable private transactions. With both the prevailing valuations and EBITs visible, it is easy to infer the multiple applied by the market to the firm. In effect, this approach to valuation "borrows" the multiple from the market, under the assumption that the market as a whole tends to be accurate in its assessment of value. That multiple is not an abstract concept: it actually has a base in the firm's realities, in particular its future expected growth and cost of capital, a direct consequence of its perceived risk level. In effect, the "multiple" is the parameter used to discount EBIT in a growing perpetuity, or

$$\text{Multiple}_0 = 1/(k-g)$$

where k is the expected cost of capital for the firm, determined by its level of business and financial risks, and g is the expected growth rate in perpetuity.

With all the pieces in hand, it is easy to understand that value (V_0) can be increased through three distinct channels:

- Operational improvements, i.e. increase EBIT;
- Multiple arbitrage, i.e. increase the multiple that applies to the EBIT;
- Leverage, or financial engineering, i.e. using more bank debt to reduce the cost of capital of the firm and leverage more effectively the equity injected into the deal.

Considering the multiple factors in the formula, value creation in private equity is driven by the ability to play on as many levers at the same time as possible to maximize the overall impact. If one is able to increase by 3 the earnings and by 2 the multiple, one should see a respectable 6× increase on the value of the firm. With adequate leverage, this could lead easily to multiples of 10× or 15× on the invested equity portion.

Operational value

The fundamental proposition in private equity is creating operational value, i.e. generating more earnings per dollar of capital. This implies robust management interventions to optimize every detail of a firm's operations. Private equity investors are known as ferocious corporate finance managers, in particular when it comes to working capital and fixed assets. Clearly though, "squeezing", i.e. reducing working capital below the firm's needs, would be counterproductive. Private equity investors cut unnecessary costs to free up resources.

Private equity also brings a long-term view to the scene, one that is often lacking in public companies, which are subject to continuous scrutiny and quarterly evaluations, and struggling private companies. Thanks to the injection of fresh capital, the private equity firm can focus on value-creating operational improvements, such as the recruitment of talent and the introduction of performance incentives and best practices.

Private equity managers also use this time to scrutinize every aspect of the company to identify potential areas of improvement: cost-cutting opportunities, repositioning of products, new markets expansion, acquisitions candidates and organic growth opportunities are examples of strategies followed to improve the company's bottom line. As Morgan Stanley describes in its note "Operational improvement: the key to value creation in private equity", a 100-day plan is often put in place, in one form or another, by the private equity firm during the due diligence phase detailing the strategy to be adopted in case of investment. Clear goals are defined in terms of market share gains, growth, cost reductions, EBITDA, return on capital and debt pay-down schedules. The private equity firm then ranks these opportunities in terms of cost and potential value creation and then typically chooses a mix that combines a few high value/high difficulty projects with some lower value ones for quicker results.[6]

Post-investment, private equity firms usually place a representative on the board of the investee company and, in the case of large syndications, expect the lead investor to play an active role on the company board. The private equity firm (or the consortium of investors) is usually the controlling shareholder, and as such has considerable voting power and influence over the strategy and corporate development, playing a hands-on role in determining such things as board composition, management compensation and incentives, selection, support and revision of management teams, strategic development and monitoring of performance. According to research from EVCA, the average private equity non-executive board member spends three times as much time on their role as the average public company director.

Private equity firms often bring on experienced people with operational background who can work closely with the portfolio companies for a few months or even a couple of years. Known as "operating partners", these partners have broad experience as senior executives across various industries. They can thus take a hands-on approach to help CEOs adapt to a challenging new role in a private equity-backed company where stronger emphasis is put on cash flow generation, where the timeframe for achieving results is greatly compressed and where CEOs need to answer to a broader set of stakeholders, including active boards of directors, banks, mezzanine funds, co-sponsors and LPs.[7] This combined set of new challenges makes the role of these operating partners particularly valuable to both the CEO and the private equity firm!

In a 2002 study, EVCA offered some very interesting insights into selective cost cutting during buyouts. Private equity investors are not blind cost cutters. Investments in areas conducive to higher profits, such as selective R&D, marketing, capital expenditure or training, on average tended to increase after buyouts, not decrease (see **Exhibit 3.1**). This again makes sense in the context of the rapid "impact" a private equity investor is trying to make on the target firm.

While non-necessary costs need to be cut, investments need to be made where earnings will be impacted. Management consulting firm Boston Consulting Group (BCG) recently analyzed[8] the operational performance of 89 US and European

---

[6] Matthews, G., Mark B. and Howland, J., "Operational Improvement: The Key to Value Creation in Private Equity", *Journal of Applied Corporate Finance*, Vol. 21, Issue 3, Summer 2009, pp. 21–27.

[7] Ibid.

[8] Boston Consulting Group, The 2012 Private-Equity Report, "Private Equity: Engaging for Growth", 2012.

Exhibit 3.1 Pre- and post-buyout key spending areas as percentage of revenues

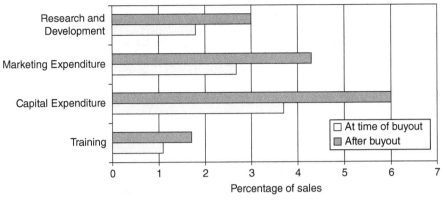

Source: EVCA Private Equity Study, April 2002

private-equity deals, and found that 70% had generated an absolute increase in EBITDA of at least 20%—and nearly half an annual EBITDA growth of 50% or more.[9]

The report also identified six different "operating models" for operational value creation, through interviews with GPs and portfolio company CEOs[10]:

Cluster 1: Private equity firms with no internal operating capabilities

- **No operating capabilities:** private equity firms falling under this category have neither internal operational capabilities nor external advisors, and hence are not involved in the day-to-day operation of portfolio companies. Interaction with portfolio companies is done through the board of directors.
- **A network of external advisors:** firms in this category rely on an external network of senior advisors, typically former CEOs and CFOs. These are given an equity stake in the portfolio companies or in the fund and serve on the board of the portfolio company and may assist in the diligence phase to build value creation plans.

Cluster 2: Private equity firms with internal operating capabilities at the partner level

- **Generalist operating partners:** firms in this category bring in, as operating partners, former senior executives and high level general managers with generalist expertise. The partners work on more than one portfolio company

---

[9] The study was conducted on deals of a value of at least €500 million that were closed between 1998 and 2008 and exited between 2005 and 2011.

[10] Boston Consulting Group, The 2012 Private-Equity Report, "New Operating Models", 2012.

at a time and are not necessarily given an equity stake, although they are on the firm payroll.

- **Functional operating partners:** same model as above, except that the operating partners are former executives and consultants with expertise in a specific functional area.

Cluster 3: Private equity firms with internal operating capabilities at multiple levels

- **Small in-house operating team:** firms in this category put in place a multilevel group of operating professionals. The team, which is significantly smaller than the deal team and has different terms of compensation, works on one company portfolio at a time throughout the entire investment process and will stay on site for up to one year.
- **Large in-house operating team:** same model as above, except that the operating team is as large as the deal team, with comparable compensation.

As we will see in the case studies below, operational value represents a significant share of the value creation potential in deals and one of increasing importance. The case studies below illustrate how private equity firms develop and implement winning strategies at the portfolio level, and how they support these strategies internally.

Case Study 9
Tumi and the Doughty Hanson Value Enhancement Group

January 2012. On a cold and dreary London morning, Doughty Hanson investment committee was discussing the future of its investment in Tumi. At stake was the definition of the proper exit strategy for the high-end luggage company Doughty Hanson had acquired in 2004 in a secondary buyout, a company that now generated some US$330 million in sales. Was this the right time to sell or should Doughty Hanson continue to build the company?

The Tumi difference

Tumi was founded in 1975 as an importer of Colombian leather travel bags and totes. The company soon expanded its product line, creating a strong brand around high quality products. It operated in the "super premium" segment of the global luggage market, investing heavily in R&D to create breakthrough inventions such as "Wheel-A-Way" wheels, the Omega closure system and the Fusion Z Nylon.

By 2000 the product categories had expanded and annual sales topped $100 million. The company relied on a multi-channel strategy to distribute its products in the US and internationally through department stores such as Harrods, Neiman Marcus, Saks Fifth Avenue, specialty stores as well as Tumi-branded stores.

Clouds forming

But the recession that hit the world in early 2001, followed by 9/11, profoundly affected the travel industry, leading to the closure of hundreds of Tumi-carrying stores in 2002. Tumi badly needed outside financing. So, in September 2002 Oaktree Capital Management, a California-based private equity firm specialized in distressed investments, became the majority shareholder of Tumi. Working side by side with the management team, it initiated a heavy turnaround plan with a clear focus on cost reduction initiatives. US-based manufacturing plants owned by Tumi were closed and production was outsourced to more than 10 Asian contract manufacturers. Tumi retained design and product development, supply chain management and sales and marketing in-house.

Under new stewardship, Tumi accomplished a complete turnaround. EBITDA more than doubled after the first year of new leadership, and then doubled again the following year to reach $22 million and a 17% EBITDA margin in 2004.

In 2004, Oaktree decided that it was time for a new "pair of hands" at Tumi—industry parlance to indicate they were keen to realize the value created and find an exit for their investment. Tumi was now a particularly attractive candidate: fast-growing and well-established across multiple channels, with 447 employees in eight locations worldwide, and more than 30 Tumi stores in key international cities including New York, Los Angeles, Chicago, London, Paris and Tokyo. A public auction was organized to find a buyer.

Acquisition by Doughty Hanson & Co.

Doughty Hanson emerged as the winning bidder and closed the deal for a reported $276 million. With Tumi, Doughty Hanson, one of the leading and most established European private equity firms, known for being publicity shy, suddenly found itself in the limelight. It had been founded in 1995 by Nigel Doughty and Richard Hanson. These two private equity veterans had worked together at Standard Chartered Bank before establishing CWB Partners in 1990, a private equity joint venture between Standard Chartered and Westdeutsche Landesbank, and then eventually creating Doughty Hanson. The firm's LPs included a diverse mix of pension funds, family offices, endowments, funds-of-funds, sovereign wealth funds, insurance groups and banks. All of the funds also included a significant investment from Doughty Hanson's own employees that ensured a strong alignment of interests with the firm's investors.

Doughty Hanson focused on the majority ownership and control of businesses at the upper end of the European middle market with enterprise values of between €250 million and €1 billion. A network of eight offices scattered across Europe allowed Doughty Hanson to build long-term relationships with potential targets many years before they were put on the market. Doughty Hanson worked in close partnership with the management teams of its portfolio companies. It went one step further by creating an in-house value enhancement group (VEG) responsible for supporting, driving and monitoring strategic and operational programmes at portfolio companies. When Doughty Hanson acquired a company, the investment team updated the VEG team on the due diligence findings and informed it about the first set of actions. The VEG then performed a joint review with the management team to identify and define potential areas that could benefit from enhancing strategies.

Doughty Hanson viewed the VEG and investment teams as a single team with two distinct focuses. The VEG was the first port of call for management teams to discuss sales growth, supply chain management, sustainability and procurement cost optimization. By contrast, the investment executives took care of the investment process, taking board seats and running financial review meetings with portfolio companies.

Tumi in the Doughty Hanson era

Doughty Hanson's plan for Tumi combined a number of growth strategies to improve operations, build the Tumi brand, develop global distribution and improve sustainability. In particular, the following strategies were carried out:

- *Supply chain and retail operations were optimized*: a new product development cycle was reduced from two years to three months, and launch dates consistently hit; planning and forecasting were improved, leading to an increase in order fulfillment from less than 80% to about 96%; the supplier appraisal system was upgraded; manufacturing quality and lead time decreased from 145 days to 70 days; logistics capabilities were opened in Asia; and initiatives were undertaken to strengthen management in retail operations.
- *Tumi was successfully positioned as a lifestyle brand*: the product breadth was significantly increased, and new products launched, leading to a diversification in product categories.

- *Global distribution was accelerated*: a global rollout of Tumi-owned stores was initiated; e-commerce was enhanced; and a strong focus was put on the expansion of the Tumi footprint in Asia Pacific.
- *Sustainability was closely integrated into Tumi's operations.*

Preparing the exit

On December 13, 2011 Tumi announced to the world that it was contemplating an IPO. Business press articles also hinted to the fact that many large luxury goods groups were also looking at Tumi, describing it as a "natural fit".

Exits are often tricky moments in the private equity investment cycle: the brand appeal has to be built to a historical high while sufficient exit options have to be created to generate competition. Was this the best time to envision cashing out of the eight-year investment? Clearly, Doughty Hanson could hold on to the investment longer, if needed. Various strategic investors had already publicly expressed an interest in Tumi. The IPO window was a bit more difficult to assess. As for a secondary buyout, many felt that Doughty Hanson had already implemented many of the most obvious value improvements, making it more challenging for the next private equity player to increase the brand value further.

On April 19, 2012, Tumi listed on the NYSE through a $389 million share offering. The IPO generated strong investor demand, with an order book 22 times oversubscribed. Eight years after the Doughty Hanson acquisition, sales of Tumi had tripled and EBITDA had almost quadrupled.

Source: Case study written by the authors and included with permission from Doughty Hanson.

MULTIPLE ARBITRAGE   A change in the EBITDA multiple between entry and exit can be attributed to different parameters, notably the re-positioning of the company, the bargaining power between the buyer and the seller or external economic and market conditions.[11]

Multiple arbitrage has often been misunderstood, a stigma from the use of the word "arbitrage" which seems to imply some form of passive value creation and hence an abuse of some form of position. Arbitrage actually takes two dominant forms:

1   A passive "timing" arbitrage, i.e. acquiring assets at the bottom of a cycle and selling them at or close to the peak. Also known as "multiple surfing", this practice actually is anything but passive since it involves putting your

---

[11] Achleitner, A.K., Lichtner, K. and Diller, C., "Value Creation in Private Equity", presentation made to the DVCA, November 2009.

money in when and where nobody else is investing. The reward is essentially the result of providing liquidity in a market that had none.

2 A more clearly active arbitrage by doing whatever is needed to justify a larger multiple, i.e. proving to the market that the firm is now on a higher growth trajectory than previously assumed. This is sometimes referred to as "multiple engineering".

Ideally, one would, of course, try to combine multiple surfing and engineering to obtain the largest possible multiple increase over the investment period, which is relatively short. There is thus a lot more to multiple arbitrage than the classic strategy of "buying low and selling high", with fund managers not doing much in between. Increased multiples are generated through repositioning the business to make it more attractive to potential buyers, injecting and capitalizing on new growth opportunities, restructuring to focus the managers on value creating segments, etc.

FINANCIAL LEVERAGE With operational value and multiple arbitrage, financial leverage is the third strategy in the GP's toolbox. However, contrary to the two other strategies, leverage is not a value *driver* per se, but rather a value *amplifier*.

In corporate finance, debt is considered fundamentally good. It improves private equity returns in three ways: (a) it amplifies the return on equity; (b) it can create value by shielding firms from taxes because interest charges are often tax deductible, whereas dividends are not; and (c) it disciplines managers, forcing them to focus on generating cash to meet the interest and principal repayment deadlines.

Leverage is abundantly used in private equity transactions for that reason, with deals typically characterized by multiple layers of debt with various seniorities. As Kaplan and Stromberg explain in their paper "Leveraged Buyouts and Private Equity"[12], the debt typically includes a loan portion that is senior and secured, and another that is junior and unsecured. A more detailed analysis was recently conducted on 1,157 buyout transactions that occurred between 1980 and 2008.[13] The sample included public-to-private buyouts, buyouts of independent companies, as well as divisional and secondary buyouts. Far from representing the entire population of buyouts, the study, however, gives a good indication of the types of financing used in buyout transactions. The authors found that 62%

---

[12] Kaplan, S. and Stromberg, P., "Leveraged Buyouts and Private Equity", *Journal of Economic Perspectives*, Vol. 22, no. 4, Season 2008.

[13] Axelson, U., Jenkinson, T., Strömberg, P.J. and Weisbach, M., "Borrow Cheap, Buy High? The Determinants of Leverage and Pricing in Buyouts", April 26, 2010, Charles A. Dice Centre Working Paper No. 2010-9; Fisher College of Business Working Paper No. 2010-03-009.

of deals in the sample included amortizing debt, which is usually held by the originating bank (debt known as **Term Loan A**) and mostly had to be paid off in less than five years, while almost 90% of deals included bullet debt, which is often securitized or sold to investors, such as hedge funds (known as **Term Loan B, C** and higher) and has longer pay-down periods. In total, Term Loan A represented about 23% of total debt, bullet debt 46.2%, while mezzanine and junior bonds about 10% each.

The authors also find that the main factors that affect the capital structure of buyouts are—rather unsurprisingly—the price and availability of debt, while the factors that predict capital structure in public companies have no explanatory power for buyouts. Term Loan A also appears to be pro-cyclical: during very liquid credit markets, when buyout leverage is generally higher, banks' share of the buyout debt is reduced while that of hedge funds, collateralized loan obligations (CLOs) and other non-bank financial institutions increases. The use of amortizing debt in buyout transactions also seemed to be declining over time, according to the study.

Private equity has attracted criticism for abusing leverage and the criticism has intensified with the credit crunch and the global economic slowdown. It is fair to say that private equity firms generally put as much debt finance into an acquisition as they can raise from banks and other capital providers. But how much is too much? For a long time, a debt-to-EBITDA multiple of three to four was considered "normal"—but from the mid-2000s this rose steadily. By 2004–2005, bankers, debt advisors and lawyers were heard saying "five is the new four" with reference to EBITDA multiples and as the decade progressed, six became the new five, followed by seven and even eight as the new "normal". For transactions in sectors considered attractive, such as telecoms, multiples in the mid-teens were not unheard of.

Was this leverage excessive? With hindsight it is easy to say it was, but large buyout funds in particular were able to generate strong returns in 2006 and 2007 by tapping into exuberant debt markets to refinance companies, managing to pay dividends to investors while retaining substantial positions in the underlying companies to boot. As with the technology bubble that came to such a spectacular end in 2001 it was a classic case of "pass the parcel": so long as you weren't holding the package when the music stopped, you were still in the game.

When the credit crunch hit, not only did the music stop, but the stereo was packed away and put in the attic. It is too early to say how this will affect returns of 2006, 2007 and 2008 vintage funds, but in the second half of 2008 through 2010, GPs took heavy write-downs on the value of their holdings, reflecting in part the trading positions of their portfolio companies and in part falls in quoted equities used as comparators. Analysis of 2008 year-end fund valuations by alternative asset intelligence firm Preqin found that private equity net asset valuations fell by just 17%, compared to the 37% decline in the S&P 500 during the year.[14] And

---

[14] www.preqin.com.

while 14% of funds were hit by write-downs of 40% or more, 19% actually saw their values increase. Buyout funds were hardest hit with a decline of 22%.

In Chapter 6: The Supporting Cast, we will devote some time to the debt providers, the banks that work in the shadow of the private equity industry to make the deals possible.

Case Study 10
Blackstone and the Celanese acquisition

It is hard to name a leveraged buyout in recent years that has proven to be as quick a success as the takeover of Celanese, the chemicals company, by the Blackstone Group. In April 2004 Blackstone, an American private equity firm, took over 83.6% of Celanese AG, over the objection of many shareholders who felt that Blackstone was underpaying for the company. Having taken well over a year to be hammered out, the deal was secured at $3.8 billion.

Celanese AG, a public German corporation, traded on both the Frankfurt and New York stock exchanges, was an integrated global producer of value-added industrial chemicals. The company produced acetyl products, as well as engineering polymers used in consumer and industrial products. Most of the company's products were used as building blocks for value-added products or in intermediate chemicals used in the paints, coatings, inks, adhesives, films, textiles, building products, and in pharmaceutical and agricultural products. Celanese operated 35 production facilities throughout the world and had indirect interests in 10 additional facilities.

Back in 2004, the deal had not been easy to formalize. Blackstone needed 75% of Celanese shareholders to accept its tender offer. Only 60% of shareholders were in favour of accepting the tender offer half an hour before the deadline, and unless Chinh E. Chu, a senior managing director at Blackstone, saved the $3.8 billion deal, the estimated $20 million Blackstone had spent on bankers, lawyers and accountants for due diligence and subsequent structuring of the deal would be lost. Among those withholding their approval were the hedge fund shareholders who wanted to exploit Germany's arcane takeover law to demand a higher price for their shares. Chu worked the phone non-stop, and when the tally came in the next day Blackstone owned 84% of Celanese, making it the largest public-to-private buyout in European history. The company was delisted, and the $3.8 billion deal was financed with debt, the company's liabilities were pushed up to $3.4 billion, and about $650 million in equity.

Just nine months after buying Celanese and taking it private, Blackstone sold 40% of it through an IPO in 2005 on the New York Stock Exchange, making reportedly in excess of $800 million. Investors who supplied Blackstone's capital more than quadrupled their investment. Blackstone's remaining stake was worth some $1.6 billion.

The global chemical industry was in a consolidation phase and without a deep-pocketed backer, Celanese had little chance of remaining independent. With Blackstone's help, Celanese bought out chemicals companies Acetex Corporation for $492 million and Vinamul Polymers for $208 million. These acquisitions meant greater job security for Celanese workers—Blackstone included $462.5 million to fund the Celanese pension obligations—repudiating claims by outsiders that Celanese's takeover by an American private equity firm could result in jobs moving to the US. Revenues had grown to $6.44 billion when Blackstone sold its remaining share in 2007, up from 5.27 billion in 2005.

According to Stephen Schwartzman,

"Celanese (at 33.5x) was a big success at a time when 5x was the norm. Chemical cycles were underestimated, as well as costs cutting, number of potential acquisitions and growth potential. These three factors were the three principal drivers of the deal."[15]

Source: Blackstone.

COMBINING STRATEGIES AND THE INGREDIENTS OF SUCCESS All three strategies—operational value, financial leverage and multiple arbitrage—are sources of value creation, and private equity firms often use a combination of the three to achieve their goal. If multiple arbitrage and leverage are viewed as easy pickings that have somehow not been earned, operational value in portfolio companies is not. As a matter of fact, private equity firms go to great lengths to play up the proportion of return generated through operational improvements rather than through the leverage effect when presenting their returns and performance to potential investors, and even shun nowadays the term LBO because of the negative connotation carried by companies supposedly buried under mountains of debt. Returns that are generated through leverage are referred to as having been created through "financial engineering", a term that arguably carries a less negative connotation.

In its 2013 Endowment Report, Yale prides itself on relying on that strategy:

"Yale's private equity strategy emphasizes partnerships with firms that pursue a value-added approach to investing. Such firms work closely with portfolio companies to create fundamentally more valuable entities, relying only secondarily on financial engineering to generate returns."[16]

---

[15] Based on interviews with the authors.

[16] Yale Endowment Report 2013.

Exhibit 3.2 Value creation drivers over the last cycle (N denotes number of transactions)

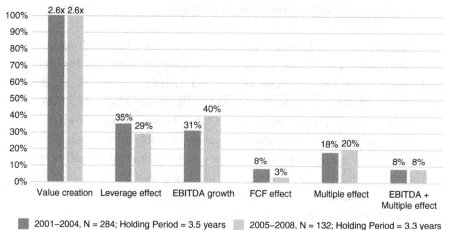

■ 2001–2004, N = 284; Holding Period = 3.5 years   ■ 2005–2008, N = 132; Holding Period = 3.3 years

Source: Value Creation in Private Equity, Joint research findings from Capital Dynamics and the Technische Universität München, Second study, June 2014

How do these strategies compare in terms of impact? What is each strategy's contribution to the overall performance of the deal? If there is no clear-cut answer to date, a few academic studies help shed some light on this fascinating topic.

In a 2014 study, Capital Dynamics and the Technische Universität München compare the value creation drivers of investments made at the peak (2005–2008) of the last buyout cycle, with those made during the years leading up to the boom (2001–2004). The results are summarized in **Exhibit 3.2**. Whereas leverage contribution declined from 35% to 29% of value creation between the two periods, EBITDA growth became the most important driver, accounting for 40% of total value creation between 2005 and 2008.

In a paper published in 2010 in the *Journal of Private Equity*, Achleitner *et al.* decompose the return IRR of a leveraged company into two components: the return on equity of an unleveraged company and the leverage effect:

$$IRR_E^l = IRR_E^u + (IRR_E^u - r_D) \cdot (D/E)$$

The leverage effect, which takes into account the cost of debt and the average debt-to-equity ratio during the holding period, is determined by solving for IRR_E^u. The IRR of the leveraged company is increased with the use of debt.[17]

Using a sample of 241 companies in Europe during the period 1989–2006, the authors find that one-third of value creation is driven by EBITDA growth, mostly through sales growth and a little through margin expansion, 15% of value creation comes from the free cash flow generated over the holding period, and

---

[17] Achleitner, A., Braun, R., Engel, N., Figge, C., and Tappeiner, F., "Value Creation Drivers in Private Equity Buyouts: Empirical Evidence from Europe" (January 12, 2010), *The Journal of Private Equity*, Spring 2010.

20% through the increase in valuation multiples between entry and exit. The remaining third is the leverage effect.

In an article published in the *Journal of Finance* in April 2011, Shourun Guo, Edith S. Hotchkiss and Weihong Song looked at a sample of 192 public-to-private buyouts of US firms with deal values of at least $100 million and announcement dates between 1990 and 2006, and compared realized returns to returns that would have been generated had profitability remained at its pre-buyout level.[18] They showed that improvements in performance accounted for 23% of the pre-buyout return, while changes in the industry total capital/EBITDA ratio accounted for 18%, and 26% in case of IPO. As for leverage, the impact on returns very much depended on whether the leverage increase was sustained after exit, though on average companies' realized annual tax benefits accounted for a median of 3.4% of the returns to pre-buyout capital.

A 2008 BCG report[19] used financial data from 32 portfolio companies in seven European private equity firms to compare the enterprise value at the time of the acquisition with the value realized upon exit, separating the contribution to realized IRR by pure sales growth and earnings improvements. As shown in **Exhibit 3.3**, out of an average IRR of 48%, 22 percentage points were attributed

Exhibit 3.3 Estimates of value drivers in 2008 BCG study

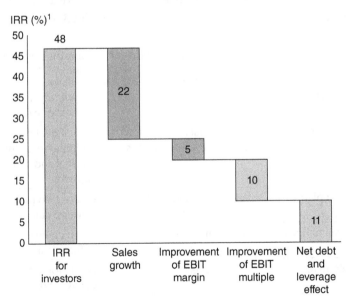

Source: The advantage of persistence: How private equity firms beat the "fade". BCG/IESE report, February 2008

---

[18] Guo, S., Hotchkiss, E. and Song, W., "Do Buyouts (Still) Create Value?", *The Journal of Finance*, Vol. 66, no. 2, 2011.

[19] "The advantage of persistence: How private equity firms beat the 'fade'". BCG/IESE report, February 2008.

to sales growth, 5 points to improvement in margins, 10 points to increases in valuation multiples and only 11 points to change in leverage.

Over the typical 10-year lifetime of a fund, the private equity firm will typically invest in 10 to 15 companies. For a few companies of the fund, most of the value will be created through financial engineering, while operational value will be the best strategy for others. Some deals will be exited fast, after two or three years, while others will take six, seven or more years to mature. Some will perform spectacularly, while others will yield mediocre results.

Research by consultancy firm McKinsey's Private Equity Practice explored the practices that distinguished great deals from simply good ones. At a time of heightened industry competition and reduced availability of leverage, private equity firms need to increasingly rely on their ability to identify value-creating opportunities. Using a sample of 60 deals from 11 leading private equity firms that had outperformed the industry, the McKinsey team first found that the main source of value in nearly two-thirds of the deals was company outperformance, whereas market or sector increases accounted for about a third.[20] In other words, it was the ability of the fund manager to increase performance in the target firms that accounted for the vast majority of the final performance, rather than "environmental" factors, such as being at the right time at the right place, or clever financial engineering manipulations using leverage. The team identified six "active ownership" strategies that were particularly well correlated with company outperformance.[21] These strategies are presented in **Exhibit 3.4**.

Exhibit 3.4 Six active ownership principles that drive company outperformance

	Common practice	Best practice
Proprietary deal insight	Due diligence	Proprietary insight from insiders or experts
Deal partner time spent	15% of deal partner time / CEO-centric interactions	45% of deal partner time / Multiple broad interactions / Internal and external support
Value creation plan	Review management plan / Review financial metrics	Create own plan / Develop customized KPIs
Management changes	Constitute board	Recruit new management before closing
Focused incentives	Widely spread equity	Equity for top managers / CEO/CFO required to invest
External support	Used infrequently	Used regularly

Source: McKinsey Quarterly, "Why some private equity firms do better than others", February 2005

[20] *McKinsey Quarterly*, "Why Some Private Equity Firms do Better than Others", February 2005.

[21] Ibid.

Proprietary deal insight: Successful deal partners sought out expertise before committing themselves. In 83% of the best deals, the initial step for investors was to secure privileged knowledge: insights from the board, management, or a trusted external source. In the worst third of deals, expertise was sought less than half of the time.

Deal partner time spent: The most effective GPs devoted more hours during the initial stages. In the best-performing ones, the partners spent more than half their time on the company during the first 100 days and met almost daily with top executives. These meetings proved critical in helping reach a consensus on the new strategic priorities, building relationships and detailing personal responsibilities. A deal partner may use the meetings to challenge management's assumptions and unearth the company's real sources of value. By contrast, lower-performing deals typically took up only 20% of the investors' time during this crucial period.

Value creation plan: Successful deal partners crafted better value creation plans and executed them more effectively. As mentioned in Chapter 2, the private equity firm usually prepared what is called a 100-day plan even before it invested in the portfolio company. The plan detailed specific goals to be achieved and listed strategic priorities for operational improvements.

Once developed, the plan was subject to nearly continuous review and revision, and an appropriate set of key performance indicators (KPIs) was developed to ensure the plan remained on track. Firms implemented such a performance-management system in 92% of the best-performing deals and only half as often in the worst.

Management changes: If leading deal partners wanted to change a company's management, they did so early in the investment. In 83% of the best deals—but only 33% of the worst—firms strengthened the management team before the closing. Later in the deal's life, the more successful deal partners were likelier to use external support to complement management than the less successful ones.

Focused incentives: Successful deal partners instituted substantial and focused performance incentives—usually a system of rewards equalling 15% to 20% of the total equity. Such incentives heavily targeted a company's leading officers as well as a handful of others who report directly to the CEO. In addition, best-practice deal partners required CEOs to invest personally in these ventures.

External support: Top fund managers did not cringe either at spending money to get the best outside support needed to evaluate deals and add value post-investment. This willingness to "buy" the best advice also indicates a more realistic attitude to the deals: creating value is a difficult endeavour at best, and one is always better off with a higher percentage of successes even if that costs a few percentage points in IRRs.

The human factor effect: Another factor which does play an important role is the characteristic of the private equity team. In the widely cited study "Corporate Governance and Value Creation: Evidence from Private Equity", Acharya *et al.* (2010)[22] show that the background of the GPs, operations (ex-consultants or ex-industry-managers) or finance (ex-bankers or ex-accountants), could have an impact on their ability to generate returns. Looking at 110 deals of large, mature private equity houses in Western Europe between 1995 and 2005, they found that GPs with an operational background (ex-consultants or ex-industry-managers) generated significantly higher outperformance in "organic" deals, where margins are improved through internal value creation programmes. By contrast, GPs with a background in finance generated higher outperformance in "inorganic" deals that focus on growing EBITDA multiples through M&As.

Apart from the GPs who lead deals, private equity firms also bring on experienced people with operational backgrounds who can work closely with the portfolio companies. As mentioned in Chapter 2, these operating partners are highly valuable: on the one hand, they can understand the private equity process, because they often have private equity experience themselves; on the other they have experience running companies, ideally, private equity-backed ones.[23]

Relationship with lenders: Good performance in turn seems to generate important benefits, directly or indirectly, because of good reputation. One example is the relationship with banks, and the resulting access to capital and good borrowing conditions. In a paper recently published by the *Journal of Financial Economics*, Demiroglu and James (2010)[24] studied 180 public-to-private LBOs and found that buyouts sponsored by the most reputable private equity groups benefited from better loan terms, such as lower spreads, longer maturities and less traditional bank debt to total buyout debt. They suggested that buyouts of more reputable private equity firms were perceived by banks as less risky with reputation serving as a substitute for banker monitoring and control… a virtuous circle that benefits the top performers.

---

[22] Acharya, V. V., Hahn, M. and Kehoe, C., "Corporate Governance and Value Creation: Evidence from Private Equity" (February 17, 2010).

[23] Matthews, G., Mark, B., and Howland, J., "Operational Improvement: The Key to Value Creation in Private equity", *Investment Management*, Morgan Stanley, July 2009.

[24] Demiroglu, C. and James, C.M., "The role of private equity group reputation in LBO financing", *Journal of Financial Economics*, Vol. 96, no. 2, May 2010.

Exiting investments

A widely held perception is that successful private equity investments are normally exited through flotation on stock markets (IPOs). In reality, IPOs are relatively rare events, and as such do not represent a large percentage of exits. **Exhibit 3.5** shows that IPOs accounted for just 16% of European buyout exits (at cost of investment) in 2012, according to EVCA.[25]

Trade sales are the most common exit route for buyouts, accounting for 38% of exits of European buyouts in 2012. Although some corporate acquisitions are paid for with shares in the acquiring company, private equity firms (and most buyers) prefer cash as a medium of exchange to avoid the complications attached to managing a new block of shares.

Write-offs made up about 7% of all European buyout exits in 2012. The number was considerably higher a couple of years earlier because of the financial crisis (40% in 2009). The numbers in Europe are very similar when we consider exit routes for private equity in general, not only for buyouts.

On a global basis, trade sales again represent the most common route for private equity-backed buyouts, followed by sales to other GPs, i.e. secondary

Exhibit 3.5   Buyout exit routes in Europe by amounts at cost in 2012

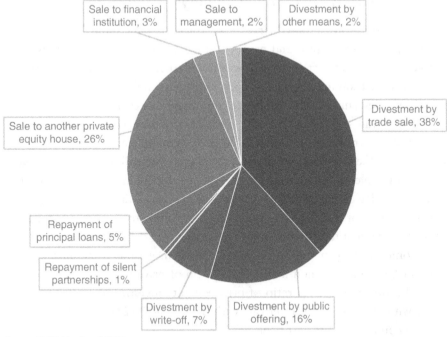

Source: EVCA Yearbook 2013

---

[25]   EVCA Yearbook 2013, www.evca.com.

Exhibit 3.6 Private equity-backed buyout exits broken down by type and aggregate exit value

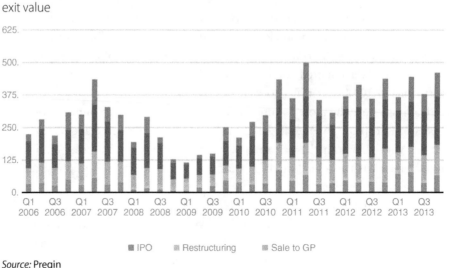

Source: Preqin

buyouts, and to a lesser extent by IPOs and restructurings, as shown in **Exhibit 3.6** from alternative asset intelligence firm Preqin.[26]

The economic impact of private equity

As private equity firms acquired larger and larger companies and whole swathes of industry, particularly in brand names and major job creators, the industry as a whole started to attract increased scrutiny. Particularly questioned were the impact of such transactions on the competitiveness and economic viability of target companies, employment, executive compensation, technology development, sustainability and social responsibility, and the economy as a whole. Is private equity primarily transferring wealth from some economic actors to others, with no net gains to the economy, or is it actually making a contribution? Does it really provide a valuable economic role, for example by disciplining all companies into a more aggressive competitive stance? Can the growth of the industry be related to an actual need or demand from the market, or simply to an overabundance or supply of investment funds with nowhere else to go?

To compare the penetration of private equity in various economies around the world, the most common metric is the ratio of private equity investment to GDP. In Europe, the average ratio of private equity investments to GDP is only 0.33%, with the UK at the forefront with a ratio of 1.12% and all the other European countries lagging far behind.[27]

---

[26] Global Private Equity Report, Preqin, 2014.

[27] EVCA Yearbook 2012.

Over the last couple of years, academics, trade bodies and research institutes have devoted much time and effort to assessing the real economic impact of private equity. The World Economic Forum (WEF), for example, coordinated the production of a much-discussed report in 2008, entitled *The Global Economic Impact of Private Equity*. The report was commissioned to complete the first rigorous, multi-country study on the impact of private equity around the world. It was prepared by a consortium of leading international scholars from institutions such as the Harvard Business School, INSEAD, London Business School, Technische Universität Munchen, Johns Hopkins University and the Swedish Institute for Financial Research, supported by an advisory board chaired by Joseph Rice, co-founder of buyout firm Clayton Dubilier & Rice, and consisting of many of the brightest minds in the industry.[28]

The WEF survey was the most comprehensive review of academic literature undertaken to date. It studied more than 21,000 private equity transactions around the world between 1970 and 2007. In direct reflection to the acceleration of investments in the later part of the period, more than 40% of the buyouts in the sample had been completed in the last three years. The total value of firms acquired in leveraged buyouts was estimated at $3.6 trillion, of which $2.7 trillion occurred in the period from 2001 to 2007. The researchers estimated that 80% of these transactions were "traditional" private equity deals (in which a financial sponsor or buyout fund backs the deal and provides the majority of the equity capital). The remaining 20% were mostly what WEF called "pure" management buyouts, where individual investors, usually the management team, led the deal and provided the equity without the need to bring in a formal, external private equity investor. These management-led buyouts were mostly smaller deals, with almost all of the larger deals requiring a financial sponsor.

We review below six claims widely used by critics regarding the economic impact of the industry.

CLAIM #1: LBOS ARE OFTEN OVER-LEVERAGED, CREATING UNDUE FINANCIAL DISTRESS   A study carried out by Axelson *et al.* (2007) found that large LBOs have an average net debt-to-enterprise value of 67% and an average net debt-to-EBITDA multiple of 5.4, considerably higher than the 14% and 1.1 multiple found in the public market sample.[29]

Given the higher level of leverage, one would expect LBO companies to be in greater danger of bankruptcy than comparable public firms, with bankruptcy

---

[28] The Global Economic Impact of Private Equity Report 2008, World Economic Forum.

[29] Axelson, U., Jenkinson, T., Weisbach, M.S., and Strömberg, P.J., "Leverage and Pricing in Buyouts: An Empirical Analysis" (August 2007), Swedish Institute for Financial Research Conference. Available at SSRN: http://ssrn.com/abstract=1027127.

accounting for a substantial portion of exits. The data somewhat supported the hypothesis—but not to the degree expected. In the WEF sample, 6% of deals ended in bankruptcy or reorganization. Excluding LBOs that were completed after 2002, which may not have been in that form of ownership long enough to be exited or distressed, 7% of LBOs ended up in trouble. Assuming an average holding period of six years, the computed annual default rate was just about 1.2% a year, compared to 0.6% for US public companies in the same period (1983–2002). While the implied default rates of LBOs was indeed double that of public companies, it was still much smaller than the average rate of default for corporate bond issuers from 1980–2002, which stood at 1.6%, according to rating agency Moody's Investor Services. To make things even more interesting, of the companies that did enter bankruptcy proceedings or required a restructuring, 10% were subject to a leveraged buyout as a means of emerging from their situation...

CLAIM #2: PRIVATE EQUITY INVESTORS ARE OVER-FOCUSED ON THE SHORT TERM Accusations that private equity firms quickly "flip" investments were found to be unsupported by the WEF survey. Although the mean hold period for an LBO was four to five years, only 42% of private equity deals had been exited five years after the initial investment, with just 12% of LBOs exited within two years and 17% within three years. The researchers observed that holding periods of private equity funds had increased markedly beyond the three-year standards of the 1990s. The median holding period stood at close to nine years, and getting longer. Back in the 1980s, the median holding period for an LBO was six to seven years.

The survey also revealed a little-known fact about holding periods in buyouts: for many companies, the LBO was actually not a transitional form of ownership at all. Of the companies that completed an LBO between 1980 and 2003, 45% remained under that form of ownership. Of LBOs completed prior to 1990, a surprisingly high 10% of companies remain under LBO conditions. That means that the LBO ownership structure was treated as almost permanent. At the end of 2007, there were 14,000 firms worldwide under LBO ownership, a huge increase from the 5,000 recorded in 2000 and the 2,000 seen in the mid-1990s.

CLAIM #3: PRIVATE EQUITY INVESTORS ARE ASSET STRIPPERS Some critics argue that private equity firms are merely asset strippers who do not invest for the long-term future of the companies. The "asset stripping" accusation is warranted to some degree, because private equity-owned companies tend to sell off assets at a faster rate than non-private equity-owned firms. However, a stricter definition of asset stripping suggests a sale of important assets without due regard to the long-term health of the remaining entity. This is not the case with private equity firms, which tend to sell non-core assets and often argue that selling at a fair price to an owner that will make better use of the assets is economically rational and usually in the best interest of all parties. For example, does a company really need to own its own office? A study of the 66 UK deals with a value of more than €100 million completed between 1996 and 2004 found that, while 13 had made significant divestments, 16 had made significant acquisitions (the remaining 37 had not made significant acquisitions or divestments).[30] Evidence from the US suggests that this active approach to managing and restructuring assets through divestitures and acquisitions is responsible for over a third of the improvement in productivity at private equity-owned companies.[31]

CLAIM #4: COST CUTTING POST-LBOS LEADS TO REDUCED INVESTMENTS IN INNOVATION The WEF study also looked at the long-term impact of private equity ownership on investments. Private equity has regularly been criticized for its short-term focus. As highlighted above, the planned three- to five-year ownership period (which often translates into much longer holding periods) could also be read as encouraging more long-term thinking than the constraints of quarterly reporting imposes on public companies. Using the number of patent citations as a proxy for innovation, the WEF study found support for the hypothesis that companies that had undergone a buyout pursued more economically important innovations than those that had not, although there was neither an increase in the overall number of patent applications nor a deterioration in the quality of innovation.[32] This suggests that companies under private equity ownership focus more decisively on the patents that yield economic benefits prior to a planned exit within the standard three- to five-year horizon. However, as Ughetto (2010) finds, what happens to innovation post-buyout could be affected by the inherent characteristics of the private equity firms and by the nature of the deals.[33]

CLAIM #5: PRIVATE EQUITY SEVERELY DISRUPTS WHOLE INDUSTRIES Bernstein *et al.* (2010), in their working paper published in the WEF's Global Economic Impact of Private Equity Report 2010[34], investigate whether private equity aggressive practices have a negative impact on industry growth. Their evidence points to the contrary: industries where private equity funds have been active in the previous five years have grown more rapidly than other sectors, whether

[30] Acharya, V.V., Hahn, M. and Kehoe, C., "Corporate Governance and Value Creation—Evidence from Private Equity", 2009.

[31] Gurung, A. and Lerner, J., "Private equity, jobs and productivity", The Global Impact of Private Equity Report 2009.

[32] Sorensen, M., Strömberg, P. and Lerner, J., "Private Equity and Long-Run Investment: The Case of Innovation", Discussion Paper, Columbia Business School, 2008.

[33] Ughetto, E., "Assessing the Contribution to Innovation of Private Equity Investors: A Study on European Buyouts", *Research Policy*, Vol. 39, 2010, pp. 126–140.

[34] Bernstein, S., Lerner J., *et al.*, "Private equity, industry performance and cyclicality", in Private Equity, Industry Performance and Cyclicality, The Global Economic Impact of Private Equity Report 2010.

measured by total production, value added or employment, and are no more volatile in the face of industry cycles than other industries. Robustness tests suggest that these results are not driven by reverse causality, i.e. that pre-existing growth brought in private equity in the first place.

CLAIM #6: PRIVATE EQUITY DESTROYS JOBS   Attempts to determine the effect of private equity ownership on employment generates the most controversy. Clearly, these are politically and emotionally loaded questions that are unfortunately also marred by methodological problems. First, data sets are often incomplete and rely on self-reporting by the private equity firms themselves, introducing potentially self-selection and non-response biases. Second, it is difficult to compare the situations at private equity-backed firms with that at firms under other forms of ownership due to the inherently complex nature of many private equity transactions. A high proportion of private deals involves acquisitions, divestitures and reorganizations, making it hard to track employment trends at the firm level. Lastly, it is sometimes difficult to track job creation precisely and in particular their geographic location. The issue is nonetheless of critical importance for policy makers, who are keen to promote domestic job creation.

The first finding in the WEF survey is that employment shrinks more rapidly in the two years following a leveraged buyout than in a control group, with the cumulative two-year employment difference being 7% in favour of non-private equity-backed companies. However, as **Exhibit 3.7** shows, employment also grows more slowly in companies that undergo LBOs in the two years preceding the transaction. This is consistent with the idea that many buyouts are of poorly performing corporate assets (variously described as "orphan" or "non-core") and makes a valid case for studying not just the employment effects of a buyout, but what would have happened had that buyout not occurred. While the rate of job creation is found to be similar in private equity-backed companies and in control groups, the rate of job destruction is greater in companies that have undergone an LBO.

Exhibit 3.7 Net job creation rates: targets vs controls before and after LBOs

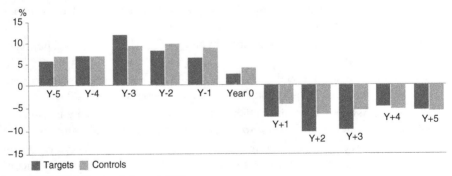

Source: WEF (World Economic Forum), 2008

Private equity ownership also affects different sectors in different ways. In the manufacturing sector, which despite its unglamorous image accounts for around a quarter of all private equity transactions since 1980, there is virtually no difference between private equity-owned firms and the control group. On the other hand, employment tends to fall sharply in companies in the retail, services and finance, insurance and real estate sectors.

A study by Steven Kaplan, of the Booth School of Business at the University of Chicago, of 76 public-to-private transactions in the 1980s,[35] found that the median company loses 12% of its employees on an industry-adjusted basis between the end of the fiscal year prior to the transaction and the end of the fiscal year that follows. This contrasts with positive data put out by industry associations—led by the British Private Equity & Venture Capital Association (BVCA) and completed by IE Consulting—that, not surprisingly, paint a rosy picture. Over the five years to 2005–2006, the number of people employed worldwide by UK private-equity-backed companies, about 8% of private sector workers, increased by an average of 9% per annum, significantly higher than the 1% recorded across FTSE 100 companies, the 2% seen in FTSE Mid-250 companies, and the 0.4% fall in general private sector employment.[36]

Research conducted by the Centre for Entrepreneurial & Financial Studies at Technische Universität Munchen for EVCA, estimates that private equity-owned companies employed nearly 6 million people in 2004, representing 3% of economically active people in Europe. Almost 5 million of those were employed in companies that had undergone a buyout, as opposed to those financed with either venture or growth capital.[37] It also found that 1 million new jobs were created by private equity- and venture-backed firms between 2000 and 2004, and claimed that a net 420,000 jobs were created at firms that had undergone a buyout. It said that the annual rate of job creation at European firms with private equity backers was 5.4% in the period 2000–2004, eight times the average 0.7% achieved across the EU 25.

Looking specifically at buyouts, EVCA found annual employment growth of 2.4% between 1997 and 2004, almost four times the EU 25 average. According to the study, employment had either stayed stable or increased in 67% of buyout situations, while in a third of instances employment had increased by more than 5% per annum. Although large portfolio companies, those with more than 1,000 employees, accounted for the majority of employment by private equity-owned companies, smaller companies were better at creating jobs, with an average annualized employment increase of 7%.

[35] Kaplan, S., "The Effects of Management Buyouts on Operating Performance and Value", *Journal of Financial Economics*, 1989.

[36] "The Economic Impact of Private Equity in the UK", British Private Equity & Venture Capital Association (BVCA), 2006.

[37] "Employment Contribution of Private Equity & Venture Capital in Europe", European Private Equity & Venture Capital Association (EVCA), November 2005.

Professor Mike Wright, at the Centre for Management Buyout Research at the University of Nottingham in the UK, has been studying the employment effects of MBOs since the mid-1980s. His studies point to significant employment loss in the immediate aftermath of more than a quarter of buyouts, but a recovery in subsequent years. In a 2007 study, he concluded that the majority of MBOs and MBIs experience long-term growth in employment.[38] This is supported by the WEF research, which finds that, while employment growth is lower in the first three years after a buyout, growth in the fourth and fifth years is slightly above that in the control groups.

The BVCA also claims that economic performance was improved, with sales growing 9% on average over the following five years (compared with 7% on the FTSE 100 and 5% for FTSE Mid-250 companies), exports grew by 6% per annum (2% nationally) and investment by 18% a year (1% nationally). Private equity-backed companies generated sales of £424 billion and exports of £48 billion.[39] The evidence was summarized by Jonathan Russell, head of buyouts at private equity firm 3i and chairman of EVCA in 2009, in the following words:

> *"Private equity is a highly effective and proven ownership structure for many businesses. It is a force for efficiency and growth across Europe. No one disputes the contributions of VC and growth capital as sources of funding and innovation. The questions are about buyouts and, particularly, big buyouts. If you study the evidence, there is no doubt that businesses grow faster, export more and are more fit-for-purpose under private equity than other types of ownership."*

The evidence collected so far, despite methodological shortcomings inherent to studies of private transactions, support the view that private equity investors do have a positive economic impact overall. As the ultimate expression of capitalism, i.e. the power of investors and capital to create value, GPs seem indeed able to bring about significant improvements in efficiency and performance, without a concurrent public loss. What will be examined in the next chapter is whether these investors were able to appropriate a significant proportion of these value gains, i.e. if they were able to consistently generate exceptional returns for their funds and investors.

[38] "Private Equity Demystified", Corporate Finance Faculty, ICAEW, 2008.
[39] "The Economic Impact of Private Equity in the UK", British Private Equity & Venture Capital Association (BVCA), 2006.

4

Private equity performance

Executive summary

In this chapter, we look at how private equity performance is measured, and how it compares to the risk and return of other asset classes. In order to measure performance, the industry relies on two main metrics: the Internal Rate of Return (IRR), which is an annualized effective compounded rate of return, and the Total Value to Paid-In Capital (TVPI), which provides a multiple of capital invested. While both metrics can sometimes provide conflicting insights on performance—the IRR takes into account the time value of money, while the multiple does not—both measures need to be considered simultaneously when analyzing an investment. On a quarterly basis, the private equity firm will report to LPs a valuation of all investments in the portfolio, whether realized or still unrealized. While realized investments have an undisputed value that is given by the exit value of the portfolio company, unrealized investments are valued in a more subjective way by the GP following guidelines which leave much room for interpretation.

Contrary to public equities that exhibit relatively low variance, private equity funds display huge performance disparities. The high variance is an indication of the level of risk of the asset class. Because of its characteristics, venture capital in particular tends to be more risky than buyouts and hence the performance gap between the top VCs and the bottom ones is likely to be the greatest. However, according to different studies, the average private equity performance is not better or worse than stock market performance as a whole, despite the high level of risk. The best-performing managers do, however, outperform the other asset classes. Manager selection is, therefore, key to successful investing. Macroeconomic conditions also play a key role, in the sense that funds launched during downturns are more likely to perform better than those launched during boom years, where competition for deals tends to generate price inflation and make value creation more difficult.

The diversification potential of private equity in an investment portfolio is often not only overstated but is quite possibly the wrong rationale to use in the first instance. Firsthand, it could be assumed that since value creation in private equity comes from operational improvements to portfolio companies, the results should hardly be correlated with the stock markets. Actually, evidence suggests that private equity returns—especially those of underperforming managers—are closely correlated to stock market returns. To make matters worse, the recent crises have shown that diversification does not work when you need it most, i.e. correlations tend to go up significantly during crises. To the extent that investors interested in private equity tend to have a fair degree of risk tolerance, they are also the most likely to have equity-heavy portfolios and hence are the least likely to benefit from the diversification benefits of adding private equity to the mix in the first place. The bottom line is that diversification should not be a major rationale for allocating capital to private equity: expected returns should be.

A positive note to investors is certainly the fact that private equity returns exhibit a high degree of persistence: fund managers who have outperformed the industry average in the past are likely to do so again in the follow-up funds. Similarly, fund managers who have underperformed the industry average in the past are likely to do so again.

The preceding chapters have shown that the private equity asset class is characterized by a long investment horizon, a lack of liquidity and a certain unpredictability of cash flows. Therefore, the possibility of portfolio diversification warrants attention. But the litmus test for the industry is its ability to deliver returns consistently over the long term. If private equity can do this, then investors can put up with the asset class' inconveniences.

Whether the industry's claim of superior risk-adjusted returns are supported or not is the subject of extensive scrutiny and endless scepticism. Is the industry's reality living up to the hype? Is it able to generate returns that more than compensate investors for the less desirable characteristics of the asset class? Without this, the very sustainability of the industry could be questioned

THE BEST AND THE REST   Before we delve into the subject of performance measurement, let us first say that there is a huge discrepancy between the performance of the top quartile managers and the performance of all other private equity managers. In a recently published study, the consulting firm Bain & Company analyzed the returns produced by more than 850 buyout, growth-capital and late-stage venture capital vintages, in the mature markets of both the US and Western Europe and the rest of the world, for the period 1995 to 2009. As **Exhibit 4.1** suggests, the bulk of managers generated reasonable but not spectacular returns around the median, while a significant share of GPs produced returns that were either catastrophic or just spectacular.

The huge variability makes extensive due diligence prior to picking a GP all the more important: what is the point of having one's capital blocked for 10 years in an asset class that is not producing any return but with heavy fees every year? In the section below, we will focus on understanding how performance is actually measured by managers.

Exhibit 4.1 Net IRR deviation from median benchmark for private equity buyout funds

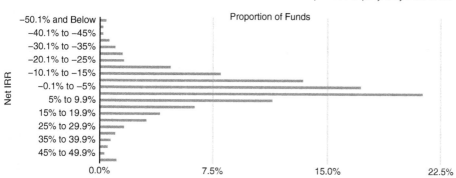

Source: Preqin

MEASURING PERFORMANCE The very long-term nature of the private equity industry, the complexity of valuing early-stage portfolio companies and the illiquidity of the underlying positions make it difficult to compare the asset class' performance to more liquid assets.

Performance metrics

How should private equity performance then be measured? The industry typically uses two types of measures: the rate of return and the multiple(s).

THE INTERNAL RATE OF RETURN (IRR) EVCA defines it as the interim net return earned by LPs from fund inception to a stated date. The IRR is calculated as an annualized effective compounded rate of return using monthly cash flows to and from investors, together with the Residual Value as a terminal cash flow to investors.[1] Fortunately, IRR has been programmed into Excel and most financial calculators, and, therefore, the real worry is the accuracy of the data.

In the initial years of the life of a fund, returns will often be negative due to the front-loading of costs such as management fees, usually drawn from committed capital, and a period of 12 months when investments are kept at cost. Over time, value creation in portfolio companies will generate gains, unrealized until an exit comes about. This creates a return profile known as the "J curve", where returns typically dip for a number of years before moving into positive territory at some point in the fund's life, when the fund's earliest investments are realized.

Although the IRR has a lot of appeal because it is a simple and easy-to-grasp concept, it presents a number of pitfalls well known in the industry. In particular, it relies on the notion that interim cash flows are reinvested in projects with equal rates of return. This means that the IRR is likely to overestimate the true return of an investment since a good investment is not necessarily followed by equally profitable ones. The numbers will be further inflated and even more misleading if investments are sold very quickly, perhaps just a few months after being made, since the early cash flows will be—in theory—reinvested for a longer period of time. This is particularly true in periods of markets' "irrational exuberance", such as the dot-com boom (c. 1998–2001) and the credit boom (c. 2004–2007), when quick profitable investments led to artificially high IRRs, which in turn helped fuel demand for the private equity asset class.

In his paper rightly titled "The Hazards of Using IRR to Measure Performance: The Case of Private Equity",[2] Phalippou discusses some of the limitations of the

---

[1] EVCA, http://www.evca.eu/toolbox/glossary.aspx?id=982.

[2] For a discussion, see Phalippou, L., "The Hazards of Using IRR to Measure Performance: The Case of Private Equity", *Journal of Performance Measurement*, Vol. 12, no. 4, Summer 2008, pp. 55–67.

IRR in the case of private equity. First, he argues, GPs might be incentivized to exit good investments early on, even if doing so might not be in the best interest of investors, only to artificially inflate their IRR. However, this would reduce their carried interest. Second, the author shows that, because of the re-investment assumption, the IRR will actually exaggerate the spread between bottom-quartile and top-quartile funds, leading to an artificially high volatility in the asset class. The author addresses those pitfalls with a Modified IRR.

THE TOTAL VALUE TO PAID-IN CAPITAL RATIO (TVPI)   The Total Value to Paid-In Capital Ratio, or TVPI, is defined by EVCA as the sum of the cumulative distributions returned to LPs and the value of the LPs' interest still held within the fund, all relative to the cumulative paid-in capital.[3] The ratio is net of fees and carried interest.

TVPI is usually expressed as a multiple of capital invested, corresponding to the sum of the Cumulative Distributions and the Residual Value:

$$\text{TVPI} = \text{Investment Multiple} = (\text{Cumulative Distributions} + \text{Residual Value}) / \text{Paid-In Capital}$$

The first part of the TVPI is often referred to as the Distribution to Paid-In Capital Ratio (DPI), measuring the cumulative distributions returned to LPs as a proportion of the cumulative paid-in capital, net of fees and carried interest. It represents a measure of the fund's realized return on investment. The second part of the TVPI is referred to as the Residual Value to Paid-In Capital Ratio (RVPI), providing a measure of the value of the investors' interest held within the fund, relative to the cumulative paid-in capital, again net of fees and carried interest. RVPI is subjective as the manager decides what his investment is worth. Bad managers usually tend to overvalue their investment, while good managers are generally conservative.

The multiple is a very intuitive measure of fund performance: it gives a simple indication of how much the initial value has grown, from inception to a certain point in time. However, it has a significant limitation: it does not take into account the time value of money. A multiple of 3, for example, means that the initial investment into the fund has now tripled in value. But it does not differentiate between a tripling of value occurring just after two years, and one that occurs at the very end of the life of the fund, a much less attractive option from a financial point of view.

The two metrics, multiple and IRR, often offer a diverging view of performance: one takes the time value of money into account while the other does not. So when good investments are held for many years, the IRR might look poor while the multiple can look very attractive. The reality is that both measures need to be considered together to get a true picture of returns.

---

[3] EVCA, http://www.evca.eu/toolbox/glossary.aspx?id=982.

Valuing realized and unrealized investments

Usually every quarter, the GP will provide his LPs with a valuation of all companies in the portfolio. This means that a specific value will be attributed to each investment, whether realized or still unrealized. While realized investments have a value that is given by the exit value of the portfolio company—whether the sales price, the value at IPO or the write-off—unrealized investments are valued in a more subjective way by the GP following guidelines which leave much room for interpretation. Although valuations should be based on a portfolio company's fair value, in accordance with appropriate industry valuation guidelines, the GP is nonetheless free to base his valuation model on the assumptions he chooses.

The subjectivity involved in the valuation often leads to one single company being valued differently by GPs who have joined forces in a so-called club deal... For investors who are used to liquid, tradable assets such as public equities and bonds, this can be very disconcerting.

Valuation of private equity funds has been the subject of heated debate since Blackstone chairman and CEO Stephen Schwartzman railed against the mark-to-market accounting rules that forced the listed private equity giant into hefty write-downs. "*What they are trying to ask you to do is value your companies as if you're going to sell them at the bottom of a recession,*" Schwartzman complained in May 2009 (*Financial Times*, Gloom hits buy-out gathering, February 3, 2009). Marking-to-market was generally seen as a step in the right direction in terms of making valuations less subjective and allowing investors to compare different positions. What it failed to integrate was the fact that there is no continuous pricing for most of those assets, nor is there necessarily a need to sell these assets at any given point in time.

Contrary to their public counterparts, private equity-backed companies are only valued at quarterly intervals. The fact that it is impossible to provide a daily value for these investments is one of the reasons the industry targets only qualified professional investors, with regulators considering that their own role is best restricted to protecting unsophisticated, private investors. Professional investors, for their part, are supposed to have more resources and competences than many regulators do to evaluate the riskiness of their investments. As a result, the only incontestable valuations in the life of a fund are at inception, when no investments have yet been made, and at termination, when all investments have been liquidated and the proceeds distributed.[4] But what happens between these two points in time is never totally clear...

---

[4] See Cumming, D. and Walz, U., "Private equity returns and disclosure around the world", *Journal of International Business Studies* Vol. 41, 2010, for a discussion on the subject.

Reporting fund performance

Detailed reporting of fund performance is critical for all parties involved in the partnership. It allows for a more transparent relationship between the GP and his LPs, lowering processing times and monitoring costs.

Approaches to reporting have become increasingly standardized, facilitating comparison across funds and over time. Industry groups such as EVCA and ILPA have been instrumental in the adoption of industry reporting guidelines. These include, for example, a recommendation to publish quarterly disclosures of the positions of the fund, including total commitments, total drawdowns, fair values of the portfolio, total net asset value (NAV), IRR and cash flows to investors, as well as a quarterly reporting detailing the current valuation of each company in the fund's portfolio and any proceeds from realized investments.[5]

Exhibit 4.2, prepared by ILPA, provides an example of what GPs should include in their reporting documents to LPs. The table—which should be ideally updated on a quarterly basis and audited annually—details for each of the portfolio companies the total committed by the fund, the total invested, the current cost, the reported value and the realized proceeds.[6]

INDUSTRY PERFORMANCE DATA   Knowing how the industry as a whole performs is critical. It allows investors to understand the risk/return characteristics of the asset class, while providing an opportunity to compare a GP's performance with that of his peers. Getting a clear image of the industry performance is nonetheless challenging.

Membership and self-reporting biases

Without the active cooperation of the fund managers and without a legal framework that requires the public disclosure of all fund activities and performance, the industry has long relied on voluntary reporting of cash flows and net asset values by the funds themselves. Performance surveys are usually conducted by organizations such as EVCA or Thomson Reuters. This manner of proceeding clearly introduces a number of biases into the reported performance statistics. The funds surveyed represent only a sample of the population as a whole. In Europe, about 70% of the private equity funds in existence are members of EVCA[7], and hence participate in the survey. The rest are funds that have elected not to belong to the industry trade group. Whether these funds are materially different from the member funds is a question of great debate. Of those 70% receiving the survey, only about 60–70% actually complete it and return the form in due time. This

---

[5] EVCA Reporting Guidelines, June 2006 (updated 2010).

[6] Institutional Limited Partners Association, Quarterly Reporting Standards Best Practices, October 2011.

[7] EVCA 2009 European Private Equity Market.

Exhibit 4.2 Sample of a schedule of investments

							Best Practices Fund II, LP - 12/31/2010											Inv. Multiple: (C+D)/A		
Company Name	Security Type	Number of Shares	Fund Ownership % (Fully Diluted)	LP Ownership % (Fully Diluted)	Initial Investment Date	Final Exit Date	Investment Data (Expressed in $)					Valuation Driver*	Period Change in Valuation	Period Change in Cost	Unrealized gains/(losses) & accrued interest	Movement Summary**		Current Quarter	Prior Quarter	Security Type IRR (SI)
							Fund Commitment	Total Invested (A)	Current Cost (B)	Reported Value (C)	Realized Proceeds (D)									
Company 1	Equity	1,250,000	55%	5.66%	3/15/2007		5,000,000	5,000,000	4,500,000	4,700,000	1,000,000	L	$0	$0	$0	1		1.14	1.09	5%
Company 1	Debt	12,789	55%	5.66%	6/15/2007		5,000,000	5,000,000	5,000,000	5,200,000	500,000	E	$297,829	$0	$297,829	2		1.14	1.09	10%
Company 3	Equity		12%	5.66%	9/15/2007		5,000,000	5,000,000	2,500,000	2,700,000	0	E	$468,019	$386	$467,633	2		0.54	0.49	-40%
Company 3	Debt		12%	5.66%	9/15/2007		5,000,000	5,000,000	5,000,000	5,200,000	1,000,000	B	-$145,546	$0	-$145,546	3		1.24	1.19	15%
Company 4	Equity		90%	5.66%	2/15/2008		5,000,000	5,000,000	5,000,000	10,000,000	0	H	$38,609	$38,417	$192	4		2.00	1.95	35%
Company 5	Equity		80%	5.66%	5/15/2008		4,000,000	4,000,000	4,000,000	0	0	A	$323,439	$323,439	$0	5		0.00	0.00	-100%
Company 6	Equity		65%	5.66%	8/15/2008		4,000,000	4,000,000	4,000,000	5,000,000	0	M	$2,333,324	$1,693,069	$640,255	6		1.25	1.20	10%
Company 7	Equity		100%	5.66%	11/15/2008		4,000,000	4,000,000	4,000,000	4,500,000	0	L	-$111,989	$0	-$111,989	2		1.13	1.08	3%
Company 8	Equity		60%	5.66%	6/15/2010		8,000,000	4,000,000	4,000,000	4,000,000	250,000	P	$418,876	$0	$418,876	4		1.06	1.01	1%
Sub Total Active:							*45,000,000*	*41,000,000*	*38,000,000*	*41,300,000*	*2,750,000*		*3,622,561*	*2,055,311*	*1,567,250*			*1.07*	*1.01*	*2%*
Company 2	Equity				4/15/2007	12/28/2010	5,000,000	5,000,000	5,000,000	0	7,500,000		0	(1,253,152)	1,253,152	7		1.50	1.50	15%
Sub Total Liquidated:							*5,000,000*	*5,000,000*	*0*	*0*	*7,500,000*		*0*	*(1,253,152)*	*1,253,152*			*1.50*	*1.50*	*15%*
Grand Total:							**50,000,000**	**46,000,000**	**38,000,000**	**41,300,000**	**10,250,000**		**3,622,561**	**802,159**	**2,820,402**			**1.12**	**1.06**	**3%**

*Valuation Driver:

A- Investment held at cost

B - Valuation has been reduced due to significant deterioration in the company's performance and potential

C - Valuation has been adjusted to the value paid by a sophisticated unrelated new investor

D - Valuation at a later round of financing (no new unrelated investor)

E - Valuation based on the closing quoted price

F - Valuation based on the closing quoted price with a discount for lock up restrictions

G - Follow-on costs of a written down investment

H - Future realization proceeds

I - Valuation based on fairness option in relation to proposed merger

J - Realization

K - Valuation based on recent transaction multiples

L - Valuation based on recent market multiples

M - Valuation based on recent market and transaction multiples

N - Valuation based on expert third party opinion

O - Valuation based on closing quoted price plus valuation of warrants

P - Revised company prospects

**Movement Summary:

1 - No Change

2 - Change in public market value

3 - Deterioration in performance and potential

4 - Future realization proceeds

5 - Follow-on financing

6 - New investment

7 - Investment write-off

8 - Realized investment

Source: ILPA, 2011

voluntary reporting could easily introduce an upward bias since underperformers are more likely to select themselves out. Industry associations also produce an increasing volume of literature and research in praise of the industry and its role in economic development, but their very position in the food chain makes them very unlikely to come out with a negative picture of the industry.

To get around the self-selection and membership biases, alternative asset intelligence firms such as Preqin and custodians such as State Street conduct extensive surveys of the industry. Preqin in particular has been tracking almost 7,500 private equity funds historically, and is confident that its research represents approximately 95% of the total number of funds ever raised. The performance information is sourced directly from GPs as well as from their LPs, increasing the chance that both strong and poor fund performance are captured equally, allowing for a much more accurate picture of the industry.

Fortunately enough for the industry, exact data exist. Under the Freedom of Information Act, state pension funds such as CalPERS are required by law to publish the performance of the private equity funds in which they are invested. This transparency did not, however, come naturally: it was rather the result of a court ruling[8] that occurred in 2002, forcing CalPERS to provide full disclosure on its private equity activities to the general public. The court ruling was, however, not welcomed by GPs, many fearing that the public might misinterpret performance data, applying the metrics commonly used for public equities to a long-term asset class. Whether some GPs have deliberately stayed away from US pension funds like CalPERS is hard to know, although one thing is clear: the ruling—which offers the general public a glimpse into a high-performing segment of the industry—has brought the issue of performance much more to everyone's attention.[9]

Academic research on private equity continues to be strongly hampered by the discrepancies that exist across the various industry databases. To address this issue, the Private Capital Research Institute (PCRI), a private equity research organization led by Harvard Business School Professor Josh Lerner and funded by the Kauffman Foundation, has recently launched a new initiative, together with some of the industry's biggest firms, to build a database of industry performance. The database would solely be for academic purposes though.[10]

INDUSTRY VARIABILITY Before looking at industry averages, it is critical to understand that the variations around the averages are high in the industry. We

[8] The ruling is known as CalPERS vs. Mercury News. See section on CalPERS in Chapter 5 for an overview.

[9] All the information on the 2002 ruling for investment transparency is taken from Chaplinsky, S. and Perry, S., "CalPERS versus Mercury News: Disclosure Comes to Private Equity", Darden Business Publishing, 2004.

[10] PRNewswire, April 4, 2012, "Leading Managers to Contribute Data to Effort to Advance Understanding of Private Capital".

mentioned it briefly at the beginning of the chapter, there are very large differences in returns among GPs and even across funds with the same GPs. Preqin in particular has been looking at the performance of the top quartile or decile funds versus the bottom ones and highlights key differences: on average bottom quartile buyout funds have the largest proportion of deals written off (6%), compared to just 2% for top quartile buyout funds' deals. Similarly, while 23% of all top quartile buyout funds' exits occur via IPOs and private placement offerings, just 16% of bottom buyout quartile funds' exits do.[11]

Performance variation is illustrated in **Exhibit 4.3** with data from the Yale Endowment fund (June 2012). In a way, the spread between top and third quartile is an effective measure of variability, or risk, within each asset class, a measure highly relevant for investors. While traditional asset classes demonstrate fairly moderate variations, buyouts, venture capital and real estate exhibit the most variability. Given this level of risk, has the industry been able to generate returns commensurate with its risk profile? That some private equity funds are able to generate significant returns is clearly not disputed: in this specific example, the top performing buyouts generate among the highest absolute returns during the period. Venture capital, by contrast, offers—in this particular case—poor results, both in terms of very high variability and low returns. The venture capital model still has merits though, with spectacular results at times, but selecting winners seems to be much more difficult than for buyouts.

Performance by segments

There are various segments in private equity, all with very different performance characteristics. Depending on the timing and the market at certain points in

Exhibit 4.3 Spread between first and third quartile managers at Yale Endowment ten years ending June 30, 2012

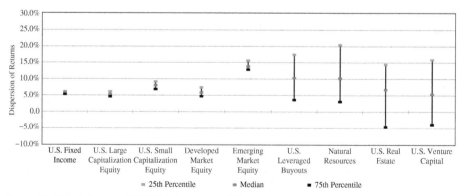

Source: The Yale Endowment 2012, Yale Investment Office

---

[11] Preqin Special Report: "Exits in Private Equity", April 2011.

time, a particular segment will outperform the others. Supply and demand for a particular segment will likely determine returns. Funds raised during periods of exuberant enthusiasm for example, when too much capital chases too few deals, tend to generate lower returns—as the IRR of venture capital funds launched during the dot-com boom illustrates.

Buyouts typically target stable companies with highly predictable cash flows: few of these portfolio companies would go bust, unless too much leverage has been added. Buyouts is, therefore, not a highly risky segment and one should not expect a high variance in performance between the winners and the losers. This sharply contrasts with venture capital, a highly risky segment in which managers face a large number of unknowns, and often invest before the market they target even exists. As a result, one can expect to find a huge discrepancy between the best venture capital deals and the worst.

Performance by fund size

Private equity funds vary enormously in size, from the very small funds with only a handful of employees to the mega funds, managing billions of dollars. Is one more likely to generate stronger returns with larger or smaller funds? There is no easy answer to this question.

First, it is clear that those who manage to raise increasingly larger funds are able to because they have been outperforming the industry with their smaller funds and earning the trust of their investors. However, a GP who has been very successful with a small fund is not guaranteed success when he subsequently raises a larger fund simply because the market in which he now operates is different. Furthermore, the incentives of larger funds, and to a large extent mega funds, are very different from the ones of smaller funds, in the sense that the share of the management fee in the GP's overall compensation is now much bigger relative to the performance fee, reducing the alignment between the GP and his LPs.

At the other end of the spectrum, one finds that very small funds are largely first-time funds. Most of these first-time funds will never raise a second fund and those who do struggle to simultaneously fundraise and look after their investments. However, the small funds category also includes some highly successful small funds that deliberately remain small. These funds usually have no problem raising funds among their loyal base of investors.

Lerner, Leamon and Hardymon[12], in a recent working paper, attempted to determine through simulation the optimal size of VC and buyout funds. Their results are intriguing. As shown in **Exhibit 4.4**, the theoretical optimum fund size for VC would be around $150–200 million, whereas for buyout funds the optimum would

---

[12] Lerner, J., Leamon, A. and Hardymon, F., "Venture Capital, Private Equity, and the Financing of Entrepreneurship". New York: John Wiley & Sons, 2012.

Exhibit 4.4 Impact of fund size on predicted relative IRRs

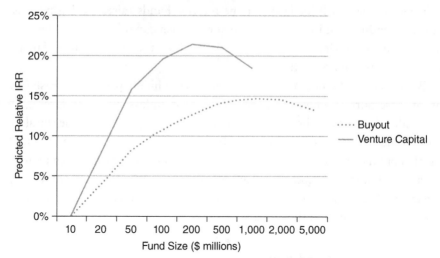

Source: Lerner, J., A. Leamon, and F. Hardymon, 2011, *Private Equity, Venture Capital, and the Financing of Entrepreneurship: The Power of Active Investing*, New York: Wiley

be around $1 billion. According to our knowledge these results were not corrected for first time funds and we suspect that optimal fund sizes may be even lower.

The study provides a rather interesting perspective on the industry. However, by looking only at the size component, it fails to take into account the complexity of private equity, and in particular the supply and demand for private equity at a given time, the competition for deals, or the experience of the management team.

The persistence effect

Do high-performing GPs have inherent skills that allow them to continue to outperform their peers in subsequent funds? Similarly, do low-performing GPs lack those skills and continue to underperform their peers in their next fund? If the answer is positive, fund selection by LPs could be made somewhat easier by looking at past performance. Although empirical research is likely to suffer from reporting biases—notably, a bias toward success as the worst performers are unlikely to raise future funds—several studies point to a persistence effect.

First, Kaplan and Schoar (2005)[13] found strong evidence of persistence in private equity returns: GPs whose fund outperforms the industry in one fund are likely to outperform the industry in the next, and more likely to raise larger follow-on funds. This relationship is shown to be somewhat concave, so that top-performing partnerships grow proportionally less than average-performing ones.

[13] Kaplan, S. N. and Schoar, A., "Private Equity Performance: Returns, Persistence, & Capital Flows", *Journal of Finance*, Vol. 60, no. 4, 2005.

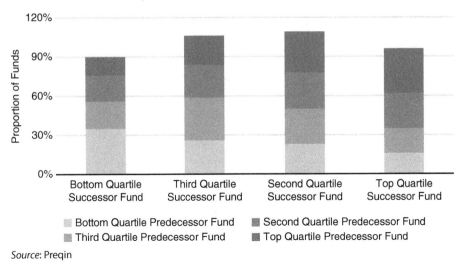

Source: Preqin

The study shows that private equity funds contrast sharply with mutual funds, which exhibit extremely low persistence: prior mutual fund performance has limited predictability value for the performance of future funds under the same manager; or in the words of the UK regulatory disclaimer on advertising: "Past performance is no guide to future performance."[14]

These results are corroborated by a study conducted by management consulting firm BCG and IESE in 2008 on the relative performance of 75 funds and their subsequent follow-up fund. The study, based on data from Preqin, shows persistence of returns to be a prevalent factor: while the top performers in the sample outperform the average by 107%, their subsequent funds outperform the average by 95%. Similarly, while the worst performers underperform the average by 75%, they continue to underperform in their subsequent fund by 50%.[15]

Exhibit 4.5, based on performance data for thousands of funds compiled by Preqin, shows that 34% of top quartile GPs are among the top quartile in their next fund. Persistence also affects the worst performing GPs: in 61% of the cases, below average managers do not reach the median in their following fund.[16]

However, if persistence seems to be well documented, its evolution over time is not clear yet. Consulting firm McKinsey & Company created a storm in 2010 when it published a report based on data from Preqin of funds between 1990 and 2005 suggesting that the phenomenon of performance persistence was declining

---

[14] FSA: Report of the Task Force on Past Performance, September 2001.

[15] Meerkatt, H., Liechstenstein, H., *et al.*, "The Advantage of Persistence: How Private Equity Firms Beat the Fade", BCG/IESE report, February 2008.

[16] Preqin.

with time. If that is indeed the case, LPs will need to conduct even more thorough due diligence when selecting their GP in the future.[17]

The timing effect

Performance in private equity is highly dependent on the timing of the initial investments. Funds launched in difficult economic environments, such as recessions, tend to deliver the best performance. This is illustrated in **Exhibit 4.6**, which tracks the median and quartile spread of all private equity funds by vintage year. Funds launched in recessionary years, such as 1990–1994 or 2000–2004, exhibited stronger performance, arguably also with a larger spread.

However, supply and demand of both capital and deals are more significant factors than the macro environment. In the periods 1990–1994 and 2000–2004, which were characterized by shortages of capital relative to deal flow, there was less competition for deals and, therefore, more attractive entry pricing. By contrast, the sheer weight of money raised in the mid-2000s places some doubt

---

[17] McKinsey & Company, "Private Equity Canada 2010, Preparing for the Next Wave of Growth."

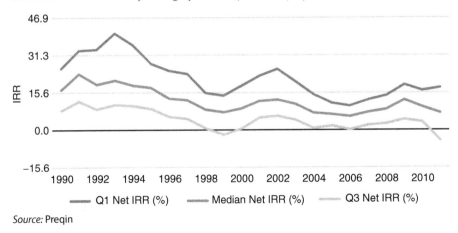

Source: Preqin

on the assumption that the current recession will prove to be as classic a vintage for private equity investors as the previous ones.

Savvy investors should increase commitments to the asset class during recessions, taking advantage of other investors' reluctance to make commitments during these troubled times.

PRIVATE EQUITY AND PORTFOLIO DIVERSIFICATION We have started this section by looking at how performance at the *fund* level was likely to be affected by the timing, existing competition, the GP's experience, etc... We now take a look at performance at the *portfolio* level, to understand the role of the private equity asset class in the LP's portfolio.

Comparison against benchmarks

The private equity industry has always been keen to support claims that the top performers in the asset class provide long-term outperformance over mainstream assets. There are a number of commonly cited reasons for this, including inefficient information, active and qualified GPs, greater use of leverage and, of course, greater and better-structured incentives for managers—as discussed in Chapter 2.

Numerous research studies have been conducted to estimate the relative performance of the buyout industry with respect to public markets, and although they differ in terms of their final conclusions, many researchers obtain inconclusive results as to the existence of sufficient overperformance to compensate for illiquidity and other private equity risks. In "Private Equity Demystified", published in 2008 by the Corporate Finance Faculty of the ICAEW in London, Mike Wright

Exhibit 4.7 Cambridge associates LLC US PE index vs. benchmarks, as of September 30, 2011

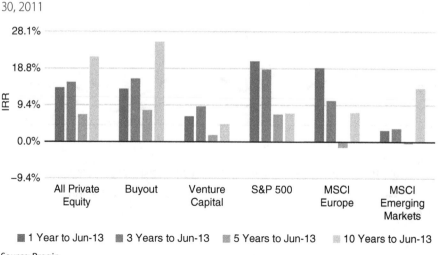

■ 1 Year to Jun-13   ■ 3 Years to Jun-13   ■ 5 Years to Jun-13   ▨ 10 Years to Jun-13

Source: Preqin

of the Centre for Management Buyout Research and John Gilligan, a partner at accountancy firm PKF, examined 15 peer-reviewed academic studies on returns and performance adjusted for risk, mainly for buyouts in the US, where data sets were more complete. Results were inconclusive.[18]

The results very much depended on the sample used, the period of time considered and the method adopted. An interesting comparative study was conducted in 2011 by Cambridge Associates LLC, comparing the performance of its well-regarded US Private Equity Index® against selected benchmark statistics, as reported in **Exhibit 4.7**. The US Private Equity Index® relies on an end-to-end calculation based on data compiled from 905 US private equity funds (buyout, growth equity, private equity energy and mezzanine funds), including fully liquidated partnerships, formed between 1986 and 2011, and measured as pooled end-to-end return, net of fees, expenses, and carried interest.

Private equity in the US seemed to deliver returns slightly superior to major equity benchmarks, especially given the huge public equities drop during the crisis. Having said that, the annual premium for illiquidity seems low considering other hassles of private equity investing. With that in mind, we review below some of the most compelling studies in the literature. For a more comprehensive overview of the literature, we recommend the paper authored by Metrick and Yasuda (2010).[19]

---

[18] Wright, M. and Gilligan, J., "Financing Change: Private Equity Demystified", ICAEW Corporate Finance Faculty, October 2008.

[19] Metrick, A. and Yasuda, A., "Venture Capital and Other Private Equity: A Survey", NBER Working Paper No. 16652. Issued in December 2010.

In a widely respected study published in 2005, Steven Kaplan and Antoinette Schoar addressed directly the controversial issue of performance.[20] Using data on the performance of individual funds collected by Venture Economics in the US from both GPs and LPs (thereby reducing the risk for biases), Kaplan and Schoar found that the equal-weighted median IRR on a basket of 746 funds between 1980 and 1997 was 12%, while the equal-weighted average IRR stood at 17%. When weighting the funds to take into account their size, the median IRR was slightly improved at 14%, while the mean was 18%, indicating that larger funds performed better. Buyout funds also fared better than venture funds. Of the 169 LBO funds studied on a size-weighted basis, the median IRR was 15% and the mean 19%.

The authors then calculate a public market equivalent (PME), which compared an investment in a private equity fund to an investment in the S&P 500. A fund with a PME greater than one is considered to outperform the S&P 500 net of all fees. The studied universe of private equity funds had a median PME on an equal-weighted basis of 0.74 and a mean PME of 0.96, indicating that private equity had slightly underperformed the S&P 500 over the period—net of fees. The authors also suggested that, on average, buyout and VC funds exceeded the S&P 500—gross of fees.

Building on Kaplan and Schoar's study, Phalippou and Gottschalg (2009) studied US and non-US buyouts and concluded that, after adjusting for sample bias and "inflated accounting" valuation of ongoing investments, average fund performance changes from slight outperformance of the S&P 500 to underperformance of 3% per annum, and risk-adjusted underperformance of 6% per year.[21] In their 2006 study, Groh and Gottschalg, on the other hand, conclude that risk-adjusted performance of US buyouts is considerably greater than the corresponding S&P index.

Despite being one of the most comprehensive studies of private equity returns, Kaplan and Schoar's work highlighted key difficulties in assessing private equity fund performance: its long-term nature and the fact that any attempt to value funds before they are fully realized is necessarily subjective. In the case of this 2005 study, the desire to only calculate funds' IRRs on actual cash inflows and outflows means that only funds established before 1994 were included. As outlined before, the industry at that point in time was radically different from the industry today. It would actually be fair to say that this was the "previous generation" of funds. Today, the Washington-based Carlyle Group has more than $97.7 billion under management; in 1994, by contrast, it was still investing from its first fund, Carlyle

---

[20] Kaplan, S.N. and Schoar, A., "Private Equity Performance: Returns, Persistence and Capital Flows", *Journal of Finance*, Vol. 60, no. 4, 2005.

[21] Phalippou, L. and Gottschalg, O., "The Performance of Private Equity Funds", *Review of Financial Studies*, Vol. 22, no. 4, 2009.

Partners I, which had raised $100 million in 1990. It was not until 1996 that Carlyle closed its second fund, Carlyle Partners II, with $1.3 billion of committed capital. The markets, structures and deals across funds of such different sizes are radically different... and likely to affect the return generation.

To address the issue of timing, Robinson and Sensoy (2011) used a larger proprietary database—obtained from an LP—that contained quarterly data on capital calls, distributions, and estimated market values for 990 funds over a period spanning 1984 to 2010.[22] The authors used the PME method developed in Kaplan and Schoar (2005) and obtained an average PME of 1.15 for all private equity funds, and 1.2 for buyout funds only. These numbers are much higher than what Kaplan and Schoar (2005) and Phalippou and Gottschalg (2009) found when restricting their analyses to funds with vintage years prior to 1995 and cash flows through 2003 only.[23]

Industry consultants have generated results very similar to academic researchers. In research published in *Investments & Pensions Europe* in 2004, Laurence Zage, then head of research at private equity placement agents Helix Associates and now managing director at Monument Group, compared returns on US private equity funds raised between 1983 and 2002 with the total return index, including reinvestment of dividends, of the MSCI USA Index, which covers 85% of the free-float capitalization of the US quoted universe.[24] To overcome comparability problems caused by the differences between public and private equity markets (particularly with regard to commitments and drawdowns and the difficulties of ensuring that the maximum amount of assets are invested while retaining sufficient free cash to meet drawdown notices) Zage constructed a public market index that matched private equity's unpredictable cash flow behaviour. Zage found that the quoted index outperformed private equity returns over the 20-year period, analyzed both on a straight and weighted basis. He also found a high degree of correlation between the quoted index and private equity. His conclusion was that if investors were looking to the private equity markets for outperformance and diversification from the public markets, they were very unlikely to find satisfaction on either count. A caveat mentioned in the research, though, is that the relative underperformance of private equity affected mostly recent vintages, possibly because of the immaturity of these portfolios and the J curve effect.

---

[22] Robinson, D. and Sensoy, B., "Private Equity in the 21st Century: Cash Flows, Performance, and Contract Terms from 1984–2010", Fisher College of Business Working Paper Series, 2011.

[23] The authors do, however, find a similar result as Kaplan and Schoar (2005) when they take the same sample period.

[24] Zage, L., "Wide of the Mark: How does Private Equity Measure up to Public Markets?", Investment & Pensions Europe, March 2004.

BCG takes a different approach to measuring performance.[25] In a research paper published in 2008 together with IESE researchers, the authors compared the IRR on a sample of 218 private equity funds with vintage years between 1979 and 2002 and with RVPIs not exceeding 20%, with an equivalent investment in the MSCI World Index. They find an average IRR of 13% in the case of the funds, and a return of about 10% in the case of the index. However, to get a risk-adjusted measure of private equity performance, the authors take into account three factors: a discount to account for the risk highly leveraged investments generate, a discount for illiquidity risk and a stability premium because private equity-backed companies are generally more stable business-wise. The authors show that the risk-adjusted returns from private equity are—on average—roughly equivalent to returns from the public capital market.

Of course, when one looks at the top-quartile funds instead of the industry average, the picture is significantly different.

Correlation to other asset classes

One of the most enduring beliefs about private equity as an asset class is that its returns are not closely correlated to the returns of many other assets. Consequently, adding private equity to one's portfolio brings material diversification benefits. The argument is not entirely fallacious, but it does fail to capture a number of significant caveats.

First of all, there is a wide variety of private equity strategies, each with different economic sources of risk and return. As explained by Goldman Sachs in a 2005 paper on private equity risk return, if a private equity-backed company does not have many new sources of risks and returns compared to public companies, its return is expected to be fairly correlated with the market. Similarly, a VC-backed technology company whose success depends more on the effectiveness of the innovation than on general market conditions might see its return correlated less with the public market compared to a buyout that relies mostly on financial leverage to create value.[26]

Although the exact nature of the correlation between private equity and other asset classes is the object of much debate, most studies show that the correlation is significant, with the asset class not being the isolated island many tend to believe.[27] In particular, as seen in **Exhibit 4.8**, private equity has historically shown high correlation to the broad stock market. On the other hand, private equity tends

[25] Meerkatt, H., Liechstenstein, H., *et al.*, "The advantage of persistence: How private equity firms beat the fade", BCG/IESE report, February 2008.

[26] Winkelmann, K., Browne, S. and Murphy, D., "Active Risk Budgeting in Action: Assessing Risk and Return in Private Equity", Strategic Research, Goldman Sachs, 2005.

[27] Van Swaay, H., "Private equity and stock markets", *Le Temps*, October 15, 2012.

Exhibit 4.8 Median public pension fund returns by asset classes (as of June 30, 2013)

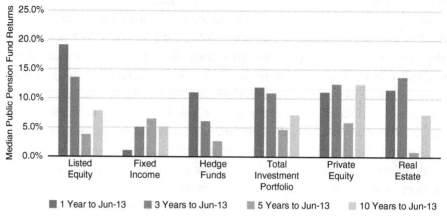

Source: Preqin

to have a low correlation with real estate or fixed income indices, such as the NAREIT Equity index or the 90-day US Treasury-Bill index. Venture capital, for its part, also exhibits a very high correlation, sometimes in excess of 90%, to the NASDAQ stock index.

JP Morgan, in a study published in 2008, found similar results when taking the 20-year track record of the Cambridge Venture Capital and Private Equity indices: the correlation between private equity and US Small Stocks was 58%, and 65% with the Wilshire 5000, and could even be underestimated due to the infrequency of private equity reporting. Other alternative asset classes, such as realty, timber or funds-of-funds, exhibit, however, much lower correlation with public markets, according to the authors, and might provide better options for diversification.[28]

The existence of relatively high correlations might be due to a number of factors. First, the financing of private equity deals relies heavily on the credit market. Second, the stock market is an important provider of exit opportunities and a trusted reference for trade sales valuations.

However, value creation in private equity comes to large extent post-investment. This value creation may not be strongly correlated with public market returns; instead, it is derived mostly from idiosyncratic capabilities and circumstances. Therefore, funds managed by good managers—those who create the biggest value post-investment—should arguably be less correlated with public markets, and hence offer a better diversification potential. Research by Laurence Zage[29] reached the same conclusion: after adjusting calculations to include only top-quartile

---

[28] Mergenthaler, K. and Moten, C., "Private Equity for Institutional Investors: Current Environment and Trends", J.P. Morgan Investment Analytics and Consulting, 2008.

[29] Investment & Pensions Europe, March 2004.

performers, persistent outperformance as well as a lower degree of observable correlation to quoted markets could be found, with a correlation coefficient to the MSCI USA Index of 0.50 for top-quartile funds, against 0.85 for all funds.

A criticism of the diversification argument in the case of private equity is that diversification seems to be particularly effective in protecting portfolios against risk—when risk is not present! Alternatively, bouts of negative volatility tend to be associated quite systematically with increases in observed correlations, hence reducing the diversification benefits when most needed. Practically speaking, the prices of various assets are more likely to track US stocks in down markets than in up markets.

Robinson and Sensoy (2011) looked more specifically at the correlation of private equity cash flows with public markets: they found that capital calls and distributions both increase when public equity valuations rise. Private equity distributions are, however, more sensitive than calls, implying a pro-cyclical asset class.[30]

The challenging task for investors is to make optimal portfolio allocations between private equity and publicly-listed equities. In their 2005 paper, Goldman Sachs' researchers adapted the standard CAPM model, commonly used for public equities, to estimate the risk and returns of private equity assets and hopefully provide a framework for investors to better understand risk.[31] Returns were typically decomposed into a risk-free rate, a return due to exposure to the equity markets—the *beta*, and a return due to deviations from the market portfolio—the *alpha* (see CAPM equation below).[32] The alpha effectively refers to the return that is not correlated with the public markets, but instead is attributable to the private equity investor skills. Recognizing the difficulty of using the CAPM model empirically for private equity investments, the authors made various assumptions on the model parameters (such as the alpha, beta, equity index selection, carry and expected information ratio) to allow investors to optimize their private equity portfolio allocation.[33] In particular, they showed that the more leveraged a company is, the more sensitive returns are to equity market fluctuations (through the impact on beta), and the more volatile they become (through the impact on residual volatility).

[30] Robinson, D. and Sensoy, B., "Private Equity in the 21st Century: Liquidity, Cash Flows, and Performance from 1984–2010", Charles A. Dice Center Working Paper No. 2010-021.

[31] Winkelmann, K., Browne, S. and Murphy, D., "Active Risk Budgeting in Action: Assessing Risk and Return in Private Equity", Strategic Research, Goldman Sachs, 2005.

[32] In financial terms, the alpha is the product of the information ratio (IR) and the residual volatility, such that the CAPM model can be written as: $(R_p-R_f)=Beta*(R_m-R_f)+IR*(Residual\ Volatility)$.

[33] See Winkelmann K., Browne, S. and Murphy, D., "Active Risk Budgeting in Action: Assessing Risk and Return in Private Equity", Strategic Research, Goldman Sachs, 2005, for a discussion on the calibration of parameters and how it impacts portfolio decisions. In particular, the authors show that one can take as equity index for large buyouts the S&P 500 Index, for small buyouts the Russell 2000 Index and for European buyouts the MSCI Europe Index.

5

The main characters in private equity

Executive summary

The macro perspective adopted so far fails to capture the incredible diversity of managers within private equity. The industry is anything but a homogeneous grouping, and will become even less so as it moves towards a greater level of maturity. A multitude of specialized fund managers have developed, not only in terms of organization, but also in terms of size, geographical reach, strategic focus and *modus operandi*. Darwin would have been proud of the evolutionary zeal of some of the sharpest minds in finance and investment...

The term private equity itself encompasses a rich variety of transactions, from seed investments of $10,000+ to $30 billion-plus leveraged buyouts. Traditional definitions and typologies of the private equity market are still helpful, but fail to reflect the latest evolutions and specializations in this complex market. In particular, private equity firms have developed idiosyncratic approaches to deal sourcing, generating post-investment value and engineering exits. Employing armies of management consultants, industry veterans and assorted advisors, they continuously seek to develop new edges to achieve superior performance. In this chapter, we employ different perspectives to segment the private equity world and attempt to reveal its amazing variety and specialization today. We investigate firm sizes, geographic reaches, styles and strategies as means to gain better insights into their value creation potential.

Limited Partners (LPs), for their part, also continue to look for diversification across sectors, segments, strategies and geographies to gain wider exposures. Their needs for returns and cash flows as well as their willingness to take risk from illiquidity or business, continuously shift as they undergo radical regulatory changes of their own. Shifting LP constraints affect the General Partners (GPs) ability to deliver, forcing them to adopt new approaches to deal making and portfolio management. LPs also develop new desires based on what is perceived as "hot" at any particular point in time, and these interests have to be taken into consideration. For example, while mega-funds were very popular before the financial crisis, LP surveys indicate that mid-market funds, distressed funds and funds focused on Asia-Pacific gained in popularity after that.

The preceding chapters were used to discuss the industry as a whole, looking at the way it functions and performs. But the industry is far from homogeneous; it actually aggregates a wide variety of players differentiating on many fronts. This chapter takes a finer comb to explore these different segments of private equity, shedding light on the extraordinary diversity of an industry that is becoming more and more specialized and differentiated. Through carefully selected case studies, we hope to gain a new appreciation for the distinct personalities of leading characters in the industry. Understanding these players in depth is a pre-requirement for any prospective investor before committing funds to the asset class.

Size matters: fund sizes, deal sizes and other dimension issues!

Most efforts at industry segmentation start with the target transaction sizes. Buyout transactions have traditionally been divided into small, mid-market, large and mega deals, but ambiguity remains as to what constitutes, for example, a mid-sized buyout, or what is really the mid-market. EVCA produced a relatively straightforward, if arbitrary, set of definitions (presented in **Exhibit 5.1**). The proposed typology is subject to interpretation though. For example, a €60 million buyout structured around a €14 million equity injection could be alternatively rated a small deal (in terms of equity value) or a mid-market transaction (based on the transaction value). During the credit-driven private equity boom that ran through mid-2007, investment banks informally labelled a deal as mid-market if its size was less than $2 billion...

Directly connected to size of transactions are the sizes of the funds themselves. EVCA again published a rather simple classification, presented in **Exhibit 5.2**. The classification, used mostly for performance reporting purposes, is also somewhat contentious in the face of the creeping up of fund sizes. A €600 million buyout fund specializing in large deals would have a hard time justifying a large fund label in 2010.

Each organization, however, has its own set of definitions. Preqin, for example, defines small funds as those below $500 million, mid-market funds below $1.5 billion, large funds below $4.5 billion and mega funds as those above $4.5 billion.

Exhibit 5.1   EVCA classification of buyout transactions by deal size

Buyout segment	Equity value (€million)	Transaction value (€million)
Small	<15	<50
Mid-market	$15 \leq X < 150$	$50 \leq X < 500$
Large	$150 \leq X < 300$	$500 \leq X < 1,000$
Mege	≥ 300	$\geq 1,000$

Source: EVCA reports

Exhibit 5.2 EVCA classification of buyout funds by fund size

Buyout funds	Fund size ($m)
Small	<250
Mid-market	$250 \leq X < 500$
Large	$500 \leq X < 1,000$
Mega	$\geq 1,000$

Source: EVCA/PEREP Analytics, in EVCA 2009 Buyout Report, December 2009

There are no accurate figures for the number of institutional private equity firms in existence, nor is there full transparency in the plethora of other organizations that, because of their style of operation and investment techniques, should be treated as such. For example, Philip Green, the high-profile UK retail entrepreneur who owns Arcadia and famously tried to buy Marks & Spencer, an icon of the British high street, has reported using private equity teams at his lawyers, accountants and banks. In all but name, his transactions can be viewed as private equity deals, even though they are not supported by investors in a fund structure. Similarly, a number of "super angels", i.e. sophisticated and often full-time venture capitalists, operate as professional investors, again without the benefit of a formal fund structure.

In the US, there are an estimated 2,800 private equity firms[1], while Europe's trade body, EVCA, reports almost 1,200 members[2] and the Emerging Markets Private Equity Association (EMPEA) counts more than 300 members.[3] These bodies, however, only attract the largest firms. Many are either too small to afford the not insubstantial membership fees or see little point in joining such organizations. Furthermore, many organizations are not private equity firms *per se*, although they take money from external parties to invest in private companies, looking to generate returns and realize their gain through some kind of exit event over a medium-term horizon. Preqin tracks about 5,200 active private equity investors worldwide[4], although China, which is relatively new to private equity, reported recently over 10,000 managers on its own.

One of the most significant developments in the private equity industry over the past decade has been the emergence of a handful of global players managing so-called "mega funds". No strict definition exists, but a number of funds of more than $5 billion have been raised since 2004, moving GPs into new, uncharted territory. Assuming that a mega fund has at least 10 investments and leverage of 2:1, this would translate into average transaction sizes of around $1.5 billion, with $500 million in equity and $1 billion in debt. Whether there are as many

---

[1] Private Equity Growth Capital Council.

[2] EVCA www.evca.eu.

[3] Emerging Markets Private Equity Association, August 2009, www.empea.net.

[4] Global Private Equity Report, Preqin, 2014.

$1.5 billion attractive buyout opportunities as there are attractive $0.5 billion ones remains to be seen. The fact is that competition among mega funds is considerably less strong than among regular buyout funds. There is only a handful of mega private equity funds on the market, and these funds may work in syndicates, as very large deals are well known. There are many more small deals than large ones.

Because those mega funds are still relatively new it is difficult to assess their performance. A number of points can be made though. As outlined by Andrew Metrick and Ayako Yasuda[5], the incentive system in place for buyout funds becomes less efficient when funds become very large. Performance related fees (carried interest) become less important than management fees.

A size effect, i.e. a positive correlation between fund size and performance, could be expected for a number of reasons:

Better managers. They generate larger management fees and potentially greater carried interests, meaning they can attract and retain the best talents. To the extent that the percentages of carry are actually difficult to negotiate, and hence do not reflect past performance, the only way to increase GP income is by raising larger funds.

Broader set of competencies in larger teams. Larger funds can recruit industry veterans as sector advisors or operating partners, an option simply not affordable to smaller funds.

Natural selection. Not all funds get the chance to grow big: only the ones that have delivered good performance usually get to attract larger LP commitments. In effect, the industry has installed its own selection mechanism based on realized performance. Fund managers that deliver high performance get rewarded with larger funds. This means that large funds are generally managed by fund managers who have been successful in the past with smaller funds and their success has allowed them to raise increasingly larger funds.

Stronger external supports. Larger funds are privileged clients for external service providers such as investment bankers, auditors, underwriters, consultants and lawyers (see Chapter 6). As such, they are likely to receive superior service, particularly at exits through IPOs or trade sales, when service providers reap handsome fees, as well as preferential treatment or early approaches on the best deal opportunities. The concept of reciprocity is extremely strong between buyout groups and the advisory and transactions support firms that service them.

Economies of scale. Many functions within the firm benefit from clear economies of scale, such as deal administration, reporting and

5   Metrick, A. and Yasuda, A., "The economics of private equity funds", Chicago GSB working paper, 2008.

fundraising. Senior people have to dedicate a substantial portion of their time to raising capital every three to four years. By contrast, the largest funds have dedicated fundraising teams and maintain a constant dialogue with investors and potential investors, while the senior managing partners focus on running the firm and delivering value.

Brand power. As with any industry, brand plays a key role in private equity. In recent years firms have invested in their brands, sponsoring and speaking at conferences, advertising, producing and distributing marketing materials and, in some cases, pursuing aggressive PR campaigns. A strong brand brings benefits in fundraising, where investors have sometimes displayed a herd-like mentality (if others are in, it must be good) allowing high-profile firms to continue to raise funds even when their performance has taken a dive.

Superior access to deals. Strong brand names also attract entrepreneurs and management teams. When picking a VC firm or a buyout firm, an entrepreneur or company manager will look for maximum signalling impact, which is usually obtained through top-tier firms. Consequently, top private equity firms often get first choice on deals.

For the purposes of providing insights into the operations of private equity firms and their approach to making, managing and exiting investments, we pool players in the following generic categories:

Direct investors:

- Global alternative asset managers;
- Regional, domestic and multi-country funds;
- Mid-market funds;
- Venture capital funds;
- Distressed funds;
- Secondaries funds.

Indirect investors:

- Funds-of-funds;
- Other Institutional Limited Partners.

Exhibit 5.3 shows the contribution of different categories to global private equity raised.

In the rest of the chapter, detailed profiles are presented of firms operating in each of these market segments. The selection of firms presented is subjective; the intent though is to select and interview firms with strong track records and outstanding reputations in the industry. There is thus no attempt at capturing

Exhibit 5.3 Global private equity raised, by type of firm

Global PE capital raised (by fund type)

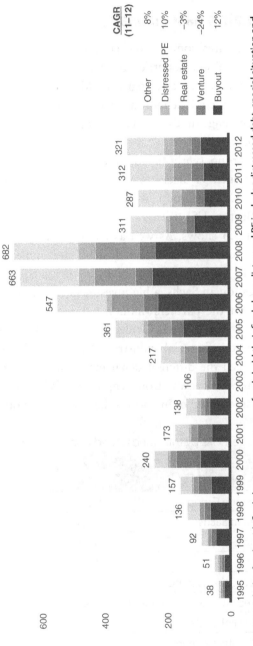

Notes: Includes funds with final close; represents year funds held their final close; distressed PE includes distressed debt, special situation and turnaround funds
Source: Bain Global Private Equity Report 2013, Prequin

the average industry player, but in effect to capture some "best practices". As explained in Chapter 4, good private equity firms tend to be very good, the bad ones very bad and the average produce only very average returns.

Global alternative asset managers

This category captures some of the largest private equity firms in the world, operating across multiple countries and with offices on all continents, from the US, to Europe, Asia and, increasingly, the Middle East. Whilst relatively young, these firms have attracted the most attention in the popular press because of their size. They often manage funds that have raised tens of billions of dollars and wield immense deal power.

This select group (with city of origin in brackets) includes, for example, industry leaders such as Blackstone (New York, US), Kohlberg Kravis Roberts (New York, US), Carlyle Group (Washington, US), TPG Capital (Fort Worth, US), Bain Capital (Boston, US), Permira (London, UK) and Apax Partners (London, UK), as **Exhibit 5.4** shows. As well as making traditional buyouts, many have expanded their product range to include debt, mezzanine and real estate.

One entity in the top 10 is not really a private equity firm, but the private equity arm of Goldman Sachs, a big investment bank. The structure was initially a vehicle to invest the partners' money, but soon expanded into a substantial manager of third party capital. Banks such as Goldman Sachs are involved in many sectors of the financial industry—therefore, "Chinese walls" have been established between the different departments; but not everybody is convinced and some investors steer away from "captive funds". "No conflict, no interest" is sometimes the description of investment banks' motivation.

Exhibit 5.4 Largest GPs by total funds raised in last 10 years

Rank	Firm	Total funds raised in last 10 years ($bn)	GP location
1	Blackstone Group	112.1	US
2	Goldman Sachs	78.4	US
3	Carlyle Group	78.1	US
4	TPG	57.5	US
5	Kohlberg Kravis Roberts	55.9	US
6	Oaktree Capital Management	55.6	US
7	Apollo Global Management	56.3	US
8	CVC Capital Partners	48.5	UK
9	Lone Star Funds	37.1	US
10	Bain Capital	36.9	US

Source: Preqin

Many of the large private equity firms have developed close relationships with the largest institutional investors. The California State Public Employees Retirement System (CalPERS), for example, has a direct equity stake in the management company of the Carlyle Group. As well as the economic benefit that can accrue to CalPERS from this stake (the fees generated by these funds are substantial), the argument is that the firm and its investors can cooperate more closely on future investment strategies to make sure interests are more closely aligned. In fact, the largest pension funds have so much money committed to private equity (even if it is a relatively small percentage of the overall funds under management) that the only way that capital can be deployed is through investing in the very largest funds. As an example, the Washington State Pension Fund, one of the largest private equity investors, was reported to have allotted $500 million to KKR's latest fund, the North American XI Fund, a fund trying to raise money in November 2012.[6] This was actually way down from the $1.5 billion commitment the pension fund had made to the KKR's 2006 pool. Similarly, the Oregon Pension Fund was reported to have pledged $525 million to that fund (which was said to have garnered some $6.2 billion as of November 1, 2012), compared to $1.3 billion for the prior fund. Part of the fundraising difficulties seemed to stem from the disappointing performance of KKR's 2006 gigantic $17.6 billion fund, which was reported to have returned only an average annual return net of fees and carry of 5.4%, short of the industry median of 7.6%.

These funds talk extensively of their ability to add value—Permira even calls its strategy "impact investing". It is, however, often difficult to sort out the reality from the hype, i.e. how much of the gain comes from financial structuring and how much from actual operational improvements.

EXAMPLE: THE CARLYLE GROUP

Founded:	1987
Employees:	890
Offices:	North America—New York, Washington DC, Los Angeles, Denver, Charlotte, Mexico City. South America—São Paulo. Europe—London, Paris, Frankfurt, Munich, Luxembourg, Madrid, Barcelona, Milan, Stockholm. MENA—Istanbul, Cairo, Beirut, Dubai. Australasia—Mumbai, Singapore, Hong Kong, Shanghai, Beijing, Seoul, Tokyo, Sydney
Funds under management:	€84.5 billion (2009)

---

[6] Chassany, A.S. and Alesci, C., "KKR struggles to lure money to a new Fund", Bloomberg News, November 1, 2012.

The Carlyle Group was the brainchild of David Rubenstein and Stephen Norris. Originally from Baltimore, Rubenstein trained as a lawyer at the University of Chicago Law School before acting as a domestic policy advisor to President Jimmy Carter in the 1970s and working in private practice. Norris is also a lawyer, qualifying at the University of Alabama Law School before becoming a VP at the Marriott Group of hotels. The two teamed up in 1987 to form The Carlyle Group, named after the hotel in the Upper East Side of New York City where the pair first met with anchor investors. They brought on board two other founding partners: Dan D'Aniello, a former VP for finance and development at the Marriott Corporation responsible for M&A, and William Conway, Jr. who had held various roles during a 10-year career at the First National Bank of Chicago, before joining MCI Communications as senior VP and CFO.

Carlyle really began to roll in 1989, following the arrival of former US Defense Secretary Frank Carlucci. In his first year he helped deliver a deal involving defence R&D company BDM International, a specialist in large projects including the US Department of Defense's Ballistic Missile Defense System. Carlyle sold BDM to TRW for $924 million in 1997 and made its investors 10.5 times their investment. In 1990 the firm launched its first buyout fund, with $100 million of commitments. Ten years after its birth Carlyle set up its operations in Europe. Today Carlyle operates out of offices in 19 countries to manage 76 funds—23 buyout funds focused on investment opportunities in Asia, Europe, Japan, the Middle East/North Africa, North America, South America and the global energy and power industry, 11 real estate funds and 10 growth capital funds that focus on investment opportunities in Asia, Europe and North America.

Carlyle has invested alongside other private equity firms in three of the 10 largest ever buyouts: the $21.6 billion takeover of Kinder Morgan in 2006 (alongside Goldman Sachs and Riverstone, itself a spin-off from Carlyle); the $17.6 billion acquisition of Freescale Seminconductor in 2006 (with Blackstone, Permira and TPG); and the $15 billion purchase of Hertz a year earlier (with Clayton Dubilier & Rice and Merrill Lynch).[7]

Norris left the company in 2006 and the three founding partners, Rubenstein, Conway and D'Aniello, are said to still own a 50%+ interest in the group and remain at the helm of The Carlyle Group. Succession is on the agenda and the recent overhaul of the management structure has certainly looked at addressing this issue. Decision-making has been decentralized, so that, instead of relying on the blessing of the three founders for every deal, there are investment committees around the firm. In this way the founders can concentrate on what they do best—Rubenstein fundraising, Conway investing and D'Aniello holding the operations together.

The rest of Carlyle is owned by a group of its employees, most of whom are managing directors, and two institutional investors: CalPERS which paid $175 million

---

[7] *Fortune*, February 25, 2007.

in 2001 to own 5.1%, and Mubadala Development Company, a strategic investment and development company from Abu Dhabi, which paid a whopping $1.35 billion for a 7.5% stake in 2007, before making an additional $500 million investment in 2010.[8]

Despite its unquestionable financial success, Carlyle has battled with its public perception. Carlyle employed some significant public figures as advisors over the years, including former US President George H.W. Bush, former British Prime Minister John Major (chairman Carlyle Europe) and former US Secretary of State James Baker, as well as Thaksin Shinawatra and Anand Panyarachun, both former Prime Ministers of Thailand, and Fidel Ramos, former president of the Philippines. The cozy relationships with political powers made the firm a target of conspiracy theorists, bloggers and radical filmmaker Michael Moore. In 2003, Dan Briody published the most famous attack on the group, *The Iron Triangle: Inside the Secret World of the Carlyle Group.*[9] Politicians may have impressed investors and brought skills to the firm, but Rubenstein acknowledges there was a downside:

> *"Carlyle was perceived as having strong political power and has had to fight this opinion. It backfired somewhat in Europe, especially as Carlyle has been identified as being close to the Bush administration. The former advisors were viewed more positively, however, in other regions such as Asia."*

Nevertheless, LPs are the centre of the business for Rubenstein, the fundraising specialist, and deserve openness and transparency at all times because they own the fund.

> *"Carlyle has been very successful with its fundraising operation. This is an ongoing and perpetual process. There is inefficiency in fundraising, as the style of the industry is to go back on the market every two years. Public/ evergreen vehicles offer a solution, as there is no need to go on the market. But LPs like the system as it is: they get more details, more information and a 'special flavor' out of the private equity fundraising methods."*

LPs certainly seem to appreciate the attention. As one said: "When it comes to fundraising and investor relations, they are best in class."

Carlyle's strategy is to leverage the local insight of its investment professionals around the world. It called this approach "One Carlyle". Its professionals collaborate across the firms' investment disciplines, from deal sourcing and due diligence to portfolio company development. The result is a broader view of potential investment opportunities and a deeper level of expertise, which helps create

---

[8] Carlyle press release, December 16, 2010.

[9] Briody, D., "The Iron Triangle", John Wiley & Sons, 2003.

value for Carlyle portfolio companies, and supposedly superior returns for Carlyle investors. Despite being risk averse and taking a "low beta" approach to investing, it claims average returns in excess of 20%.

> "We are pretty conservative and do not aim for home runs. On a quantitative dollar/profit basis, Dex Media was probably the most impressive (with a $2–$2.5 billion profit). The conservative approach has also led to the firm's worst deals—the ones it didn't do: These are the deals we passed on, such as Netscape, ATT Fiber Optics, Amazon. Internet investments in Europe were probably our worst financial experience."

Case Study 11
Carlyle and the AZ-EM carve-out

With strong industry expertise in semiconductors and specialty chemicals for the electronics industry, the Carlyle Group naturally zoomed in for a possible buyout of AZ-EM, an operating division of Clariant, global leader in specialty chemicals. At that time, Switzerland-based Clariant had operations on five continents, over 100 companies around the world, and over 21,000 employees, generating sales of around CHF 8.5 billion in 2003.

Clariant had a strong tradition of growth through acquisitions as well as targeted divestitures to streamline operations. In 2003, due to a significant downturn in some of its key product lines, the company was unable to realize the full potential of its disparate businesses, and the AZ-Electronic Materials (AZ-EM) business was quickly identified as a strong candidate for disposal. In addition to helping raise much needed cash for the group, the sale would help give greater focus to the remaining business lines. While it was not a household name, AZ-EM had manufacturing facilities in North America, Europe and Asia and employed about 750 people globally who contributed to the manufacture of many of the technologies used by consumer electronics companies such as Samsung, Texas Instruments, Intel, Toshiba and LG-Philips. It served broadly three main markets, flat panel displays, industrial chemicals and printing chemicals, and generally designed and built new products in close partnership with its customers.

Clariant engineered an auction amongst its closest competitors, but because no suitable buyer was found, it had to resort to the second best option—a negotiated sale to a qualified private equity buyer. The Carlyle Group's managing director for Europe, Dr Robert Easton, knew this was a good opportunity: the possibility of an exclusive deal; a seller in dire need of cash; Carlyle's industry expertise in semiconductors and electronic materials through its buyout and venture activities; and the attractiveness of the buyout target, namely a high growth, cash generating business that was not too capital-intensive. He had been scouting for new ways to apply Carlyle's expertise and funds to new companies. His background ensured that he felt comfortable with the industry and since the semiconductor market was not for the fainthearted, many potential investors would be kept at bay and valuations in check. He wanted to act quickly to secure an exclusive agreement with Clariant. In the cutthroat private equity world of 2004, proprietary deals were the only way to make money.

He got on an airplane to meet with the other managing directors at Carlyle, fully aware that each of them had the power to veto his proposal. In February 2004, The Carlyle Group submitted a preliminary non-binding offer for AZ-EM, valuing the business at approximately CHF 500 million on a debt- and cash-free basis. Soon after, following a meeting with the CEO of Clariant, a 70-day exclusivity agreement was signed. Third party specialists were hired in all key areas and given very specific instructions by the team to uncover the upside potential as well as all downside risks. At the end, Easton recommended that Carlyle make a bid and, through a unanimous vote, the investment committee gave the go-ahead to make a firm offer. The deal was signed in July 2004 for a reported €338 million.[10]

Carlyle's focus moved to creating value for the company by streamlining operations, bringing margins up to industry standards and managing working capital more aggressively. Its industry expertise was very valuable, and its global presence with teams across Asia, the US and Europe helped develop AZ-EM's business internationally. AZ-EM's management team remained largely intact after the sale. In the first few months, Carlyle conducted a strategic review of all product lines to increase profitability by either getting rid of ailing businesses or giving the promising ones more time to develop. AZ-EM also successfully carried out the carve-out from Clariant: within nine months, it moved from being fully reliant on Clariant's central administration, finance, HR and IT support services to operating on a standalone basis, with a new centrally reporting financial SAP system, one of SAP's most successful customer stories. The results were immediate: working capital was being managed tightly and significant cash flows were generated in the first year. Consistency in all parts of the supply chain was quickly attained with a big focus on quality, which earned the company the "Preferred Quality Supplier" award from Intel.

Equity participation by management added a true ownership stake and significant upside potential while aligning incentives with Carlyle's. Initially

---

[10]   The average 2004 Euro to CHF exchange rate was €1= CHF 1.54.

sceptical about this scheme because they had to pay for their equity stakes, top management quickly bought in once bonus targets were successfully met. By 2008, most had generated significant wealth from their equity stakes.

Carlyle finally considered exit routes. It had acquired the company with a mixture of €112 million of equity and €226 million of debt for a total consideration of about €338 million. Three years later, in 2007, the acquisition debt had been completely paid off when it decided to sell 50% of AZ-EM's equity to Vestar Capital partners, another leading private equity firm, for €1.4 billion, a 10× multiple on the original equity investment on the realized part of its investment. AZ-EM went public in October 2010, giving a chance to Carlyle and Vestar Capital Partners to gradually reduce their stakes over time. The remaining 11.6% stake was sold in March 2012 for $208 million. In December 2013, Merck AG, the German drugs and chemicals company, put together a premium offer for AZ-EM for $2.6 billion.

Source: Case study written by the authors and included with permission from the Carlyle Group.

EXAMPLE: BAIN CAPITAL

Founded:	1984
Employees:	700+
Offices:	Boston, New York, Chicago, London, Munich, Mumbai, Hong Kong, Shanghai and Tokyo
Funds under management:	$57 billion

In 1984 three partners from Boston-based management consultancy firm Bain & Company—Mitt Romney (and a group of colleagues), Thomas Coleman Andrews III and Eric Kriss—founded Bain Capital. Romney, who began his career with the Boston Consulting Group in 1974, joined Bain & Company in 1978, rising to VP before leaving at the inception of Bain Capital. He was at the helm of the company for 14 years when he returned in 1990 to a financially troubled Bain & Company as CEO, leading a successful turnaround and returning to Bain Capital in 1992. After leaving Bain Capital in 1998 he took on the first of his public service roles as president and CEO of the 2002 Winter Olympics in Salt Lake City. In 2002 he was elected the 70th Governor of Massachusetts, and after standing down in 2006, ran unsuccessfully for the Republican presidential nomination for the Republican Party in 2008, following in the footsteps of his father, George Romney, who lost in the nomination race to Richard Nixon in 1968. Romney finally secured the Republican presidential nomination in 2012, bringing the whole private equity industry into the spotlight in his face-off against President Obama.

Joining Romney as founding partners were Thomas Coleman Andrews III, who came from a Virginian family steeped in politics—his grandfather (of the same name) stood as an independent presidential candidate in 1956. He joined Bain & Company in 1978 and became partner in 1982, before becoming chief executive of South Africa-based World Airways. Eric Kriss was founder and CEO of MediVision, a network of eye surgery centres, and then between 1993 and 1998 CEO of MediQual Systems, a healthcare information company. A blues pianist, he has written three books on the subject and in 2004 released his appropriately titled debut, "Initial Public Offering". Also in the start-up team were Josh Berkenstein, Bob While, Geoff Rehnert and Adam Kirsh, who all stayed with the firm for between 13 and 20 years and helped develop its strategic approach to private equity investing.

Bain Capital's maiden fund raised $37 million. Some of its first investments were in early-stage and start-up companies, including $650,000 in a fledgling office supply retailer named Staples Inc. In 1989, having invested a total of $2 million, Bain Capital sold its stake for $13 million. From opening its first store in Boston with financial and strategic support from Bain Capital, Staples grew to 1,700 outlets in North America and Europe, now worth $16 billion.

Despite the success of early venture investments, Bain Capital began to see a broad mix of opportunities in mature companies as well. Strategic repositioning and the application of earlier consulting experiences became the core of Bain Capital's strategy, which recorded an average 113% growth per annum in assets under management under Romney's 15-year stewardship. The focus shifted increasingly toward LBOs in the retail and consumer products, information technology, communications, healthcare and manufacturing sectors.

From its foundation in 1984 to 2010, the firm closed 10 funds and made investments in more than 250 companies, growing to over $64 billion in assets under management. In 2010, its holdings included stakes in Domino's Pizza, pharmaceuticals group Warner Chilcott, Toys 'R' Us, Warner Music Group, Dunkin' Donuts, Brakes Food Distribution and SunGard Data Systems.

Bain Capital prized its very flat management structure, with all its managing directors subscribing fully to its consensus-oriented partnership ethos. Dwight Poler, who headed the European operations, said the consensus was due in large part to the fact that Bain Capital's professionals were, as a group, the largest investor in each of the Bain Capital funds, so the shared responsibility of the co-invest culture permeated all firm activities globally. This approach helped the firm attract—and more importantly retain—some of the industry's most talented investment specialists, with a depth of experience in all areas of the corporate capital structure.

"The level of co-invest is core to our culture of alignment, and thus to our returns. The minimum co-invest by GPs is 1%," said Poler, "and I would say a majority of GPs are in the 1–2% range. When your fund sizes increase substantially it

becomes harder for GPs to have more meaningful stakes, because even 1% is a lot." He kept the exact figure close to his chest, but noted: *"We are larger than any other LPs. Our LPs are very supportive of this alignment. They say: 'We trust you. You Bain Capital professionals have more money in than we do. Find good investments and we want to invest alongside you.'"*

In 1998 Bain Capital upped the ante with its sixth fund and reportedly raised a few eyebrows amongst its US investors when it hiked its rate of carried interest to 30%, a level unheard of in the leveraged buyout space. Silicon Valley's top tier early-stage venture funds, including Sequoia Capital and Kleiner Perkins Caulfield & Byers, charged 30% carried interests, but the standard LBO carry was around the 20% mark. The higher level was attributed to the seniority of the staff working on the fund, according to Geoffrey Rehnert, Bain Capital MD at the time. Yet 30% remained the standard Bain Capital carry over to the next seven funds to 2010—and investors went with it. Whether this carry can be maintained in the post-crisis marketplace, with some rebalancing of the power attempted between GPs and LPs, is, literally, a million-dollar question.

The founders' consulting experience had shown that a combination of strong management, sound fundamental business analysis, focused strategy, and

> *"At least 50-60 % of our time spent on due diligence is just on strategic and business due diligence – we cannot settle for just a static picture of a market or competitive position. Getting a very dynamic view about how markets will change, looking for dislocations or inflection points, looking for changes in competitive strategy or resources, and then understanding how well the target company is geared to adapt its own business model – its strategy, fixed/variable cost structure, resource deployment – as the market changes. That's where we look for differential insights of both opportunity and risk."*

Support for portfolio companies is also a clear differentiating factor. The firm has more than 60 executives worldwide focused solely on post-acquisition support of its companies—although this focus is increasingly being copied by rivals, since the financial crisis removed the ability to generate significant returns through mere financial engineering.

> *"At its core, our strategy has been similar to what we used to do for our consulting clients: focus on how to improve strategic positioning and operating performance,"* says Poler. *"At Bain & Co. we used to measure the change in client stock price from date of our engagement as a proxy. So what the founders of Bain Capital did was to take that philosophy, but put our own money behind it. And, with a more direct feedback loop where we can apply the right people and financial resources to ensure the optimal strategy*

is supported, as well as learn from our successes and mistakes, we have seen tremendous results. That approach is 100% the same now as it was then."

Critics of the firm asked whether the firm would be able to maintain its performance as it raised larger funds, and became involved in the biggest deals seen during the boom years of 2005–2007. Consortia deals potentially reduced their ability to control and direct investments, but also raised questions about how they could maintain a competitive edge over rivals and, perhaps more significantly, why an investor would put money with Bain Capital and pay a 30% carried interest when it could invest with a KKR or a Blackstone Group at a 20% carry.

Case Study 12
Bain Capital and the turnaround of Samsonite

In 2002 luggage maker Samsonite Corp. had been through the mill. The company, which started in Denver in 1910, had, for much of the prior decade, been majority-owned by Apollo Management, which had rescued the business in 1993 from the verge of bankruptcy. Highly leveraged by Apollo, its shares had plummeted from $44 in 1997 to $5, at which point, in 2001, it was delisted from the NASDAQ small cap market. The group, which also owned the brands Timberland, Lacoste and Tourister and was renowned in the US and Europe, took a devastating hit when global travel fell in the wake of 9/11.

"Samsonite," said Poler, "had gone through a dividend re-cap and been left highly overlevered as a public company. Then it hit a whole range of problems – 9/11, SARS and the Gulf War – travel, and the sale of luggage, was just decimated. Before we invested, the company had just too much debt and, even after the junior creditors had swapped their debt for equity, management survived only by cutting advertising and all investments just to make the interest payments. We felt Samsonite still had a good strategic position – it was very much a market leader, with a great market share relative to competitors, but it was falling behind. We also noted that a significant change in the industry was just taking place where specialty luggage retailers, which had fuelled the growth of specialist manufacturers, were now struggling as mall-based retail declined. So in a world without specialist salespeople to support small brands, we thought the value of a big brand would prevail."

In 2003 Bain Capital stepped in, acquired the company and de-leveraged it, with $106 million contributing to paying down the existing bank loans. The company was left with a single bond outstanding. With a more stable capital structure, manufacturing was moved to low-cost countries, the product was redesigned from the old hard-set luggage to soft side, which proved more popular. In March 2004, Marcello Bottoli, a veteran of luxury-brand bag maker Louis Vuitton, became CEO. A new management team was brought in and the retail strategy revamped after product and manufacturing goals were met. With Bain Capital's support, the company focused more on upscale products, taking that approach first to Europe and Asia and later to the US. In 2007 Bain Capital sold the business in a deal worth $1.7 billion to private equity firm CVC Capital Partners, which planned to expand the business to China and India.

Says Poler *"We left the company much healthier than it had been and back to being a market leader."*

Source: Case study written by the authors and included with permission from Bain Capital.

Regional, domestic and multi-country funds

Contrary to the global players described above, regional funds tend to operate in a single region, country or collection of adjacent countries. Investments typically range between $250 million and $2 billion, and often have a cross-border element or involve expansion into new geographies. With a well-developed private equity market, Europe is home to many regional players, such as 3i and CVC Capital, both based in London, PAI Partners in Paris and EQT in Stockholm. The US harbours firms such as Advent International in Boston and HIG Capital in Miami.

Multi-country funds tend to operate at a slightly smaller scale than the regional funds, generally targeting companies with an enterprise value between $75 million and $500 million, though many have the capacity to complete larger transactions if they find suitable opportunities and co-investors. Their office networks are, on the whole, slightly smaller than the pan-regional funds and cover a part of a larger area, such as, for example, the Nordic countries, German-speaking countries (Germany, Switzerland, Austria) or Southern Europe. In some instances, they will invest in a selection of countries that may not share physical borders, but where there are opportunities to transfer skills developed in one market into another with comparable characteristics, such as between the UK and Germany. In fact, UK private equity investors long ago took a liking for the famous Mittelstand companies in Germany, SMEs that are the competitive backbone of Germany's manufacturing sector, and for some world leaders in their niche technology market. Many now face succession issues as their founders retire, and are likely to need capital as Germany's once generous banks will lend much less under Basel III.

EXAMPLE: EQT PARTNERS

Founded:	1994
Employees:	200+
Offices:	Copenhagen, Frankfurt, Helsinki, Hong Kong, London, Munich, New York, Oslo, Shanghai, Stockholm, Warsaw and Zurich
Funds under management:	€11 billion

EQT Partners was founded in Stockholm in 1994 by Investor AB, the Swedish investment and industrial holding company founded in 1916 and still controlled by the Wallenberg family. At first, EQT was effectively an investor club for the Wallenberg family and their contacts and all the initial meetings were held in Swedish, unusual in the English-speaking private equity world. The firm was established with the help of US private equity pioneer AEA, which had been founded in 1968 by the Rockefeller, Mellon and Harriman family interests.

Conni Jonsson, who had worked for Investor AB for seven years, was part of the original team and has been managing partner since its foundation. Thomas von Koch, now head of EQT Equity, and Jan Ståhlberg, deputy CEO and chairman of EQT Partners, were part of the founding team. At the heart of their approach was a belief that the way to generate above-average returns for investors was through operational improvements at the portfolio companies.

"It took a lot of education and luckily enough we had AEA who joined in the venture with us," said Jonsson. AEA *"had the sort of philosophy we were trying to develop here in the European environment. Being able to refer to them helped us."*

"The successes of the existing private equity players were evident so people asked us: 'why do we need to do more?' The old models were very financially driven and we had to convert investors to our way of thinking. We had to explain that as the industry was developing, competition would increase and there will be a need to create value through improving the companies we support," recalled Jonsson.

EQT I was launched in 1995 and its commitments of SEK3.2 billion were fully invested in medium-sized companies in Sweden, Norway and Denmark by 1999. The fund was wound up in January 2007, having delivered a gross IRR of 88% to its investors and 5.3 times the money. EQT II, launched in 1999, raised SEK6.2 billion, was fully invested in 2000 and closed in 2007 with an IRR of 25%.

The firm began to look at geographies beyond its immediate Nordic environments, and started to expand to German-speaking countries with a focus on the acquisition of larger medium-sized enterprises, the prized Mittelstand. Senior advisors were quickly brought on board: Dr Mark Woessner (former CEO of Bertelsmann and president of Bertelsmann Stiftung); Dr Peter H. Grassmann (former CEO of Carl Zeiss); Harald Einsmann (former CEO of Procter & Gamble Europe); Dr Günter Rexrodt (former German Minister for Economic Affairs); and Dr Eckhard Cordes (head of group development at Daimler Chrysler).

In 2000 EQT began a foray into Asia, with offices in Hong Kong and Shanghai, followed by an office in New York in 2007 and more recently offices in Central and Easter Europe.

> "We could have grown faster but we like to grow under control and we like to bring in local people and then train them and allow them to develop. It takes time to grow."

EQT Partners organizes its operations into four business lines corresponding to the investment focus of the funds advised—EQT Equity, EQT Expansion Capital, EQT Opportunity and EQT Infrastructure. In total there are approximately 200 employees at EQT, half of which are investment professionals. The 30 partners jointly own 69% of the shares, with Investor AB holding the rest. In 2007 Investor AB reduced its stake. As the funds grew in size, it had to cast its net further into European pools of capital, progressively becoming less reliant on Sweden and the Nordic region for investors.

EQT invested in all sectors and companies in which the funds could stimulate change to achieve improvements. It had access to sector-specific knowledge through its extensive network of senior industrialists, which were closely engaged in acquiring, managing and exiting investments.

> Jonsson says: "we apply whatever is needed to manage the company and to allow it to be developed—in some cases it is strategy, in others structure, operating efficiency or product or market development. It's different from case to case. The challenge for us is to convince people that the model of applying an industrial approach to a project would be successful."

Each portfolio company is equipped with a "managing Troika" of a CEO, a board chairman and an EQT representative, which allows for an active dialogue with— and acts as a sounding board to—the CEO on a continuous and informal basis. This Troika, at the core of EQT's corporate governance model, is evaluated once a year in a 360° appraisal process, ensuring that relevant competencies are always present at the board level, that all board members add value and that governance is carried out in accordance with EQT's principles.

"Most firms buy companies, hold them for a while and then sell them," says Jonsson. *"We don't operate that way. We buy companies and then we manage them and then we sell them. And if you do not have a complete understanding of how you govern a company, how it functions, the legal framework, how to work with unions and the management and the board, you are not able to manage a company, you can only watch over a company. We are here to manage companies, not only watch them."*

Case Study 13
EQT's investment in Tognum

In March 2006 EQT Fund IV acquired 100% of German engine manufacturer MTU Friedrichshafen, including the off-highway part of Detroit Diesel in the US, from DaimlerChrysler. The business was one of the world's leading suppliers of off-highway diesel engines, propulsion systems and decentralized energy systems, with turnover in excess of €2 billion and employing more than 7,000 people worldwide. The deal was reportedly worth €1.6 billion[11], with approximately €1 billion of equity going into the business.

The business was renamed Tognum and the first thing EQT did on assuming ownership was to invite the Maybach family to reinvest in the business after EQT realized they shared a common view on the potential for development of the company. Apart from the eponymous Maybach company, which had been founded in 1909 by Karl and Wilhelm Maybach, EQT also appointed a heavyweight team of four industrial members to the supervisory board: chairman Rolf Eckrodt, formerly executive president and COO of Mitsubishi Motors Corporation; Sune Karlsson, who was formerly executive VP of ABB; Giulio Mazzalupi, who was president and COO of the Atlas Copco Group; and Jürgen Grossmann, who was CEO and sole shareholder of Georgsmarienhütte Holding, which comprised 43 companies active in heavy industry. Two representatives from EQT Partners and six executive members from Tognum completed the supervisory board.

"We made some serious investments in a new engine range and pushed the company aggressively to enter Asian markets and move production to Asia to get costs down," said Jonsson. *"We had some fortunate timing with the cruise ship market, the energy market, the off-road market, infrastructure and Eastern Europe. The new board was very constructive and made sure management really went there and exploited those opportunities."*

---

[11] *Financial Times*, May 2, 2008.

Tognum's shares were listed on the Frankfurt Stock Exchange in July 2007, raising €2.07 billion, the biggest German IPO since Postbank in 2000. EQT made €268 million from the IPO. Two months later the company was listed on MDAX. In July 2008, just two years after it had taken the firm over, EQT sold its last shares in Tognum to Daimler. Sales had grown almost 50% to €3.2 billion, while EBITDA had grown 143%, from €213 million to €517 million. Daimler's minority stake valued the business at €2.7 billion, effectively valuing EQT's restructuring of the business at €1.1 billion. As an editorial in the *Financial Times* put it: *"EQT took a decent asset and made it hum, in what turned out to be a good advertisement for private equity in Germany."* Jonsson attributed the successful exit to EQT doing the groundwork and planning the process clearly in advance.

Volker Heuer, CEO of Tognum, was happy with the restructuring and the future of the company at the time of the final sale to Daimler:

> *"With its industrial approach, EQT has been a perfect owner and shareholder through our recent expansion phase. Tognum has flourished as an independent company, and we welcome Daimler as a long-term investor that provides stability to the shareholder base and remains a reliable cooperation partner."*

Not surprisingly, Jonsson was also pleased:

> *"This was a good deal, because everything worked out perfectly in terms of what we did with the company—how we were able to buy it, with the support of the union and the management, how we could put in a board that had a huge impact on the way the company was managed, and then what we did with the company and how we exited it. It was pretty much a perfect deal from all perspectives. What made it a bit unusual is that it was a very cyclical industry, so in addition to all things that went right in the company, every external factor also worked in our favour. We were able to get the energy in the company focused on the right things and their execution was top notch."*

Source: Case study written by the authors and included with permission from EQT.

Mid-market funds

Mid-market funds are structured to capture opportunities in the mid-market space, a segment they claim as less competitive than the market for larger deals (which tend to be broadly advertised and generate expensive bidding wars) and with better economics than small cap deals (where smaller amounts of capital are put to work while due diligence and value enhancement activities are very much size independent). The definition of what constitutes a mid-market deal is somewhat loose and definitions have been shown to vary depending on the stage of industry development. Preqin, for example, currently defines mid-market deals as deals ranging from $250 million to $1 billion, although for older vintages the threshold used to be lower. EVCA for its part defines a mid-market deal as one with a market value between €50 and €500 million, or equity values between €15 and €150 million.

Target companies often require significant interventions to professionalize their management team and processes and prepare them for the next stages of growth. Specialist firms, like Doughty Hanson & Co.[12], have made that active ownership approach a distinctive feature of their value proposition. Their internal Value Enhancement Group (VEG) operates very much like a dedicated internal consulting group providing support to the management teams. In line with the required interventions post-deal, the firm developed more cooperative relationships with the prior owners, to the point of defining the transactions as "cooperative" with management teams. In the case of their investment in TMF Equity Trust[13] in October 2008, Doughty Hanson Fund V acquired only a significant majority stake, leaving a significant ownership stake to the company founders. Headquartered in Amsterdam, TMF is the world's leading independent provider of corporate compliance outsourcing solutions. Founded in 1988, it provides specialized administrative services such as bookkeeping, reporting, HR, payroll, domiciliary, structured finance and fund administration services. Under Doughty Hanson's ownership, the company has completed 13 add-on acquisitions with a total enterprise value of almost €50 million. In January 2011 Fund V acquired Equity Trust, a global provider of non-advisory trust and fiduciary services to multinational corporate clients, financial institutions, high net worth individuals and intermediaries. TMF and Equity Trust merged in June 2011 to create TMF Group, the world's leading provider of outsourced back office administrative services. With operations in 75 countries, TMF Group provides services to more than 35,000 clients including nearly half of the Fortune 500 companies.

According to Preqin, mid-market funds raised $22 billion in 2012[14], 60% in North America and 30% in Europe. By contrast, small funds raised $10.2 billion, large funds raised $19.4 billion and mega funds raised $30.3 during that same period.[15]

---

[12] http://www.doughtyhanson.com/.

[13] http://www.doughtyhanson.com/private-equity/our-portfolio/tmf-group.aspx.

[14] For January–December 2012 YTD.

[15] Preqin Private Equity Spotlight, Prequin, December 2012.

EXAMPLE: H.I.G. CAPITAL

Founded:	1993
Employees:	250 investment professionals
Offices:	Miami, New York, Boston, San Francisco, Chicago, Dallas, London, Hamburg, Paris, Madrid, Milan, Rio de Janeiro
Funds under management:	$15 billion

H.I.G. Capital was founded in 1993 by Tony Tamer, previously a partner at Bain & Company, and Sami Mnaymneh, who brought hands-on deal-making expertise, having been a managing director advising private equity clients at heavyweight Blackstone Group. Before his spell at Blackstone, Mnaymneh was VP in the M&A department at investment bank Morgan Stanley & Co., where he devoted a significant amount of his time to leveraged buyouts and served as senior advisor to a number of prominent US private equity firms. Tamer brought extensive operating experience, particularly in the communications and tech industries, having held marketing, engineering and manufacturing positions at Hewlett-Packard and Sprint Corporation.

From the very beginning, H.I.G. set out on a different path to most private equity firms. For a start, the firm shunned New York, where most of the major players were based, with the two founding partners heading for Miami.

> *"If you take the entire south east of the United States and study the small cap end of the market, then back in 1993 there were just a couple of small private equity funds established there,"* said Tamer. *"I was based in Boston, Sami in New York and we both decided we would go somewhere in the south east where we thought we would get a lot more visibility and a lot more attention from the deal flow sources and the wider business community because of the lack of competition. It turned out to be one of the best things that we did. The attention we received was even more than we expected."*

It took the team 12 months to raise their first fund – H.I.G. Capital Partners I – a hybrid leveraged buyout fund, with an investment strategy which would draw on the backgrounds of the two founding partners. Its final close was $75 million. The investors were widely spread, with Tamer and Mnaymneh calling on the contacts they had built up during their time at Bain and Blackstone respectively – entrepreneurs, institutions and high net worth individuals.

> *"For the first fund you have to rely quite a bit on people who have seen you and trust you and know you have a good business mind,"* said Tamer. *"I had*

a couple of ex-clients I had done consultancy work with, and Sami had some he'd worked with at Blackstone. As an entrepreneur you have to call on every relation you have. It took us a little while but we were determined and it worked out well for us."

The firm by 2010 was a leading global private investment firm with over $8.5 billion of capital under management. Specifically it was the world's premier small to mid-cap buyout house, focused on North American and European buyouts. The firm had invested in more than 200 companies and employed more than 150 investment professionals. It had offices in Miami, Atlanta, Boston, San Francisco, London, Hamburg and Paris. The European offices were part of its European affiliate H.I.G. Europe, which was founded in 2006. H.I.G. was attracting less publicity because it was operating at the lower end of the market, below the media and government radars. Its investments covered a very broad spectrum of industries.

H.I.G.'s US family of funds was divided into five business lines: H.I.G. Private Equity, whose funds focused on leveraged buyouts, equity, debt and other investments in small and mid-sized companies; H.I.G. Ventures, which partnered with entrepreneurs to provide growth capital, expertise and the relationships necessary to build market-leaders; Bayside Capital, which focused on investing in mid-market companies that could benefit from operational enhancements, improved access to capital and balance sheet realignments; Brightpoint Capital, its public securities investment affiliate, which invested primarily in small and mid-capitalization publicly traded companies; and H.I.G. Realty, H.I.G.'s real estate investment affiliate, which made opportunistic investments in small and mid-size real estate properties in the United States.

The founders remain the firm's managing directors. Apart from their close involvement in fundraising and investing, they remain closely involved with the recruitment of H.I.G.'s investment professionals.

"Sami and I spend a lot of time on recruitment. The investment professionals that get hired here go through a pretty rigorous interview process. It is very important from a cultural standpoint – you want to make sure people have not just similar philosophies in terms of not having big egos and being very team oriented, but that they are folks who have backgrounds we believe we can relate with. A lot of people at H.I.G. come from a nicely mixed background of both financial, operating and strategy," said Tamer.

One of the defining features of H.I.G. Capital is its flat management structure.

"From the start we pursued a philosophy of having a very flat organization," said Tamer. *"People here don't have big egos, they love what they do, and really believe in the platform, the engine and the advantages we have."*

"We have a lot of ex-strategy consultants and operations people here as well" said Tamer. *"The reason I think strategy/operations experience is very relevant is that we are very proactive, very focused on results when we work with our portfolio companies – we seek to identify 20% of the action that is going to result in 80% of the results. This is particularly crucial for smaller companies, because it is very easy for anyone to come up with a long list of what can be improved, because everything can be improved – products, quality, customer service, distribution channel, efficiencies. For smaller companies you do not have the luxury of working on a long list of things. You really need two or three key initiatives given the limited bandwidth and the limited resources that a small company has to drive the best results. To be able to identify these priorities you need to have that general management hat."*

H.I.G. has remained steadier than most firms which dramatically increase the size of their funds.

"We have grown at a reasonable pace and mostly horizontally and not vertically. Instead of having one buyout fund that we grow to become a $10 billion fund where you are forced to do major cap deals, we continue to focus on the same size transactions but adding a distressed capability, an ability to do further growth equity, or the ability to expand to Europe", said Tamer. "And we grow our companies to become middle market companies."

Its investments take a variety of forms, from leveraged buyouts, management-backed recapitalizations and industry consolidations, to minority investments. The company uses finance from its different funds for each investment, and allows for a comfortable cushion to accommodate fluctuations in company performance.

H.I.G. Private Equity structures its investments in various ways:

1 **Management buyouts and recapitalizations**, where the team works closely with the management team and the company owners who wish to sell a stake in their company while staying involved and retaining operational control of their business.
2 **Add-on acquisitions**, where the team provides strategic and financial resources to enable company owners to acquire other companies which they have identified as attractive acquisition candidates.
3 **Industry consolidations**, where the team provides expertise in backing consolidations of fragmented industries.
4 **Turnarounds**, where the team is active in the investment of underperforming businesses and financially and / or operationally distressed companies.
5 **Corporate divestitures**, where the team brings the resources and experience needed to complete the divestiture of non-core or non-strategic assets of corporations.

6   **Public-to-private transactions**, where the team partners with the management teams of micro-cap public companies to take their companies private, in situations where the cost of public ownership far exceeds the benefit.

7   **Growth and development capital**, where the team provides growth capital to promising high-growth companies, typically by acquiring a meaningful minority stake in them.

"There is a huge overlap between our funds, which do 80% the same thing and have a specialty for the remaining 20%," said Tamer. *"We see the overlap in the deal flow we are calling on, the types of CEOs we are calling on, the type of lenders we work with, and the initiatives we are implementing. Our great network, and the many offices both here in the US and Europe give us the ability to tap into the network of the executives within the companies we own, or being able to make a customer introduction to one of our companies. I believe LPs see the power of that synergy. What explains our returns is the advantage the platform gives us combined with the discipline we have."*

Case Study 14
H.I.G. and Thermal Industries

Thermal Industries, based in Pittsburgh, Pennsylvania, was the leading US manufacturer of vinyl-framed windows for the replacement and remodelling segment, when H.I.G. took a stake in 1997. Its company's windows were primarily sold to remodelling or home improvement contractors and window replacement specialists for use in residential remodelling. Thermal also manufactured and distributed other vinyl-based products including patio enclosures, patio doors, outside decks and marine docks.

As Tony Tamer, co-founder of H.I.G. Capital said:

"Thermal Industries was a very high quality business but it was not making the most of its potential. The owner manager still owned 55% of the shares even though the company was listed on the NYSE. The owner accepted a price of $12 per share from H.I.G., which was lower than a strategic buyer offered for the business, but the owner elected to stick with H.I.G. because he believed in their plans and vision for the business. The only reason he did this was he said: 'I'm going to get to see this company do what it deserves to do and the employees will see it continue with a better future.' It is amazing to see these types of dynamics. It made us proud to see that our work was so appreciated by somebody who could have easily got out and sold the company for more."

Source: Case study written by the authors and included with permission from H.I.G.

Venture capital funds

It all started with venture capital, which targets early-stage, high-potential and often high technology companies that can grow into hugely successful businesses, if they get it right. Some of today's greatest companies like Google, eBay, Genentech, Apple, Amazon.com, PayPal, Yahoo!, Dell and Facebook were all originally backed by venture capital. Venture capital is the most difficult sector of private equity. It tries to create value by growing companies very fast. This can be done through new technologies, if there are new and fast growing markets for these technologies. Unfortunately there are many examples of brilliant solutions looking for a problem. Fast growing markets also change fast and are much less predictable than the buyout environment. On top of that a small, fast-growing company will be continuously teetering on the edge of bankruptcy, as it eats into its cash. Until it slows down, becomes sufficiently large and starts generating cash, it will have to rely on the next round of venture capital funding. Small early-stage companies and venture capitalists alike will try to spread the risk by having several investors in a syndicate. Typically such an investment round will be enough to get a company to the next milestone like a patent, a first client or regulatory approval. After reaching a milestone, a company will normally be worth (much) more and the next financing will be at a higher valuation. Whereas buyout houses have to buy low, sell high, make their companies a little better and then amplify these effects with leverage, venture capitalists have to do all that and possess a "nose" for the next big idea. They may also have to change the team several times along the way. Developing a prototype requires different skills from obtaining regulatory approval or from setting up production in the Far East. If you are lucky and good enough to get to an IPO, you will need a CEO who can put on a tie and be fluent in "Investor Speak".

Venture capital is cool and a lot more fun, as it works with fresh and sometimes outrageous ideas from young and creative people. However, the failure rates are much higher and the difference between good and bad venture capitalists is much greater than in buyouts. Venture capital does not scale very well unlike buyouts. It is hard to spend much more than $5–10 million sensibly in a typical start-up. During the dotcom bubble some start-ups raised much more and the extra money was spent on Porsches, which did not increase their success rate.

Contrary to the other segments of the private equity industry that rely massively on debt, VC relies principally on equity. The main reason is that VC-backed companies generally do not have tangible assets or stable cashflows that could allow them to get a bank loan. As a matter of fact, many do not even have a product or a service to sell when the deal is made, and many will require many years before they eventually do.

Gompers and Lerner (2004) traced back the origins of the VC industry to the aftermath of World War II, when the American Research and Development

(ARD) was formed in 1946 by MIT President Karl Compton, Harvard Business School Professor Georges F. Doriot and local business leaders to commercialize the technologies developed for World War II, particularly innovations undertaken at the Massachusetts Institute of Technology (MIT).[16] The US Congress soon followed by creating the US Small Business Investment Company (SBIC) programme to help small US businesses access capital not available through banks or other private capital sources.[17] The industry grew quickly in the 1950s, 1960s and 1970s—first in Boston and New York, then in California—although the annual flow of money into new venture funds never exceeded a few hundred million dollars at that time.[18]

The late 1970s were, however, a defining moment. First, the 1978 Revenue Act decreased the capital gains tax from 49.5% to 28%. Second, the Employee Retirement Income Security Act (ERISA) was clarified: up until 1978, pension funds did not invest in VC, the ERISA's prudent man rule clearly stating that pension managers had to invest with the care of a "prudent man". The year 1979 was a turning point when the Department of Labor implied that a small fraction invested in VC was not considered imprudent.[19] This clarification had a tremendous effect on fundraising, with annual pension fund commitments to VC rising dramatically from $100–$200 million annually during the 1970s to almost $70 billion by the end of 2000.[20] Whereas individuals accounted for the largest share of investments in new VC funds in 1978 (32%), their share fell to 11% by 1998, pension funds' investments representing 47%.[21]

The industry grew fast, especially in the 1990s: returns were strong, the IPO market was flourishing and the internet boom seemed to last forever. Between 1991 and 2000, new capital commitments increased more than 20-fold[22]... until the disastrous burst of the dotcom bubble put the brakes on an emerging industry.

The industry partially recovered a few years later with annual aggregate commitments amounting to $50 billion in 2007 and 2008, and more than 300 new funds were launched annually.[23] Today, since the recent recession's ravages, the VC industry stands firmly on its feet, attracting about $30 billion annually.[24]

---

[16] Gompers, A. and Lerner, J., "The Venture Capital Cycle", MIT Press, 2004.

[17] http://www.sbia.org.

[18] Gompers, A. and Lerner, J., "The Venture Capital Cycle", MIT Press, 2004.

[19] Ibid.

[20] Harvard Business School, "A Note on the Venture Capital Industry", July 12 2001.

[21] Ibid.

[22] Ibid.

[23] Global Private Equity Report, Prequin, 2012.

[24] Global Private Equity Report, Prequin, 2013.

EXAMPLE: TVM CAPITAL

Founded:	1983
Employees:	30
Offices:	Munich, Montreal, Dubai
Funds under management:	€1.3 billion

TVM Capital is a group of globally acting venture capital and private equity firms with an operating track record of 30 years. Investment teams have financed more than 250 emerging companies since 1984. During the last 15 years the firm has become increasingly specialized in the most attractive and high-growth verticals in the broader healthcare markets, with focus areas in financing innovative products and technologies in the European and U.S. biopharmaceutical and medical device markets, as well as healthcare services in the Middle East and India. TVM Capital funds operate globally with dedicated life science venture capital funds advised by group members TVM Life Science Management in Montreal and TVM Capital in Munich, and its healthcare private equity fund managed by TVM Capital Healthcare out of Dubai.

Founded as Techno Venture Management in 1983, as one of the first venture capital firms in Germany, TVM Capital raised its first venture capital fund in 1984. Headquartered in Munich, TVM Capital built strong representation in North America focusing on transatlantic investment models on IT and Life Sciences. In 2010, TVM Capital Healthcare started operations in Dubai and closed its first Shari'a compliant private equity fund TVM Healthcare MENA I. In May 2012, TVM Capital Life Science celebrated the start of operations of its new Montreal investment office and the first closing of fund generation VII. Today, the firm is one of the very few true international private equity and venture capital firms, counting numerous global deals with investments across many continents and countries, and with former portfolio companies listed on stock exchanges in Europe and the U.S. (including NASDAQ, London Stock Exchange, Frankfurt Stock Exchange, NASDAQ Europe and the Swiss Stock Exchange).

- 1996 TVM Capital portfolio company Qiagen is the first German company to go public on NASDAQ. TVM Capital was a lead investor in the company.
- 2001 To offer a higher degree of flexibility to investors, TVM Capital's fifth fund generation consists of two dedicated industry-specific fund entities — TVM V Life Science Ventures, raised in 2001, and TVM V Information Technology, raised in 2002.
- 2002 TVM Capital surpasses $1 billion in investment funds raised and under management.
- 2005 TVM Capital raises EUR240 million for TVM Life Science Ventures VI to focus on biotech and biopharmaceutical investment opportunities in the U.S. and Europe.

- 2010 TVM Capital Healthcare starts operations in Dubai with a Shari'a compliant fund focusing on private equity investments in healthcare businesses in the Middle East and North Africa region, as well as in India.
- 2012 TVM Capital Life Science starts operations in the Montreal investment office. An investor syndicate led by Teralys Capital and pharmaceutical company and strategic partner, Eli Lilly and Company invest US$143 million in the first closing of TVM Life Science Ventures VII, a new fund dedicated to investments in the life sciences sector.
- 2013 TVM Capital announces that its activities in information technology have come to an end, and its investment focus will be exclusively on financing innovation in biopharmaceuticals and medical technologies through its venture capital team based in Munich and Montreal, and investing in innovative and fast growing businesses in the broader healthcare market through its private equity team based in Dubai.

Despite having been involved in technology venture the firm did not get its fingers burnt when the technology bubble burst in 2001. The firm invested only in technologies it understood, from science to commercialization.

> *"At the time of the tech boom our LPs urged the investment managers to invest in dot-com," said general partner Stefan Fischer, who joined TVM Capital in 2000. "But the people here decided against it because they said they did not believe the new business models would be sustainable for most of the companies in the long run, and hence they could not create value and make a decent return from these investments."*
>
> *"We only had one dot-com investment in our technology portfolio, an internet provider," said Fischer. "All the other investments were outside the internet world. The bubble did not affect us directly, but indirectly because venture capital became less attractive as an asset class, LP's did not invest as much in venture capital anymore and the market for fund managers got smaller."*

TVM Capital restructured in 2013 and now has two teams – finance (corporate finance and fund administration), life science venture capital (operating from the Munich and Montreal office) and healthcare private equity (operating from the Dubai office). The finance team is a shared resource of the firm, interfacing with the industry-focused teams on all aspects of portfolio management and maintaining close contact with the LPs regarding fund administration and reporting.

Fischer explained the roles in their inter-disciplinary team approach:

> *"In most venture capital firms, an investment manager will cover everything related to a particular portfolio company. Here, we really split it up. I take care of all the financial, tax and legal aspects of the transaction and also later on I look after the company's monitoring systems and its preparation for exit."*

Dr Hubert Birner, based in Munich and Montreal, is responsible for the TVM Capital life science practice. Dr. Helmut Schühsler is the Chairman of TVM Capital and heads the healthcare private equity practice in Dubai.

With 30-years of operating track record, TVM Capital has invested in more than 250 emerging companies in technology and life sciences, in a mixture of seed and later-stage ventures.

"On the one hand you have to be a specialist, as you have to deeply understand the business and science of the company, but on the other you also have to be a generalist because it's not only the science, it's all the strategic aspects of a company you have to be able to cover," said Fischer. *"You have to look left and right and forward and backward, see what's around you and analyze it. You need analytical skills and decision-making skills. Then you have to also be able to implement on an operational basis."*

"Buyout funds and the hedge funds have delivered fantastic returns over the last few years, whereas VC, because of blocked exit routes, was not that favorable," said Fischer. *"We had to come up with a new investment model that met our LPs' interest: capital efficiency. Hence, our most recent Life Science Venture Capital Fund, focuses on a new investment approach to developing pharmaceutical assets in a capital efficient fashion, to a human proof-of-concept in single asset companies. TVM Life Science Ventures VII is a unique collaboration between TVM Capital Life Science and Lilly to finance and access innovation outside the Lilly walls and as a way to manage risk and share reward. This strategic relationship with Lilly enables the project-focused companies of the fund to reach clinical proof of concept efficiently and cost effectively. Each project-focused company can choose to work with Chorus, Lilly's efficient and cost-effective development engine for early- to mid-stage molecules. Chorus, which is part of Global External Research and Development at Lilly, designs and executes lean and focused drug development plans that specifically test key scientific hypotheses to progress molecules from candidate selection to clinical proof-of-concept."*

Case Study 15
TVM and the Jerini deal

In 2002 TVM made its first investment in Jerini, a pharmaceutical company whose core business was the discovery, development and commercialization of novel peptide-based drugs. The company pursued disease indications that had limited or no treatment options. It also established several in-house development programmes that addressed indications within the therapeutic areas of ophthalmology, oncology and inflammatory disease.

Jerini was nurtured as an investment for six years, and in July 2008 sold to global specialty biopharmaceutical company Shire. The sale came as Jerini's symptomatic treatment for acute attacks of hereditary angioedema (HAE) in adults, Firazyr, was about to go to market. According to Angus Russell, chief executive of Shire:

> "Jerini had successfully developed Firazyr, a first-in-class compound, which satisfied a high unmet medical need and treated a morbidly symptomatic disorder. With orphan designation in both Europe and the US and a launch in Europe in the second half of the year, the acquisition would bring near term revenues as well as contribute to Shire's longer term growth."

The deal also highlighted the importance TVM placed on staying close to big pharma companies, particularly when IPOs appeared less of an option.

> "Definitely, Big Pharma are facing serious problems: their pipeline will continue to shrink, so they need to replenish it and add to their revenue stream. It was the right time to sell because Shire was looking for acquisitions. Jerini had gained IMEA approval and was in discussions with the FDA, and Shire was convinced that they'd get the approval. So that was the right timing and the right candidate for Shire."

Source: Case study written by the authors and included with permission from TVM Capital.

Distressed private equity

Distressed private equity injects capital into companies that are going through tough times, in the hope that they get back on track. Preqin regroups three types of private equity funds under this umbrella: distressed debt, turnaround and special situations vehicles, and defines them as follows[25]:

- Distressed debt involves purchasing debt securities that are trading at a distressed level, in anticipation that those securities will have a higher market valuation and generate profit at a future selling point, or taking a position to potentially gain control of an asset.
- Turnaround investments focus on purchasing equity in companies that are in distress, and aiming to subsequently restore the company to profitability.
- Special situations investments focus on event-driven or complex situations, where a fund manager may be able to exploit pricing inefficiencies due to an expected or actual significant event.

[25] Preqin Special Report: Distressed Private Equity, Prequin, October 2011.

Contrary to the other segments, distressed private equity is counter-cyclical, a feature that many investors exploit to better diversify their portfolio. Adverse economic conditions help generate investment opportunities: indeed, two periods of economic downturn—namely the post-dotcom boom and the economic crisis that started in 2008—have created vast opportunities for distressed financing. These periods also saw a significant increase in the share of funds raised by distressed private equity funds, as a proportion of all private equity raised.

The distressed financing segment supposedly started when Chapter 11 of the US Bankruptcy Code was adopted in 1978. The law finally provided a framework for helping ailing companies, putting the focus on restructuring rather than on liquidating them. The junk bond boom of the 1980s then helped trigger many opportunities for distressed debt and restructuring deals.[26]

Because it requires an intimate knowledge of local bankruptcy laws, distressed financing is a complex segment, which makes cross-border investment challenging. The largest distressed private equity firm by far is Oaktree Capital Management ($46.3 billion raised in the last 10 years), a firm encountered earlier in the case study "Tumi and the Doughty Hanson Value Enhancement Group" (see **Exhibit 5.5**).[27] In that case, Oaktree Capital entered Tumi's capital in the aftermath of 9/11, a disastrous event for the travel industry in which Tumi was operating. In two short years, it engineered the required changes to weather the storm and start growing again, mostly by focusing the firm away from wholesale distribution in the US only to their own retail stores internationally.

Exhibit 5.5 Largest GPs by total distressed private equity funds raised in last 10 years

Rank	Firm name	Total funds raised in last 10 years ($bn)	GP location
1	Oaktree Capital Management	46.5	US
2	Avenue Capital Group	17.6	US
3	Centrebridge Capital Partners	11.6	US
4	CarVal Investors	10.9	US
5	Sankaty Advisors	10.2	US
6	Cerberus Capital Management	10.0	US
7	Fortress Investment Group	9.9	US
8	Sun Capital Partners	8.4	US
9	GSO Capital Partners	8.3	US
10	WL Ross & Co.	8.2	US

Source: Preqin

[26] DePonte, K., "An overview of the private equity distressed debt and restructuring markets", Probitas Partners.

[27] Global Private Equity Report, Preqin, 2013.

EXAMPLE: CERBERUS CAPITAL MANAGEMENT LP

Founded:	1992
Employees:	275+
Offices:	New York, Atlanta, Chicago, Los Angeles, London, Baarn, Frankfurt, Tokyo, Osaka, Taipei
Funds under management:	$25 billion

Stephen Feinberg founded Cerberus Capital Management in 1992 at the tender age of 32. The firm started life as a small hedge fund, with four partners trading distressed debt instruments such as high-yield bonds. By 2000 its funds had grown to $5 billion and it moved into private equity, focusing not just on picking up bits of corporate debt, but on taking control of distressed companies in order to turn them around.

The obsessively private Feinberg is not the archetypal leveraged buyout hotshot. Son of a steel salesman, he was born in the Bronx and brought up in the relatively poor suburb of Spring Valley. In 1982 he left Princeton with a degree in politics and worked as a trader at Drexel Burnham and Gruntal & Co. He founded the firm in New York with William Richter, who at 49 was the director and co-chairman of Rent-A-Wreck, a discount car-rental firm. The pair started out with just $10 million under management. Feinberg has been at the helm of the firm ever since, seeing its assets under management grow to $25 billion by 2007. *"Everything runs through him, full stop,"* said an (obviously) anonymous lawyer who has worked with Cerberus on several deals told *Fortune* magazine. *"Cerberus is Steve Feinberg."*[28] Richter is senior managing director and president. The other 275 employees of the firm are equally bordering on the reclusive. Outside of Richter, Snow and Quayle there was little in the public domain on the other partners, directors or employees. The firm's public relations professionals had a hotline for urgent, deal-related inquiries but no names were mentioned.

As with most of the large US buyout firms, Cerberus had strong political connections, in particular to the Republican Party, and Feinberg's notorious secrecy had allowed conspiracy theorists to run amok on the internet. In October 2006, John Snow, President George W. Bush's second US Secretary of the Treasury, was named chairman of Cerberus. Dan Quayle, who was VP under his father, President George Bush, was also chairman of Cerberus Global Investments.

Cerberus once suffered a reputation as Wall Street's scrappy pitbull, investing in ailing companies no one else wanted. But Feinberg refashioned the firm into a gargantuan do-it-all firm that controlled companies with sales topping McDonald's

---

[28] *Fortune*, August 5, 2007.

and Coca-Cola. It beat KKR to buy out GMAC, General Motors' lending arm, and snatched up iconic brands such as the Albertsons grocery chain, a business that ran a raft of Burger King outlets and, going back to Richter's roots, Alamo Rent-A-Car. For Cerberus the demarcation lines between a hedge fund, a buyout firm and private equity were always blurred, with the underlying strategy of a turnaround fund employing whichever tactics and financing instruments were needed to get the job done.

Despite being an extremely active acquirer of businesses since its foundation, Feinberg had managed to largely shun the spotlight. By 2007 Cerberus had more than $22 billion of assets under management, one-third of them being through its private equity funds. However, since 2007 it had to manage two serious problems in its portfolio, GMAC, the auto-financing arm of the Detroit car making giant GM, and Chrysler, which was acquired for $7.4 billion in 2007 before being sold to Fiat with a 81% hammering.

In January 2009, with two serious government bailouts in its portfolio, Cerberus was rumoured to be cutting 10% of its workforce.[29] In a typically guarded statement, the firm announced:

> *"Cerberus, like every responsible business, is constantly evaluating its cost structure to ensure alignment with the available market opportunities. In today's challenging economic environment, we, like many other private investment firms, are considering a variety of options."*

A banal statement made interesting by the fact that challenging economic environments should bring out the bullish side of turnaround funds.

Cerberus, tellingly, did not call itself a private equity firm or a hedge fund— it prefers the term "private investment firm". It has raised four buyout-type funds, each of which figure in the top quartile of distressed funds, according to research firm Private Equity Intelligence.

Unlike most private equity firms, which only took public companies private in the hope of reselling later at a profit, Cerberus used its enormous war chest— it raised $8 billion for its newest fund—for pretty much any asset it believed was undervalued. That included equity stakes, debt and real estate. The firm had a long-term investment horizon with the aim of creating industry leaders in the global marketplace. Operating in the environment of distressed companies meant Cerberus was very focused on modelling the downside risk of an investment—Feinberg's love of chess and all its permutations no doubt helped him evaluate plans B to Z. According to John Snow: *"Unlike many purely private equity firms, Cerberus did not invest with an exit strategy in mind. It invested with a 'buy, build and hold' strategy."*[30]

He added:

---

[29] *Financial Times*, January 19, 2009.

[30] John Snow to the Detroit Economics Club, July 11, 2007.

"The prescription we offer is patient capital. The solution we offer these companies is freedom. We can free a company to focus on what it does best and provide them with resources to do it. For a starved enterprise with a sound strategy, we can offer much-needed investment in products and people, freeing captured value. We are able to inject equity directly, and also efficiently raise capital in the debt markets."[6]

This was obviously back in 2007.

Cerberus liked deals most other private equity firms really did not—complicated deals that involved lots of hard-to-assess risks, some kind of finance business and unions. Not all Cerberus deals possessed those attributes, but a surprising number did, with Chrysler the most famous—or, rather, infamous. Other notable acquisitions included Bayer's plasma products business (2004), MeadWestvaco's paper business (for $2.3 billion in 2005), later renamed NewPage Corporation, Torex Retail, a retail solutions provider in troubled waters (for approximately $400 million), AerFinance, an aircraft leasing business, North American Bus Industries, Optima Bus Corporation and Blue Bird Corporation in the bus manufacturing sector, as well as bus companies Coach America and American Coach Lines, which it acquired from the UK's Stagecoach Group. In the financial services sector, aside from the acquisition of GMAC in December 2006, Cerberus acquired Austrian bank Bawag PSK for €3.2 billion.

Case Study 16
Cerberus and the car rental industry

One of the deals Cerberus built its reputation on was the buyout in 2003 of ANC Car Rental, the parent company of Alamo Rent-A-Car and National Car Rental. The deal was a turnaround and drew on Richter's deep sector knowledge of car rental businesses, having spent almost two decades with Rent-A-Wreck. ANC filed for bankruptcy in 2001, and after 18 months in Chapter 11, in came Cerberus. The business was acquired through the Cerberus vehicle Vanguard. The firm put in $240 million of equity and assumed what had been an overwhelming $3 billion debt burden. It added a further $2.2 billion of leverage.

Cerberus's approach was operational. One of the first steps post-acquisition was to evaluate the sites and the leases on the sites, with a view to renegotiating terms or finding cheaper alternative locations. An annual saving of $8 million in rent from the renegotiation of 14 leases in mission-critical locations, including New York, Boston and Los Angeles, set the business back on the road to profitability. The headquarters of the two operating companies were merged in Tulsa, with offices in Boca Raton closed as a cost-saving measure. There were 850 lay-offs.

By 2006 Vanguard—the new name of the company—had returned to profitability and was increasing its market share. Cerberus took a $126 million dividend and in the summer of that year announced plans for an IPO. But when interest was not forthcoming for the IPO, it switched to plan B. Vanguard's European business was sold to Europcar in 2006 for $862 million for a four times return on the original investment, while US operations were sold to Enterprise Rent-A-Car in 2007 for a healthy, but undisclosed return.

Source: Cerberus.

Secondary funds

The continued development and maturation of the secondary market over the next two decades is likely to be one of the most important developments in the private equity market for LPs. Historically, the secondary market has been something of a fire sale environment, with sellers often in a weak position and to some extent grateful for whatever they could get out of their private equity commitments. From a seller's perspective, the market had a number of significant drawbacks, among which was cost. This is especially true when supply is very large, as was the case in 2008 and 2009, when many LPs wanted to liquidate their commitments but faced heavy discounts on the market, often in excess of 20%.

As we explained above, the past 10–15 years saw the emergence of a relatively active secondary market for private equity and venture capital commitments, with three of Europe's biggest investors in the buyout and venture capital secondary market—namely Coller Capital, Axa Private Equity and Pantheon Venture—announcing in October 2010 they were raising almost $12 billion to launch secondary funds, anticipating that banks and financial institutions would be willing to sell a significant share of commitments made during the 2005–2007 boom years.[31]

The secondary market remains fragmented, with large players including AlpInvest, AXA Private Equity, Coller Capital, HarbourVest Partners, Lexington Partners, Pantheon Ventures, Partners Group and Paul Capital (see **Exhibit 5.6**). A mid-tier of managers, including Adams Street Partners, Greenpark Capital, Landmark Partners, LGT Capital Partners, Newbury Partners, Pomona Capital and W Capital Partners, manage between $1 billion and $3 billion, with major investment banks including Credit Suisse, Deutsche Bank, Goldman Sachs, JP Morgan Chase and Morgan Stanley running active secondary investment programmes. More recently, a clutch of specialist firms has emerged to buy direct investments in portfolio companies (known as "secondary directs"). These include Industry Ventures, Lake Street Capital, Saints Capital, Vision Capital and W Capital, focused on purchasing portfolios of direct investments in operating companies.

---

[31] *Financial Times*, "Investors seek $12bn to grab private equity assets", October 7, 2010.

Exhibit 5.6 Largest GP secondaries: GPs by total secondary funds raised in last 10 years

Rank	Firm	Total secondary funds raised in last 10 years ($bn)	GP location
1	Lexington Partners	14.6	US
2	Ardian	13.4	France
3	Coller Capital	12.9	UK
4	Goldman Sachs AIMS Private Equity	11.5	US
5	Strategic Partners Fund Solutions	11.5	US
6	Partners Group	8.8	Switzerland
7	HarbourVest Partners	7.5	US
8	Pantheon	6.3	UK
9	AlpInvest Partners	5.4	Netherlands
10	Landmark Partners	4.9	US

Source: Preqin

The secondary market is also less intermediated than the primary one, though an increasing number of boutiques are trying to muscle in on what is perceived as a growing market. There are also a number of initiatives to develop electronic exchanges for private equity commitments, such as NYPPE and SecondMarket, though these have yet to achieve critical mass.

EXAMPLE: COLLER CAPITAL

Founded: 1990
Employees: 100+
Offices: London, New York and Singapore
Funds under management: $8 billion

In 1990 Jeremy Coller left his role as sector fund manager at ICI Pension Plan to set up secondaries investment firm Coller Capital. The industry was very much in its nascent stage—in 1988 there were just a handful of such firms, all less than $50 million in size. As a secondary investor, Coller Capital was set up to acquire existing private equity portfolios of venture capital, leveraged buyout and mezzanine capital funds, together with portfolios of privately held companies or direct stakes in companies. Sellers of these interests ranged from financial institutions, corporations, government entities and family offices. It was in this fledgling sector of the market that Coller saw great opportunities for his new firm. He set up shop on Cavendish Square, just behind Oxford Street in London, and set about shaking the secondaries industry. In 1994 the firm launched Coller International Partners

I (CIP I), which comprised six investment entities advised or co-advised by Coller Capital, and had total investor commitments of $87 million. In 1995 Coller drew the media's attention to the secondary market when it paid $20 million to acquire Standard Life's portfolio of US venture and buyout funds.

Coller was fully dedicated to acquiring portfolios of private equity interests—both LP fund positions and direct investments in companies or corporations—from their original investors, who typically were financial institutions, corporations, government bodies, family offices or charitable foundations.

The firm's individual investments have an enormous range—from $1 million to $1 billion or more. In 2001, the fund purchased the Bell Labs corporate venture portfolio from Lucent Technologies. This transaction was often credited for kickstarting the market in direct private equity investments—also called directs or synthetic secondaries, a major feature of today's secondary market. Coller Capital's $900 million Abbey National transaction in 2004 was again, at the time, the largest ever secondary investment by a single firm. In 2006, Coller Capital made the first ever secondary investment in India, acquiring LP interests in a fund managed by ICICI Venture. And the firm's $1 billion joint venture with Royal Dutch Shell, completed in 2007, represented the largest ever secondary investment in corporate venture assets.

Partner Erwin Roex explained the simplicity of their offering:

> *"What we do is we provide liquidity to private equity investors, which can be at certain points in the private equity cycle important to a number of investors. One of the main reasons is that investors do not get any liquidity out of their current portfolios and that creates issues for those investors who were counting on distributions from the investment part of their portfolio to fund capital calls on their other existing commitments."*

Jeremy Coller very much remains at the helm of Coller Capital, as both CEO and chief investment officer. His role over the last 20 years in developing the secondary industry could not be underplayed. He was named in 2010 the fifth most influential figure in private equity by *Financial News*. His early career was spent as head of research at Fidelity International before he moved on to become sector fund manager at ICI Pension Plan, where he was an early investor in Dayton Carr's Venture Capital Fund of America, one of the early secondary firms. He attended Carmel College, and holds a master's degree in philosophy from the University of Sussex, as well as a bachelor's degree from Manchester University School of Management.

The firm has 10 partners alongside Coller himself. Veteran private equity lawyer Frank Morgan is president of Coller Capital in the US. Having worked with Coller Capital from 1991 as an external advisor, he formally joined the firm in 2003. He was previously partner at law firms Dewey & LeBoeuf, Mayer Brown and Gaston & Snow, advising international private equity funds and portfolio companies on legal and business issues.

Case Study 17
Coller and the Abbey Bank deal

In 2004, Coller Capital closed what had become a typical deal style—buying a private equity portfolio from a bank. In this case it was the $900 million portfolio from Abbey bank. The deal involved the acquisition of 41 fund positions with 32 different managers, 16 direct investments and around 850 underlying companies.

It was Coller Capital's ability to provide a complete liquidity solution which was most attractive to Abbey, and the firm's track record gave the bank a high confidence of closure—even in the face of a very tight deadline. Providing liquidity was the whole essence of the secondaries market. Abbey announced in early 2004 "a fair deal, at a price in line with our expectations". At the time it was the largest secondaries investment by a single firm.

The sale price represented a $105 million discount to the holding value, but this was net of provisions and prior capital returns. *Financial News* reported that Abbey lost "up to £286 million" on the deal.[32] But Abbey was looking to focus on personal finance and get rid of its non-core assets, preferably in exchange for liquidity. The purchase consideration was cash plus a secured loan note with £165 million principal amount.

Of the deal, Coller himself said:

"This sale is evidence of the increasingly mainstream role that secondaries are playing in providing portfolio liquidity to the private equity marketplace. Abbey is typical of the new breed of sophisticated seller in the secondaries market—an investor with a high-quality private equity portfolio from which it decides to exit in due course."

Funds-of-funds

Private equity funds-of-funds vehicles, as their name indicates, are vehicles that pool investors' capital to invest in a variety of private equity funds. Their role is very much one of intermediary, connecting investors who lack the knowledge and the experience to select private equity fund managers with private equity funds. They are used by investors who invest in private equity for the first time, for small investors who cannot afford an in-house team to conduct direct investments, as well as for investors who look for diversification across different vintages and sectors. Funds-of-funds invest in a wide range of funds, typically between 10 and 50, with some adopting an opportunistic approach to fund selection while others focusing on a specific region, sector or strategy (see **Exhibit 5.7**).

Many investors, however, find the cost of investing in private equity through funds-of-funds particularly high, as layers of management fees are incurred.

---

[32] *Financial News*, January 12, 2004.

Exhibit 5.7 Largest GPs by total private equity fund of funds raised in last 10 years

Rank	Firm	Total fund of funds raised in last 10 years ($bn)	GP location
1	HarbourVest Partners	20.2	US
2	Goldman Sachs AIMS Private Equity	17.3	US
3	Pantheon	15.2	UK
4	Adams Street Partners	15.0	US
5	Commonfund Capital	14.0	US
6	Pathway Capital Management	9.8	US
7	JP Morgan Asset Management— Private Equity Group	9.8	US
8	Horsley Bridge Partners	8.3	US
9	Siguler Guff	8.3	US
10	BlackRock Private Equity Partners	7.9	US

Source: Preqin

Indeed, aside from the management fee and the carry of the fund-of-funds (around 1% and 5% respectively), the investor incurs the fees of the underlying private equity funds as well. Funds-of-funds benefit strongly from net new inflows to the industry and suffer when volumes decline. The 1% and 5% model is inevitably under pressure when the market shrinks as it has done since the Lehman crisis. Some, like Partners Group, claim to increasingly focus on direct deals becoming direct competitors to the funds they invest in.

Listed private equity funds-of-funds offer investors the possibility of committing small amounts to the asset class, without the need to lock up the capital for a long period of time.

EXAMPLE: PANTHEON

Founded:	1982
Employees:	198 (as at September 2014)
Offices:	London, San Francisco, Hong Kong, New York, Seoul, Bogotá
Funds under management:	$30.5 billion (as at March 31, 2014)

Pantheon is a leading international private equity fund investor. Founded in 1982, Pantheon has invested in private equity funds on behalf of institutional investors on a primary basis across the US, Europe and Asia since 1983, in private equity secondaries since 1988 and in co-investments since 1997. Pantheon also launched its infrastructure investment program in 2009. As at March 31, 2014, the firm managed $30.5 billion for over 400 clients.

Pantheon has developed a strong reputation and track record in primaries, secondaries and co-investments across all stages and geographies. In September 2014, Pantheon had 198 employees, including 74 investment professionals, located across its global offices. The 74 investment professionals combine over 750 years of private equity experience, 20 nationalities and 22 languages.

Over the last three decades, Pantheon has evolved into one of the most established private equity investors in the world. The firm was originally formed in London in 1982 by Rhoddy Swire, as the private equity investment division of GT Management. Pantheon's management acquired the business in 1988 through a management buyout.

Pantheon's investment philosophy since its establishment has been that private equity has the potential to outperform other asset classes by fundament-ally improving businesses. This philosophy is underpinned by a shared set of beliefs: first, private equity ownership could improve businesses by a long-term approach, active ownership, close alignment of interests and good corporate governance; second, maximizing performance within private equity requires deep global experience, extensive research and vision, combined with appropriate risk management; and third, sustainable success for Pantheon depends on relationships with clients and fund managers, all regarded as partners.

> *"We prefer managers who tell us: 'Well we did this and it worked, but much more importantly, we did this and this and it didn't work and we've taken these lessons from that experience.' That is to us a more positive indicator than a manager who may try to pass off an unsuccessful deal as simply bad luck in an otherwise performing track record,"* said Swire.

Swire, senior partner and founder of Pantheon, joined GT Management to oversee and manage unquoted investments. He qualified as a chartered accountant with Peat Marwick Mitchell & Co. (now part of KPMG) before working as an executive and getting hands-on experience of running a business at the family firm John Swire & Sons, one of Hong Kong's great trading houses, in Hong Kong, Sydney and London.

The two other senior partners were Carol Kennedy and David Braman. Kennedy joined Pantheon in 1990 after four years with Prudential Venture Managers making direct private equity investments with a European focus, and 11 years prior to that at Procter & Gamble. David Braman joined Pantheon in San Francisco in 1987, after spending many years developing and managing US West Inc.'s private equity investment programme.

In 2010, senior members of the Pantheon team, alongside Affiliated Managers Group Inc. ("AMG"), an asset management company, listed on the New York Stock

Exchange, acquired Pantheon. Pantheon retains full operational independence and today exercises management authority through its Partnership Board, which is comprised of six Pantheon Partners and a representative of AMG who acts as a non-executive director.

Case Study 18
The Pantheon deal

In August 2006 funds managed by Pantheon acquired a secondary portfolio of over 90 venture capital funds and eight direct investments from an Italian listed company, Cdb Web Tech SpA. The underlying funds ranged in value from $200 million to over $1 billion, and the individual fund positions themselves ranged from $2 million to $20 million. The transaction value—price plus unfunded follow-ons—was in excess of $400 million and with just one buyer it was one of the largest secondary transactions completed in the venture space.

"We had been researching the Italian market since the mid-1990s and knew it well through traditional private equity primary fund investing," said Elly Livingstone, global head of secondaries at Pantheon Ventures. *"Cdb Web Tech was founded and 51% owned by Carlo de Benedetti, who made his fortune building Olivetti and had gone on to build a significant conglomerate. Cogent Partners, a secondary advisory firm we had previously worked with, knew Poli & Associati, another boutique, which was close to de Benedetti's organization. In Italy deals are very much relationship-driven, so how you approach people is very important."*

After the tech boom and subsequent bursting of the bubble in 2001, Cdb Web Tech's share price trundled along at around €2 a share. De Benedetti had originally intended to do more co-investing through the vehicle, but now in his 70s and still very active, he wanted to focus more on direct company restructuring.

"The first contact with de Benedetti's organization was in September 2005 and our first meeting with him was January 2006. We signed on an Italian bank holiday in the middle of August 2006 after the exchange had closed for the long weekend. It was large, complex and we had to leverage the resources of the whole firm."

"This was a truly proprietary deal—we were the only people speaking to de Benedetti," said Livingstone. *"It was an Italian listed funds vehicle—very*

thin trading in a very volatile and rumour-driven market. We were worried about our discussions leaking in the market—€2.40-a-share would suddenly become €5-a-share. They were equally worried, because they knew that would be a deal-stopper. We had coverage of more than 1,000 funds. Our work was based upon our pre-existing knowledge of the funds and the general partners—a huge piece of work to keep secret from the market. That we pulled this through was a testament to the seller, the advisors and our team."

EXAMPLE: ALPINVEST PARTNERS

Founded: 1999
Employees: 100+
Offices: Amsterdam, New York, Hong Kong, London
Funds under management: €40 billion+

AlpInvest Partners was effectively founded in Amsterdam in 1999 as NIB Capital Private Equity, under the leadership of Volkert Doeksen. NIB was the first exclusive and independent manager of the private equity investments of two of the world's largest pension funds—ABP and PFZW (formerly PGGM), both based in the Netherlands. While ABP and PFZW had successful histories as private equity investors, it was decided that an independent, dedicated and full-scale private equity firm would best serve their interests.

"Separating the entity from the rest of the pension fund was expected to bring about important benefits. One concerns the ability to build a stable investment team. In many captive structures we see quite a bit of fluctuation in terms of investment professionals. The two pension funds believed that for an asset class that takes a very long-term view it was better to have a separate entity working specifically on their behalf", said Peter Cornelius, research economist at AlpInvest.

In 2000, listed private equity firm AlpInvest with €700 million assets under management was acquired and combined with NIB. In 2004 it was spun off from ABP and PFZW as AlpInvest Partners. The enlarged entity has since grown to be one of the largest private equity investment managers globally with over €40 billion of assets under management at the end of 2007. By 2010, it had more than 100 employees in four offices around the world, including New York (opened in 2001), Hong Kong (2006) and London (2008). At the beginning of 2011, APG and PGGM agreed to sell AlpInvest Partners to The Carlyle Group and AlpinInvest Management, with APG and

PGGM continuing to be the anchor clients of AlpInvest. As part of the transaction, both funds decided to extend their commitment as clients by granting additional investment mandates totalling more than $13 billion for the period 2011–2015.

Volkert Doeksen, the managing partner and CEO, formerly headed Dresdner Kleinwort's private equity investment team in New York. Paul de Klerk is CFO and COO, while Erik Thyssen and Ian Leigh head co-investments and mezzanine, in Europe and the US respectively. Wim Borgdorff, a founding partner, heads fund and secondary investments. He was previously managing director of alternative investments at ABP, and before that a managing director at ING Real Estate.

AlpInvest is one of the few private equity sponsors with the financial scale and global reach to partner with the world's largest private equity firms as well as specialized high-performers.

> "We apply four principles to portfolio construction – market neutrality, correlation analysis, market timing issues and finally the probability density functions of different asset classes. So first, we start with market neutrality – we look at the relative market size of sub assets and formulate expectations about their growth over the next years", said Peter Cornelius. "Then, we develop proprietary views about the return outlook for these market segments that may lead us to deviate from a market-neutral allocation. In this context, we look at performance correlations to understand diversification gains and the risk in individual asset classes. Then we look at market timing issues. Although we aim at building robust portfolios over many vintage years, we do take into account that commitments made to funds in recession years tend to outperform those raised in overheating markets. Furthermore, we factor in the cyclicality of special sub-assets, such as mezzanine, distressed debt and secondaries. Finally, we look at return distributions, to use the technical terms, the probability density functions in different asset classes. Some asset classes are closer to normal distributions, in particular the more mature asset classes such as US buyouts. There is less risk, but also limited upside potential. This contrasts with asset classes such as US venture capital, for which there is statistically speaking a long, fat tail, providing upside potential, which inevitably comes with increased risk. If you can identify and you have access to these outliers it gives you quite a bit of upside potential."

In June 2011, AlpInvest announced that MERS, a US-based independent, statewide public retirement system with more than $6.5 billion in assets under management, had awarded it a $500 million private equity investment agreement. The agreement, tailored to the specific needs of MERS, had a five-year investment period and covered the full range of AlpInvest's investment strategies including fund, secondary as well as co-investments.

AlpInvest's portfolio consisted of 250 funds, with around 150 managers, out of around 1,500 funds in the market. It had 100 core general partner relationships. AlpInvest's investment committee, which is composed of partners from around the globe, meets weekly and makes all investment decisions. It had a smaller portfolio of co-investments, and still smaller portfolios of mezzanine and direct investments. Twice a year the investment team conducts a top-down analysis of the general characteristics, size and growth of all private equity market segments. Once segments are identified, the investment team then identifies the best-in-class general partners based on the team's desired geography, industry focus and stage of life focus.

Institutional limited partners

We talked in much detail about limited partners and the role they play. Below, we briefly describe one of the most important limited partners in the world.

EXAMPLE: CALPERS (CALIFORNIA PUBLIC EMPLOYEES RETIREMENT SYSTEM)

Founded:	1932
Employees:	2,571
Offices:	Fresno, Glendale, Orange, Sacramento, San Bernardino, San Diego, San Jose, Walnut Creek
Funds under management:	$242.7 billion

CalPERS is the US' largest public pension fund with more than a million and a half members in California. It is also one of the largest private equity investors. A third of its members are state employees, another third school employees and the last third local public agency employees. While the market value of the pension fund was below $35 billion in 1985, it approached $100 billion a decade later and exceeded $200 million two decades later in 2005.[33] The financial crisis dramatically decreased the fund's assets from $253 billion in 2007 to $183 billion a year later, although by October 2012 CalPERS' total assets had rebounded to $242.7 billion.[34]

The fund's strong allocation to private equity is without doubt a reason behind the spectacular growth of the portfolio: indeed, since inception in 1990 until June 2012, CalPERS' private equity programme has generated more than $21 billion in profits.[35]

The CalPERS Board of Administration has investment authority and sole fiduciary responsibility for the management of CalPERS assets, while the CalPERS

[33] CalPERS, Facts at a Glance, January 2013, www.calpers.ca.gov.
[34] Ibid.
[35] CalPERS, PE Program Fund Performance Review, June 30, 2012, www.calpers.ca.gov.

Investment Committee and Investment Office carry out the daily activities of the investment programme. As of December 2012, the total assets of the fund were allocated among various asset classes, with "growth"—namely public and private equities—attracting 62% of the capital, "income" 18% and "real" 10%. The allocation to private equity represents 13% of the whole capital, amounting to $32 billion, with buyouts occupying the lion's share at 60%.[36]

As mentioned before, CalPERS publishes every quarter the list of private equity funds in which it invests as well as the return. Such transparency, however, did not come naturally. Instead it is the result of a court ruling initiated in 2002 in a context of increasing pressure to disclose information on private equity performance. As Chaplinsky and Perry (1999)[37] revealed, such pressure started when the *Houston Chronicle* published an article citing a potential conflict of interest between the University of Texas Investment Management Company (UTIMCO) and Austin Ventures, the largest VC in Texas, in the sense that the former might channel the endowment funds to the latter because one of its regents was the partner of the VC fund. Facing mounting pressure after the Enron scandal, UTIMCO finally disclosed the IRR of the funds in which it was invested. Soon after, the *San Jose Mercury News* sued CalPERS for similar information, but CalPERS refused to disclose. Several reasons were behind that decision: first and foremost, CalPERS had made huge efforts over the years to develop and cultivate relationships with GPs, even by— as we noted earlier—taking an ownership stake in Carlyle, one of the industry's most notable GPs, to align incentives. It feared that those precious relationships would be damaged if it decided to disclose confidential information related to performance. CalPERS also feared that the public might not be able to fully understand the subtleties of private equity, with its J-curve performance and long-term perspective, adopting instead the same lens used to analyze public equities.

A lawsuit followed, with *Mercury News* proclaiming that the public had a right to know CalPERS' performance and to hold its officials accountable. The court ruled in favour of the newspaper, requiring CalPERS to disclose the IRR on its private equity investments; without, however, imposing that the individual portfolio company holdings within each fund and their associated valued be disclosed— such information being considered "trade secrets". Very quickly, investors in other states in the US filed suits, under the Freedom of Information Act to force their state pension funds to disclose similar information.

Left without much choice, CalPERS announced in December 2002 that it would comply with the ruling. CalPERS now (mid-2014) provides private equity performance information on a quarterly basis.

---

[36] CalPERS, "Facts at a Glance", January 2013, www.calpers.ca.gov.

[37] All the information on the 2002 ruling for investment transparency is taken from: Chaplinsky, S. and Perry, S., "CalPERS versus Mercury News: Disclosure Comes to Private Equity", Darden Business Publishing, 2004.

6

The supporting cast

Executive summary

Private equity firms tend to be relatively lean economic animals, relying on a small dedicated staff primarily focused on executing deals and possibly creating post-investment value at portfolio companies. For all other activities, they prefer to punctually acquire external resources to bring to bear on specific situations. Consequently, a very fluid and dynamic ecosystem has appeared around private equity firms, with numerous providers offering specialized teams and services to eager clients.

With the industry maturing, a bewildering array of services has become available to private equity firms, including: fundraising, fund administration, financial, legal, commercial and environmental due diligences, structured finance, M&A advisory, accountancy as well as recruitment and public relations. These services are often required at specific times in the life of a fund, in particular during fundraising and deal closing phases, i.e. "transaction" times.

Banks have also carved out a nice operating niche serving the industry. They generate private equity-related income through at least three different activities: advising private equity firms on M&A, structuring syndicated loans to support acquisitions and providing leveraged finance. During the credit bubble of the mid-2000s, bankers often "double-dipped" by also generating generous initiation and management fees out of the repackaging of LBO-related debt into Collateralized Loan Obligations (CLO), the functional equivalent in the world of buyouts of the Collateralized Mortgage Obligations (CMO) that plagued real estate during those years.

This system, like all ecosystems, is subject to constant evolution. With its environment changing rapidly, private equity had demonstrated a phenomenal ability to rebound and recreate itself in the face of adversity. In this chapter, we provide an in-depth, dynamic picture of the inner workings of the private equity ecosystem, with its multiple layers of interacting players and systems, from bankers to consultants, to placement agents, due diligence specialist providers, lawyers and accounting firms. To do this, we offer to follow the fee trail, a most entertaining and educating walk down private equity alley...

Private equity is a team sport: winning requires professional support, support that requires skills and talents that are highly specialized and not commonly available. This has naturally led to the development of specialized ecosystems and niches, to which mutually dependent organisms have gravitated for the benefit of all. Silicon Valley in California, Route 128 in Massachusetts, Research Triangle Park in North Carolina or Silicon Alley in New York are all US representatives of that clustering tendency of venture capital, bringing together entrepreneurs risk investors, intellectual property experts, research institutions and specialized financial services firms. In Europe, similar forces have generated similar patterns of concentration, although at times driven by the heavy hand of the state. Sophia Antipolis, for example, situated north of Nice on the French Riviera, was meant as France's response to Silicon Valley, but the top-down approach failed to convince over the long term. Silicon Glen, around Edinburgh, Scotland, gained some traction but suffered from over-dependency on a limited number of technologies and large corporate players. On the other hand, areas around Oxford and Cambridge in the UK and Lausanne and Zurich in Switzerland have been able to hatch dynamic venture systems, usually centred around world-class research centres, respectively Oxford University, Cambridge University and the two campuses of the Swiss Federal Institute of Technology.

Private equity, despite its lower dependency on leading edge technology, has generated the same centripetal forces, bringing actors to a common location for ease of service. New York, Washington, Chicago, Boston, Houston, Los Angeles have all claimed their piece of the action in the US. In Europe, the fight between London, Paris and Frankfurt as to who would reign supreme to serve the Kings of private equity seemed to have been settled in the 1990s, when London established its supremacy in European merchant banking. But evolution prevails in all ecosystems, and no dominant position is ever permanent. Recent measures on taxes and the treatment of bonuses on financial firms in London have generated an interesting exodus of professional competences to places such as Zurich and Geneva, proving once again the ability of the system to cope with changes in its environment.

Given the predominant modus operandi of the industry, involving mostly infrequent idiosyncratic transactions, the most efficient way for private equity executives to gather the necessary skills and resources is to "rent" them when needed. This has led to the creation of a vibrant cast of "supporters" all too willing to supply these services to private equity clients. What started as a natural arrangement became somewhat blurred and possibly corrupted by the very size of the money to be distributed, leading at times to questionable relationship amongst key players, in particular between lenders, investment banks and private equity partners.

The distribution of roles and responsibilities, the duties of care and professionalism, the nature of compensations, the visibility and transparency are constantly shifting and responding to pressures from the public and the regulatory authorities. As every living organism, private equity has developed an uncanny ability to adapt to changing circumstances. As a pocket of wealth that until recently was relatively free from regulation and oversight, it had the ability to attract the best and brightest and make a contribution to society as a whole. As the ultimate embodiment of the "invisible hand", it disciplined firms and managers in extracting the most value out of the assets handed over to them by shareholders and investors. To do this, it built on some of the most fundamental forces of human nature, combining strong financial incentives with personal risk exposure to extract the best out of people. In a way, private equity could be described as a form of "capitalism on steroids", pushing to the limit the basic recipes for leveraging human, operational and financial resources...

In this chapter, we describe in depth the inner workings of the private equity ecosystem, with its multiple layers of interacting players and systems. As we point out, the system can at times appear incestuous and self-serving. This may be one of the costs to pay for efficiency. In all instances, gaining a fine understanding of the interactions between all actors is key to understanding the functioning of the industry and developing an ability to navigate its complex waters.

London as European centre of gravity

When the giants of the US private equity industry landed in London in the late 1990s, it was not in the traditional base of finance—the City—that they looked to set up shop. Instead, they sought to "out-establish" the banking establishment, opening their offices in areas such as St James's and Mayfair. Not only was Mayfair the most coveted location in the game of Monopoly; it also commanded some of the highest commercial rents in the real world.

The economic benefits of clustering and being close to the people they do business with—bankers, lawyers, accountants—did not seem to be the only criterion applied. Instead, the firms opted for the prestige of the area, developed into a predominantly aristocratic residential enclave by the 1st Earl of St Albans, Henry Jermyn, with the permission of King Charles II in the 1660s. Famous residences in the area included St James's Palace, the administrative centre of the monarchy, and Clarence House, the official residence of the Prince of Wales. BP's global headquarters was in St James's, as is Christie's, the famous auction house, surrounded by many up-market art and antique dealers and designer shops.

Sometimes referred to as "Clubland", St James's was also the home of many of the best known gentlemen's clubs in London: the Athenaeum Club, the Carlton Club, St James's Club, the RAC Club, the Reform Club and the East India Club. The smell of Cuban cigars and Chesterfield hide mixed, as the Barbarians mixed with English gentry, clearly gave the Americans the air of respectability they craved for...

Kohlberg Kravis Roberts (KKR) took space in Stirling Square in Carlton Gardens, as did Texas Pacific Group. When KKR moved to its 847sqm office in June 1999, the rent of £700/sqm was reported to be the most expensive in

London.[1] Carlyle Group chose Lansdowne House on Berkeley Square, a stone's throw from the US Embassy. Clayton Dubilier & Rice went for King Street, just off St James's Square and within sight of Clarence House.

This choice of St James's was not a navigational error on their part either, but was born of astute calculation and an unwavering assessment of their own position in the local ecosystem. Rather than getting near the City, where deals were done and where advisors and financial backers went about their business, they elected to set up shop in (desirable…) locations where people would actually have to come to them. In a way, this was making very clear who would be pulling the strings in the relationships to come…

According to research by the BVCA, for every private equity investment executive investing in UK companies, there were 2.2 full-time equivalent supporting executives providing specialist advice and financial services in 2006.[2] As serial dealmakers, private equity firms are indeed amongst the biggest consumers of professional advisory services in London. Whilst there is some debate as to whether or to what extent private equity ownership creates jobs in the wider economy, it is clear that businesses operating in the private equity "ecosystem" have seen significant growth in the amount of work referred to them by private equity firms as the industry has grown.

The private equity ecosystem: follow the fees

In order to analyze the private equity ecosystem, it is convenient to use an approach similar to the one used to investigate biological ecosystems, i.e. following the food chain. In the case of private equity, the analogy is all too easy to make between the "Food Chain" and the "Fee Chain", i.e. who lives off whom. The private equity "ecosystem" is indeed made up primarily of services firms whose fees either stem from deals transacted by the private equity industry or from the ongoing maintenance of the industry's investments. All in all, following the fees may prove the most insightful walk down private equity alley…

According to research on fees by the BVCA[3], the private equity industry generated £5.4 billion in fees for the financial services sector in the UK alone in 2006. This equates to a staggering 12% of the turnover of the financial services sector, which in turn is the biggest sector in the UK economy. The £5.4 billion in fees, which corresponds to annual fees of £580,000 per executive working on UK private equity-related mandates, was shared between the different service providers in the following way:

[1] Building Design, November 1999.

[2] The Impact of Private Equity as a UK Financial Service, BVCA, 2007.

[3] www.bvca.co.uk.

- £1.7 billion for accounting and corporate finance services;
- £1.2 billion for banking and finance services;
- £1.2 billion for legal services;
- £270 million for specialist due diligence;
- £126 million for fund placement agents;
- £130 million for property agents;
- £153 million for stockbrokers;
- £560 million for fund administration, data, research and consultancy, marketing and recruitment.

Let us proceed now to review the key players in the supporting cast of private equity and their roles in the system. This will be done by order of public visibility, which may at times not necessarily match the importance of the fee pool generated. Private equity is, after all, a game of robust egos...

Investment banks

Private equity has been an extremely lucrative source of fees for investment banks, through more channels than one would suspect at first glance. This is not a case of double dipping, as often portrayed, with banks on the one hand advising private equity firms and on the other partly financing their deals, but a case of multiple dipping, with clear potential conflicts of interest...

Dealogic estimates that financial sponsor investment banking fees paid totalled a staggering $12.3 billion in 2012, with Carlyle topping the list of financial sponsors with fees paid to banks totalling $644 million (see **Exhibit 6.1**), and

Exhibit 6.1 Financial sponsor revenue ranking—full year 2012

Rank	Financial sponsor	Fees paid $m
1	Carlyle Group	644
2	Apollo Global Management	519
3	KKR	487
4	TPG Capital	394
5	Goldman Sachs Capital Partners	386
6	CVC Capital Partners	331
7	Bain Capital Partners	326
8	Warburg Pincus	300
9	Blackstone Group	264
10	Thomas H. Lee Partners	244
	Total	12,318

Source: Dealogic

Exhibit 6.2 Bank revenue ranking, full year 2012—fees paid by financial sponsors

Rank	Bank	Revenue $m
1	Credit Suisse	1,086
2	Goldman Sachs	1,008
3	Bank of America Merrill Lynch	960
4	Deutsche Bank	936
5	JP Morgan	884
6	Barclays	869
7	Morgan Stanley	835
8	Citi	681
9	RBC Capital Markets	453
10	Jefferies & Company	388
	Total	12,318

Source: Dealogic

Credit Suisse topping the list of banks with fees received from financial sponsors exceeding $1 billion in 2012 (see **Exhibit 6.2**).[4]

Out of the $12.3 billion generated in 2012 by investment banks for servicing the private equity industry, M&A advisory fees accounted for $3.1 billion, loan financing fees accounted for another $4.8 billion, fees from debt capital markets (DCM) accounted for $2.4 billion while fees from equity capital markets (ECM) reached $2.1 billion, according to Dealogic.[5]

As some of the strongest supporting casts of the private equity ecosystem, investment banks collect their fees for servicing private equity clients from different sources.

M&A advisory fees

M&A advisory fees have traditionally been a rich source of income for the banks, with private equity making up a significant proportion of global M&A transactions. Private equity firms engage investment banks both as *buy-side* M&A advisors to source new investment opportunities, and as *sell-side* M&A advisors to prepare exits of their portfolio companies.

According to Thomson Reuters, global private equity-backed M&A activity accounted for about 12% of worldwide announced M&A, and is valued at about $320 billion for 2012.[6] Before the financial crisis, the proportion exceeded 20%

---

[4] Global Financial Sponsor Review, Full Year 2012, Dealogic.

[5] Ibid.

[6] Mergers & Acquisitions Review, Financial Advisors, Full Year 2012, Thomson Reuters.

Exhibit 6.3 Annual private equity-backed M&A activity

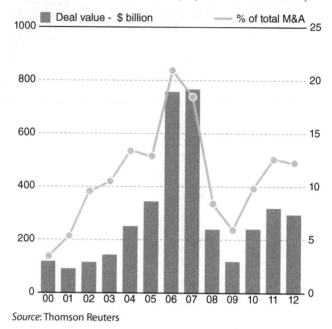

Source: Thomson Reuters

in 2006, when annual private equity-backed M&A activity almost reached $800 billion, before dropping considerably in 2008 and 2009 (see **Exhibit 6.3**).[7]

Arrangement fees

A second source of income from private equity transactions comes from arranging the structured finance to support the buyouts. The "underwrite and distribute" business is lucrative, especially during the credit boom that ran to late 2007. The bank—or a syndicate of banks—would underwrite a loan package that would then be sold on to investors with different risk profiles. With the credit crunch, this business has come under heavy criticism for its potential conflicts of interest. In particular, by disconnecting the debt arrangement from the long-term debt holding, it puts the arranging bank potentially at cross-purposes with the clients, where the issuing fee benefits (accruing to the investment bank) would outplay the long-term underperformance (accruing to the client).

Securitization fees, or the price of turning frogs into princes

A third layer of fees could also be generated by investment banks by repackaging multiple buyout-related loans into diversified debt packages and then slicing them into tranches with various cash flow and risk profiles. The securitization business, i.e. the creation of novel, original securities for sale to mostly investors, was one of the richest niches born of the credit boom. For the investment banks, it was meant

---

[7] Mergers & Acquisitions Snapshot, December 2012, Thomson Reuters.

again as a pure fee-generating business, with the packaging bank passing on the ultimate risk of the underlying instrument to its investors.

When the music stopped, the true risk exposure of the originating banks was finally disclosed to a gasping public, as was another embarrassing finding: it had become very difficult to identify the ultimate holder of the exposure to the buyout debt risk! To understand the quagmire created, one needs to distinguish the origination risk from the credit risk monitoring.

While the repackaging process is indeed almost risk-free, it does take a significant amount of time for banks to assemble a broad enough panel of loans to integrate into a particular CLO, or Collateralized Loan Obligation. During that "assembly" period, the loans, often in the billions of dollars for a single CLO, are effectively sitting on the investment bank's balance sheet, until its constituent tranches are sold to the ultimate investors.

Securitization, for the most part, was a great facilitator for the private equity industry: it provided liquidity to the originating banks, which could easily resell their buyout-related loans to other investors, with generous fees for the investment banks arranging the securitizations. The newly acquired liquidity reduced the perceived risk of providing the loans in the first place, and, therefore, of analyzing risk in a particular loan (it was going to be sold off rapidly anyway...). This eventually reduced the lending rate. Nadauld and Weisbach (2010)[8] found support for the assertion that the practice of securitizing bank debt actually reduced the cost of such debt for borrowers in the primary corporate debt market—all in all a good thing.

But the process also gave rise to a serious credit risk monitoring issue. With the original loans, assessed by the originating banker, being sliced and diced every possible way, it became very difficult—even impossible in some cases—to figure out which party was in charge and responsible for the monitoring of the credit risk. To a large extent, investors fell under the spell of multiple layers of diversification, in essence believing that diversification, by some magic trick, had in fact extinguished risk altogether. The reality was much different: diversification among buyout debts was actually minimal, and when some loans started to go bad, many did. As was learned during the LTCM debacle, correlations between the returns on various asset classes tend to go to 1 in periods of crisis, nullifying the benefits of diversification when they are most needed...

As an example of how deep securitization affected the buyout markets, one can look at ownership of European buyout-related debt before the financial crisis. Back in 1999, close to 90% of European buyout-related debt was held by banks, European or not. The rest was held by various forms of investors. By 2007, with securitization in full bloom, less than 40% of buyout-related debt was actually held directly by banks: the vast majority was held by CLO managers and

---

[8] Nadauld, T.D. and Weisbach M.S., "Did Securitization Affect the Cost of Corporate Debt?", Working Paper Ohio State University, August 25, 2010.

hedge funds.[9] Considering the lack of familiarity of these investors with credit monitoring, it is not surprising things were quickly heading for the wall...

Fund management fees, or how to compete with your best clients

With such rich pickings, investment banks soon became enamoured with private equity as a whole. The industry had everything to make it exciting, including glamour. So why not go the last step and develop an internal private equity arm altogether to grab the next layer of profits still captured by the private equity funds? Many investment banks jumped to that conclusion and developed their own private equity arms, pitching themselves into competition with one of their most important customer groups. What were initially run as bonus pools to give high-flying staff access to some of the best deals that came through their pipeline were turned into fully-fledged fund management businesses.

In 2007, Goldman Sachs closed its latest fund, GS Capital Partners VI, after having raised $20.3 billion. Apart from GS Capital Partners, its corporate equity investment arm, Goldman Sachs has a number of other private equity vehicles. Real Estate Alternatives focused on the management of targeted real estate-related funds and on making strategic real estate investments for Goldman Sachs. GS Mezzanine Partners became the largest mezzanine fund family in the world with over $17 billion invested since 1996. Technology Principal Investment invested in early- to late-stage technology companies. Infrastructure Investment Group made direct investments in infrastructure and infrastructure-related assets and companies. Urban Investment Group focused on providing long-term capital for both corporations operated or owned by ethnic minorities and real estate developers targeting urban communities. Finally, and the more directly connected fund, the Goldman Sachs Private Equity Group co-invested in direct investments and provided liquidity and capital solutions to limited and general partners.[10]

The presence of such substantial private equity operations within large investment banks led, of course, to accusations of serious potential conflicts of interest, greatly upsetting some of their biggest customers. When the private equity arms of Credit Suisse First Boston and JP Morgan won a bidding contest for British drugs group Warner Chilcott in 2004, bidding against a consortium that included Blackstone and Texas Pacific, David Blitzer, European co-head of private equity firm Blackstone, told a Reuters Corporate Finance conference:

---

[9] Meerkatt, H. and Liechstentein, H., "Get Ready for the Private Equity Shakeout", IESE working paper, December 2008.

[10] http://www2.goldmansachs.com/services/investing/private-equity/index.html.

"It's a fact of life that we compete with banks on certain transactions. On Warner Chilcott, we had two of our larger relationships (banks) beat us on the deal. That can strain relationships, but it is largely unavoidable".[11]

In the 1990s, the trend for banks to do more business with other banks and offer them financial advice led to the growth of FIGs (Financial Institutions Groups) within investment banks. By 2003 around a quarter of the European and US investment banking fees came from financial institutions[12], so it is little surprise that the investment banks created groups dedicated to servicing the sector. As M&A took off again in 2003, with private equity firms leading the charge, FIGs began to focus on the sector.

FIGs typically tapped into the investment bank's understanding of the financial, regulatory and competitive dynamics within the financial services industry to provide a comprehensive analysis of the strategic options available to their clients, from mergers, acquisitions and divestitures to capital-raising and specialty transactions. And private equity was not coy at tapping into this service. For instance, Houlihan Lokey, a mid-tier investment bank, created a FIG that offered the bank's clients, including private equity, a broad array of corporate finance, financial advisory, valuation and financial restructuring services.

FIGs are usually not only found among the bulge bracket investment banks, but also among the universal banks. Credit Suisse spent two years building its FIG, which offered clients the full range of transactions services, trade finance, trading products and asset management. When Carlyle launched its FIG group to make investments in the global banking and insurance sectors in June 2007, the pulling power of private equity was highlighted when it poached Olivier Sarkozy, the half-brother of French President Nicholas Sarkozy, from UBS, where he was the highly-regarded co-head of its global FIG.

Lending banks

Originally, it was the banks that put the L into Leverage, providing debt for the deals. The amounts borrowed every year, and the origination and servicing fees attached to such deals, provide considerable revenue streams to a number of top banks. **Exhibit 6.4** presents the top 10 debt financing providers to private equity firms in 2012.

---

[11] Reuters, October 15, 2005.

[12] *The Banker*, August 4, 2003.

Exhibit 6.4 Top 10 debt-financing providers to private equity firms in 2013 by deal value (aggregate value of deals for which financing was provided)

Name	Aggregate deal value ($bn)
Barclays	74.2
Credit Suisse	65.3
RBC Capital Markets	56.4
Bank of America Merrill Lynch	45.1
JP Morgan	43.6
Morgan Stanley	32.3
Wells Fargo Bank	32.3
Nikko Citigroup	29.1
Deutsche Bank	22.3
UBS	20.2

Source: Preqin

Accountancy firms

International accountancy firms are also major providers of advisory services to the private equity industry. Their cumulative wealth of experience advising on management buyouts (MBOs), management buy-ins (MBIs) and development capital deals across all industries is invaluable to the private equity players. Their vast global network of resources also means they can offer a wide breadth of advice in terms of industry sectors and territories worldwide. Their cost structure is also such that they are often able to advise on transactions that are below the radar of big investment banks.

The "Big Four", as PricewaterhouseCoopers (PwC), Deloitte, Ernst & Young and KPMG are generally known in the industry, have all developed private equity practices to attract and service their clients. Taken together, they took 67% of the total $165.4 billion in fees which the sector earned in 2012, a staggering amount which prompted many to believe the industry was too concentrated.[13] Precise numbers about how much of their income comes specifically from private equity sources are hard to find, although it is generally assumed that private equity has accounted for more than 20% of their advisory fees in recent years.

With increasing competition between private equity firms to get deals, the Big Four have expanded their services, increasingly offering private equity services focused on building value and managing performance and on offering one-stop services to the bigger deals. In that sense, the Big Four started to eat into territory once the preserve of the investment banks. By being well positioned at

---

[13] *International Accounting Bulletin*, "World Survey 2013: A profession adapting to a changing world", 2013.

the inception of deals, the Big Four knew what services private equity firms were likely to require as the investment strategies unfolded...

Law firms

Like the Big Four accountancy firms, law firms have set themselves up to advise private equity clients throughout the deal phases. Freshfields Bruckhaus Deringer, which had more than 2,500 lawyers in 16 countries, was typical of the approach. The firm, which was voted the private equity "Transactional Team of the Year" at the Awards for Excellence in Private Equity Advisory Services, Europe 2010, aims to give private equity clients access to lawyers in international tax, competition, securitization, corporate and M&A, as well as to specialists in employee-related matters (management incentives, employment and pensions), real estate, intellectual property and information technology.

Besides private equity and venture capital funds, Freshfields' clients in this field include investors, banks, financial advisors, start-ups, private buyers, sellers and a wide range of international corporations. The firm gives its customers legal advice on acquisitions to both domestic and cross-border buyers, as well as on take-private transactions (including those that cross national boundaries and often encounter conflicting securities laws and takeover regulations), on IPOs and trade sales, on structuring of funds (including feeder and parallel funds and co-investment arrangements), on fundraising and investing in funds, as well as on senior and mezzanine debt financing and bond issues, structured finance, tax optimization of acquisition and investment structures, and venture capital investments and private placements.

As a partner of one of the leading law firms in Europe mentioned:

> "We have extensive experience in acting on private equity transactions where we have represented investing funds, vendors selling businesses to financial buyers, lenders providing debt financing and companies raising equity. We have also acted on a number of public-to-private transactions in Europe, for acquirers, financial advisers, lenders and targets. Transactions include all sizes from venture capital investments to large cross-border transactions."

The same partner added:

> "Private equity firms are absolutely focused on getting solutions to problems and getting answers to questions. We have a golden rule within our private equity group—the Blackberry Rule—if you cannot fit the core of your advice onto one screen of a Blackberry you have to go away and rewrite it until you can. It is about knowing exactly what the core message is that you want to get across. On any private

equity deal the private equity sponsor team will be tiny compared with the corresponding team at a corporate: on a corporate deal you may have three people dealing with one aspect of a deal, whereas on a private equity deal you will have one person dealing with four aspects of the deal, so the difference is effectively 12:1. Private equity investors are much less tolerant of lawyers who indulge themselves in explaining things at great length without explaining the relevance of the information to the deal."

Due diligence specialist providers

In the not so distant past, outsourced due diligence was broadly limited to two aspects: the financial review of the target company's historical performance and the legal review of all its contracts and intellectual property. Over the years, due diligence as a service developed to address other specific transactional risks. Commercial due diligence, for instance, was one of the first and most direct extensions of the financial due diligence service, and projected earnings became an increasingly important part of target valuations.

In making an acquisition or backing an MBI or an MBO, private equity firms need to understand not just the specific performance of the intended target. They have to explore how historic performance relates to performance forecasts and how performance forecasts in turn are affected by projected market conditions and competition. They have to understand how a whole range of factors, such as technology, customers, legislation, buyers, and even the emergence of new markets, will impact the competitive state of a market, and, therefore, the valuation of the target company.

Specialist providers have appeared, such as Javelin Group, Armstrong Transaction Services and AMR International, as well as a host of sector-specific specialists that provide due diligence. AMR, for example, had performed more than 850 commercial due diligence projects in more than 40 countries and claimed that commercial due diligence acted to de-risk the deal, helping private equity investors plan and prepare for the issues that surface post-transaction.

One area of due diligence that has seen a significant growth in demand is environmental due diligence. While it had long been a major issue in the US, with investors seeking to avoid any liability under the Comprehensive Environmental Response, Compensation, and Liability Act, commonly referred to as the "Superfund law", it progressively became an important issue in many other regions. The growth in environmental due diligence business can be highlighted through the growth of Environmental Resources Management (ERM), a global environmental consultancy with 3,300 employees in 137 offices across the world. In 2005, European private equity firm Bridgepoint Capital backed a secondary buyout of ERM from private equity firm 3i, who had invested in ERM in 2001. As a regular user of the service,

Bridgepoint Capital was well positioned to see the growth potential, from $425 million in revenues in 2005 to over $600 million in 2010.

Strategy consultants

Private equity never existed in a bubble and its practitioners have always been aware of their need to seek expert advice, even on strategic matters. Management consultants offer a confidential sounding board on pre- and post-acquisition strategy, as well as on exit strategy. Their expertise in many of the sectors in which private equity firms invest, combined with their in-depth knowledge, make them valuable advisors. The big global consulting firms all recognize the need for a private equity offering—McKinsey & Company, the Boston Consulting Group (BCG), Bain & Company, Booz Allen Hamilton and AT Kearney. Other specialist firms, such as Wood MacKenzie in the oil and gas sector and Monitor in the telecoms space, have developed private equity offerings.

When the credit crunch hit the global economy, the nature of the consultancy services demanded by the private equity industry changed. The overnight loss of easily available and cheap debt removed the opportunities for over-leveraged buyouts. When prices fell off, private equity houses found themselves with no choice but to improve their portfolio businesses operationally. In April 2009, in an article entitled "The Future of Private Equity", Conor Kehoe wrote in the highly regarded and widely-read *McKinsey Quarterly*:

> *"With an estimated $470 billion in committed but unused funds, the sector faces an enormous challenge just finding ways to invest. Finally, its portfolio companies, with their high debt levels, may become financially distressed and default in the event of only small downturns in sales and EBITDA. Recent bankruptcies of several private equity-backed companies hint at how dark the future may be."*[14]

McKinsey & Company, which was founded in 1926 in Chicago and had been ranked the top management consultant by vault.com in its 2011 ranking, offers a bespoke service to private equity firms and to their portfolio companies. Apart from giving private equity firms advice on developing and implementing their strategy, it also offers what it calls "opportunity scans", which amount to using the information gleaned from its 90 offices across the globe to identify potential investments in specific industries and geographies. Strategic due diligence and deal assessment are slightly higher level and more strategic than the due diligence provided by accountants and law firms, more on a par with the commercial due diligence provided by specialists. Its services to portfolio companies include "growth

---

[14] http://www.mckinseyquarterly.com.

strategy", "go-to-market strategy", "business positioning", "organizational effectiveness", "product development", "operational improvement" and "business building". This is where private equity firms really look to McKinsey and others for assistance, because they know all too well that they cannot have a deep knowledge of all the sectors and industries they invest in.

Boston Consulting Group, like its competitors, provides private equity firms with a full spectrum of services covering the entire private equity value chain: working with portfolio companies to improve EBITDA, working with the buyout firms to identify targets for add-on acquisitions, and offering them insights on industry dynamics and due diligence support. The private equity practice consists of more than 130 partners and 500 trained professionals, with experience at all BCG levels worldwide. Its core private equity team works closely with experts from the functional and industry practice areas, as well as with turnaround specialists.

Bain & Company has the biggest private equity consultancy practice, almost three times larger than the next-largest firm. Since 1997 it has advised on more than 3,500 deal evaluations and 1,000 portfolio company projects, many of which come from Bain Capital, the investment firm founded by Bain partners in 1984. Bain claims to have advised on more than half of the global deals over $500 million in the past decade and has even put its own money in clients' deals, generating returns on invested capital that were allegedly 2.9 times higher than the industry average.[15] Bain helps clients across the entire value-creation spectrum: from fund strategy and operations, to sector specialization and strategic due diligence, to achieving value creation in portfolio companies following acquisition, and planting the seeds for portfolio companies' future growth to successful exit planning.

In many respects the work that consultants do for private equity houses is much the same as for any traditional client contemplating an acquisition or looking for advice on reviving a recently-acquired or existing business. However, the private equity firms tend to be far more focused on execution and prioritization. Indeed, private equity firms are increasingly looking for consultants with in-depth market, commercial and technical understanding of the industry, consultants that could be credible in front of portfolio companies. In 2007, Peter Bertone, lead partner in London for private equity at Booz Allen Hamilton, contradicted the premise of a feature entitled "Buy out firms favor Jacks of all trades"[16]:

> "[consulting firms] don't want just newly-minted MBAs, but want access to people who really know their industry. By combining the young, financially-oriented MBA types with industrial expertise you can reach deeper insights during due diligence than you could just with MBAs."

---

[15] www.bain.com.

[16] FT article: "Buy-out firms favour Jacks of all trades", November 19, 2007.

Consultancy fits perfectly with the private equity business model that relies on low internal resources, primarily focused on doing deals. Consultants can be brought in to fill gaps as and when required. They are not cheap but they could be turned on and off as needed and kept keen by the healthy fees, like all the other members of the supporting cast.

Placement agents

Placement agents are an integral part of the private equity fundraising cycle and are seen by some in the industry (especially by themselves) as being influential in shaping the direction of the industry. They are engaged by private equity firms to help raise funds and act as facilitators of capital flows between the LPs and general partners.

Placement agents pride themselves on their contacts and their understanding of the investor market, experience and knowledge they gained from having repeated contacts with the investors that GPs value. Fees vary according to the role and level of involvement. A rule of thumb is that a placement agent takes around a year's management fee spread over a number of years. For a $1 billion fund with a 1.5% management fee, the placement agent would typically collect a respectable $15 million over the life of the fund. In lean times, some placement agents are willing to change their model from a pure success fee to a mix of retainer and success fee, fearing that they would not be too successful at finding the funds...

Good placement agents make some due diligence and point out ways of packaging the product in terms of fees and legal structures to make the new fund more appealing to investors and more in line with market trends. They also help fund managers get a better deal for themselves and more importantly help them save time and resources next time they are on the road. As one placing agent complained, the more successful he is the more he makes himself redundant...

The biggest private equity firms have dedicated investor relations teams and, in some rare cases, their past successes mean their new funds are often closed to new investors altogether. The Carlyle Group, for example, listed 17 investor relations contacts on its website in Atlanta, Dubai, London, New York, San Francisco, Sao Paulo, Singapore, Tokyo and Washington. These people and their support teams are in constant contact with investors, thereby reducing the need for placement agents. Some of the mega funds still rely though on agents for specific geographies or niche markets.

According to research firm Preqin, 47% of funds used a placement agent in 2012, although that number drops to 10% for managers having already raised 10 or more funds.[17] Location also seems to matter, with funds focusing on Asia and the Rest of the World using placement agents more often than those focusing on North America or Europe.[18]

---

[17] Global Private Equity Report, Preqin, 2013.

[18] Ibid.

Historically, many placement agents were units of investment banks. The vast majority of their efforts focused on public equities, while private equity was just a small part of their work. The placement agent would work with the general partner at the private equity firm to draw up a private placement memorandum (PPM), and distribute it widely to anyone and everyone who might be interested. This model still exists and is sometimes used by funds after they have tapped their mainstream investors and reached a first close. Over time, the limited partner market evolved and placement agents evolved with them, positioning themselves as advisors to GPs, rather than mere salespeople. *"The mass selling approach was not in tune with the nature of investors, who were setting up teams of dedicated professionals to invest in private equity,"* explained Mounir Guen, who spent 13 years in Merrill Lynch's private placement team before setting up MVision in 2001, one of the largest independent placement agents with a staff of 50 and offices in London, New York and Hong Kong. MVision helped Swedish buyout firm EQT on its product expansion and geographic expansion, to China in particular. It also convinced EQT, a firm which had always kept a low profile, that it was in its best interest to increase its visibility, since greater public scrutiny was becoming inevitable. The result can be seen on EQT's website, which now has a section on the firm's approach to corporate governance, complete with case studies and a description of value creation strategies.

> *"It is a good way for us to explain to the target company management, to our investors, to the community, and to journalists what we are all about. We could not hide any longer, we needed to be much more transparent to the market place,"* said Conni Jonnson, chief executive of EQT.

The industry also includes a large number of mid-sized boutiques, such as Helix Associates, with 13 executives and offices in London and New York. Despite being bought by Jeffries & Company in 2005, Helix continues to operate independently, counting Swedish firm Altor Equity Partners, pan-European firm Bridgepoint and Chicago-based Madison Dearborn Partners as clients.

It is often said of placement agents that they are only as good as the last fund they helped raise. Successful placement agents, like Helix, find themselves in a virtuous circle: their good track record attracts quality GPs, leading to further successful fundraisings and more clients.

Fund administrators

Over the past decade, a number of highly skilled and structured third-party private equity fund administrators have emerged, offering comprehensive middle and back office services to funds. These administrators claim to have made a valuable contribution to the private equity industry's effort to be more institutionalized and transparent in the execution and management of its funds. The increasing industry regulatory demands have also forced administrators to continually improve the services they provide to GPs.

Most administrators started out as small teams of highly skilled and highly knowledgeable professionals having close relationships with private equity houses. Key success factors in those early days were the qualifications and experience of team members. Then, as the industry matured, specialized software systems became available, allowing GPs and their service providers alike to both significantly increase the efficiency of execution and to handle more complex structures and transactions in a transparent and controlled manner.

The European private equity industry counts a rather comprehensive set of standards such as the EVCA Code of Conduct, Corporate Governance Guidelines, Governing Principles, Reporting Guidelines and the International Private Equity & Venture Capital Valuation Guidelines. Most GPs are committed to consistently apply these industry standards and increase the transparency of the industry. The increased pressure and scrutiny following the credit crisis was probably material in reinforcing the need to open up to the outside world.

Recruitment consultants

Recruitment consultants, also known as headhunters, have targeted and built up close relationships with private equity firms. For most general partners, the recruitment of executives for portfolio firms starts with their own personal networks, sometimes including poaching advisors they worked with on successful transactions. When the internal network is insufficient, external recruiting organizations are brought in to fill the management needs. Because of the nature of the assignments and the compensation packages, private equity firms tend to recruit at fairly senior levels. Their lean structure often makes it difficult for them to train internally, so they often prefer to rely on other service firms, such as accountants and investment banks, to provide basic skills training that are then honed on the job.

The demand for senior executives has been increasing over time for full-time positions as well as part-time advisories. A good example of high profile hires is Clayton Dubilier & Rice, a US-headquartered global buyout fund. In June 2008 it continued a tradition of bringing on board senior industrialists when Fred Kindle, the former president and CEO of ABB, joined the firm as a partner. He followed the illustrious footsteps of Jack Welch, who joined the firm as a special partner in 2001 after completing his term of duty at the helm of General Electric. The same year Bob Quarta, the respected CEO of engineering group BBA, also joined the firm in London.

On top of the recruitment of general partners, there is also demand for recruitment of senior managers for portfolio companies. Whilst private equity investors are prone to cite a mantra of "management, management, management" as the key success factors in deals, the strengthening of the existing team, particularly in the finance function, plays a key role in the ultimate success of transactions.

Public relations agencies

Private equity is often viewed as somewhat shy and retiring in some quarters and downright secretive in other less sympathetic ones. Typical of the old-style approach was Doughty Hanson, the firm founded by Nigel Doughty and Richard Hanson in 1985, with over €23 billion invested across more than 100 deals. Mr Doughty was notoriously private, reputedly engaging PR consultants during the early years to simply kill stories involving the firm. But when he became chairman and owner of the football club he supported as a boy, Nottingham Forest FC, in April 2002 his photo finally appeared in the press.

In the US, private equity firms were forced into the public gaze by the scale of companies they were acquiring. Kohlberg Kravis Roberts & Co. (KKR) bounded into the US public psyche when it completed the leveraged MBO of RJR Nabisco— home of the best-known cookie and snack brands in the US, and of RJ Reynold's Tobaccos. At $31.4 billion, the 1989 deal became the largest ever buyout, and it retained the title until 2006. As KKR's website explained:

> *"As we moved into the 1980s, the scale of our investments increased even more and media interest in buyouts had become front-page news— particularly when well-known retail and consumer brands became KKR portfolio companies."*

In 2007, KKR's £12.4 billion buyout of the third-largest pharmacy chain in Europe, Alliance Boots, became the largest-ever European buyout. It was also one of a handful of high-profile deals in the UK that led to the industry's heavyweights having to explain themselves to a parliamentary select committee. KKR's buyout of the US electricity generator, distributor and retailer Energy Future Holdings currently holds the title of the largest buyout in history. All of these facts were proudly displayed on KKR's website under its "landmark achievements".

It is clear that bigger deals for more famous target companies tend to raise visibility and scrutiny. With scrutiny comes the need to manage communication and PR more professionally. Ultimately, this scrutiny, if handled professionally, can turn into an asset, raising the profile of the firm and bringing funds and deals. This would certainly appear to be the case at KKR, which had a significant media team. In the US it used one of the most experienced communications firms, Kekst and Company, founded in 1970. Apart from the four Kekst PR consultants working on the US account, KKR also retained six consultants from Finsbury for the UK account, two from Hering Schuppener for Germany, three from Image seven in France, another three from Citigate First Financial in the Netherlands and finally two from Bersay Communications in Turkey. Gavin Anderson managed KKR's publicity in the Asia Pacific region, with four consultants in Japan, three in Hong Kong, three in Singapore and three in Australia.

In total 33 PR consultants from seven firms managed KKR's PR worldwide and the firm recruited Peter McKillop from Bank of America as director of global communications in November 2008. He reported to Kenneth Mehlman, managing director and head of global public affairs, who said of the appointment:

"Today, more than ever, companies have a responsibility to engage with the public. Peter will play a critical part in telling the KKR story and communicating how we create value for investors, improve companies, and benefit multiple stakeholders."

Jon Moulton, founder of UK private equity firm Alchemy Partners, enjoyed his time in the spotlight. An outspoken character, Moulton moved from the financial pages to the front pages when his firm put in an offer for struggling carmaker Rover. He has since presented television programmes and has been a regular commentator on private equity matters. He said:

"It's part good for the ego, part a waste of time and part good for the business. It's simply that I think I've been around a long time and have actually a pretty fair understanding of most of the basics of what drives all this [private equity] lot. And that makes me a minor media figure, which I'm not really sure I could be terribly fussed about."

In 2004, financial PR specialist Piers Hooper formed Equus, a communication agency with a specific focus on European private equity, alternative asset and debt markets. The Equus team worked on more than 150 transactions and supported the brand development for a range of private equity players including large-end and mid-market GPs, turnaround specialists, industry experts, secondaries fund managers, LPs, debt providers, lawyers and investment banks.

"Five years ago the attitude of private equity to PR mirrored what happened historically with public equity. GPs wanted a plain vanilla offering, because they were not sophisticated buyers of services," said Piers Hooper. *"They just wanted someone on the end of the phone to intercede when there was an issue with the media, to advise them and keep them out of trouble. But more enlightened people saw communications as an important piece of the deal origination and LP investor validation jigsaw. Those that have been buying these services for a while have become more sophisticated. What we offer has much more to do with brand and marketing support. If you are active in communicating to all parties with whom you do business, and you hit a problem, you are likely to get a better reception than those who have taken a closed-door approach to the media and communications more broadly."*

In the true spirit of openness of communications, Equus did not disclose its client list, but offered a comprehensive palette of services, from classic brand management and media relations to transaction support, exit and crisis management, investor relations, annual reviews, publication of corporate brochures and websites and conference services. Hooper said their help was of particular importance because of the increasing competition between GPs for good quality deal flow and equally increasing competition among LPs for access to the best performing funds.

7
Investing in a fund

Executive summary

Investing in private equity is the easy part; getting results is the difficult one! This, in facetious terms, summarizes the dilemma facing investors in this asset class. While investing can indeed generate very interesting returns, it does so only to those that have invested enough time and effort to understand the inner workings of the industry. Like many alternative asset classes, private equity does not avail itself easily to common mortals. In this chapter, we try to extract simple rules of engagement that should improve one's abilities to navigate rather treacherous waters.

First of all, private equity is not an exclusive club *per se*. The only prerequisite to join is a sufficient fortune to create a level of diversification among fund investments where entry tickets can be as high as $10 million and a preferred investor status means the ability to commit hundreds of millions to a fund. Once an investor passes the investable wealth criteria, the question becomes how to invest that money with the highest chance of generating high returns. A vast array of investment vehicles exists, both for direct and indirect private equity investing, whether the investor wants to manage the GP selection and investment process himself, or whether he prefers to outsource to another organization. In all cases, private equity fund managers are not created equal. Actually, contrary to many other asset classes, very few actually perform at all... but when they do, the returns tend to be not only stellar but also relatively persistent, i.e. superior performers tend to remain superior performers over successive generations of funds, if they avoid so-called strategy drift.

That generates an interesting quagmire. If fund managers indeed persist in their performance, then investors would simply flock to the funds in the highest performance deciles, flooding them with money and making the repeat of the performance highly unlikely. The GP winners are really the choosers, and fund managers need to screen new investors to ensure consistency, reliability, value added and expertise. Past investors usually get privileged access to the next fund generations, in effect crowding out potential new investors. If not belonging to the lucky few already invested in the best performing fund families, then the task switches to detecting the next likely top performer, a much more difficult exercise requiring intensive due diligence on the investment teams.

In all instances, investing well in private equity is time-consuming and expensive and entails a level of long-term trust in the GP not found in many other asset classes. Moreover, the fund governance is such that active intervention by investors is normally not possible. And the fees incurred for the privilege of belonging to the Club are large: management fees and carried interest do pile up over 10 years, while other fees such as establishment fees, transaction and monitoring fees, underwriting fees and broken deal costs also creep into the system.

Finally, as for many other asset classes, private equity goes through cycles. As such, investors should really think about private equity commitments in terms of multiple generations of funds.

Earlier in this book, we highlighted the desirability of private equity as an asset class. The return characteristics have indeed been quite unique, in particular the stellar returns generated by the top quartile funds. But we also highlighted the severe limitations and caveats to that generic statement. First and foremost, the asset class remains fairly illiquid and exhibits an unpleasant pattern of cash flows over the life of a fund. The cash calls over the investment period as much as the random cash distributions when investments are realized create unpredictable cash flows over the life of the fund. Second, the distribution of superior performances is strongly concentrated in a very small number of funds. Because of the strong persistence in the returns across successive generations of funds, these top performing funds also happen to become larger, leading to a peculiar size effect on performance and difficulty in accessing these high performing funds. Finally, the layers of fees imposed on most funds lead to net returns that are seriously lower than the gross generated returns.

With these limitations clearly understood, it is possible to turn the attention to the practical issues to consider when investing in private equity. The fundraising process used by private equity funds is relatively primitive compared to the well-oiled machine used by public companies. It is time-consuming, requiring a lot of personal handholding with prospective investors. It is not uncommon for the process to last months and even years in tight markets or for a first-time fund. Whereas big private equity groups have dedicated teams permanently on the road meeting prospective investors and maintaining relationships with existing ones, smaller ones cannot afford this and will temporarily take part of their team off investments to fundraise.

The private equity game

To play the game one needs capital, a lot of capital. Contrary to popular belief, private equity is not really an "exclusive" club, in the sense that stringent criteria for admission apply. But how much are we talking about? Typically $5 million or $10 million, although many fund managers tend to accept lower amounts. Let's assume that to get access to a desirable fund one would need to commit a minimum of $5 million per fund. To obtain a broad diversification in a private equity portfolio, such as geographic coverage, vintages and strategies, it probably takes investments in 15 to 20 funds. Practically, that involves committing somewhere between $75 and 100 million. An allocation of 10% of an overall investment portfolio is a reasonable figure. Taking 10% as an example, it would thus take a $750 million to $1 billion portfolio of investable capital to be able to put together a "reasonable" portfolio of private equity investments.

Without drifting into the philosophical debate as to the role of financial regulators, regulation is there and imposes a heavy burden on firms and fund managers. Private equity always treasured its freedom of action and elected early on to operate outside the realm of regulation, choosing instead to deal directly with the most sophisticated investors. Since the fundraising process is very intensive, requiring one-on-one interaction with investors, it is also time-consuming and expensive, so fund managers have to impose minimum commitment levels.

Fundraising is critically important to fund managers, who are willing to invest much time and effort in the process. At times, it even appears that fundraising takes precedence over investing... Witness the huge amounts of money raised during the dotcom bubble and the buyout bubble a few years later. During both periods, much more money was raised than could be wisely invested, resulting in sub-optimal portfolio allocations. Venture capital in the US in 2000 is the perfect illustration. Some $100 billion were reportedly committed to VC funds in that year alone, according to NVCA data published in 2001. Assuming the investment period was four years and the average VC investment was around $5 million, spread over a number of rounds, it meant the industry essentially had to find some 5,000 industry-defining, breakthrough-technology ventures that could grow into $ billion companies within 5–10 years... each year! That number was, on the face of it, ridiculous but that did not deter investors from committing capital to these funds. So were the heady days in venture capital... This led to many undeserving managers/entrepreneurs getting funding and to deserving ones getting far too much to spend on perks. In the world of buyouts, excess capital led many private equity managers to increasingly buy from each other (through secondary buyouts) in order to spend money, as they could not find enough "virgin" deals. This contrasts with lean years, when every cent is turned over twice before being invested and the supply of deals outstrips available money.

Very few managers have the discipline to limit the size of their fund when large amounts of capital are available in the market. The larger the fund, the more fees collected, so managers are strongly motivated to raise as much as they can when the money is available. This dangerous flaw in the private equity remuneration system was elaborated on earlier. Those managers that can say "no" are usually those that are not only general partners but also significant LPs in their own funds, i.e. the fact that they are investing their own money realigns their interest with that of their investors.

In the rest of the chapter, we will discuss each and every step prospective investors go through in the life of a private equity fund and offer our advice.

The decision to invest

The decision to invest in private equity involves often a mix of rational and emotional drivers. The latter often includes some romantic notion that one should support new technologies, entrepreneurs and management teams and be a little more involved in "real" business, rather than investing in fancy sets of graphics and financial ratios. In extreme cases, this leads to the common mistake of going for direct investments in new ventures, rescue operations or local investments. Such direct investments often turn into disasters, with lack of experience, knowledge and dedication, and usually a combination of all three, very much guaranteeing an unpleasant outcome.

The rational analysis would be based on a deep understanding of a firm's or individual's ability to take risk, investment horizon and return requirements. To illustrate the process, let us take a deep look at the strategic analysis conducted in 2002 by ATP, the supplementary pension fund system in Denmark, that led to the decision to significantly increase its allocation to alternative assets, and in particular to private equity. During the next decade, ATP-PEP established itself as one of the largest investors in Europe.

Case Study 19
The Danish pension fund system

ATP ("Arbejdsmarkedets Tillægs Pension", or Danish Labor Market Supplementary Pension), Denmark's largest and most extensive supplementary pension scheme, was introduced in 1964 to provide a supplement to the state-funded old-age pension. Like all pension fund managers in the world, ATP was starting to feel the pinch of the impending demographics crunch: with a greying global population, there were fewer workers supporting each retiree.

The ATP scheme was capitalization-based, as opposed to redistribution-based, with each member receiving a pension reflecting his/her contributions over time. For every DKr[1] 396 (US$47) a member contributed to the scheme, he or she would earn the right to an annual pension benefit of DKr 100 ($11.87) for the rest of his or her life. This ratio was based on the assumption that ATP would be able to achieve a long-term return on investments of at least 4.5% after tax, a return guaranteed to members. However, such a long-term return did not protect the contributor's purchasing power: in order to retain the **real** value of its pension commitments, ATP had to achieve a long-term return of 4.5% *after* taxes and inflation, possibly even more if pensions were to track wages and salaries.

---

[1] DKr stands for Danish kroner. At the time of the case, DKr 1 equalled €0.1345, US$0.1187 and 0.1968 Swiss Francs. The equivalent US$ numbers are provided as often as possible.

In 2001, 80%+ of the Danish population between the ages of 16 and 66 paid contributions to the ATP scheme, with average annual contributions of DKr 2,683 ($318), around 1% of an average Danish salary. However, only a small proportion of the pensioners received the full pension since the ATP scheme had only been launched in 1964 and was still a long way from maturity. In addition to the basic pension, a bonus was also paid in years where "excess" returns were generated by the fund. ATP was not expected to reach its "steady state" before 2040: for this to happen, all ATP pensioners would have to belong to generations paying contributions throughout their entire working years. In 2010, the first generations that had been able to pay ATP contributions throughout their working years were retiring, with a full pension of around DKr 30,000 ($3,561 per year), compared to the DKr 20,000 in 2001.

As the scheme was maturing, total payments were set to rise considerably and would eventually reach a level that exceeded the annual contributions by a wide margin. In the long term, a relative equilibrium would be established in which total payments, on the one hand, and the sum of contributions and investment returns, on the other, would balance. Upon maturity, the ATP system would be the most important source of supplementary pension income for close to 50% of all Danish pensioners, and would be particularly important to those least well off. In other words, ATP had to be seen as a "socially responsible" asset manager, temporarily facing revenues significantly higher than its obligations but huge pension liabilities in the future.

ATP investment mandate

The most important task for ATP management was to generate the highest possible returns on available assets without exposing them to undue capital losses—a social mission as well as a financial one... The critical social responsibilities of ATP warranted close scrutiny by the political world. In recent years, a number of regulatory changes had been implemented to provide ATP with the tools to increase returns while at the same time diversifying the fund's risk exposure. For example, recent amendments allowed ATP to increase its allocation to equities from 50% to 70%,[2] but still prohibited ATP from holding controlling interests in any individual companies. As part of the strategy review, ATP decided to significantly increase its allocations of capital to unlisted equities. The "normal" market return on equities was expected to be two percentage points above the yield of a 10-year government bond and ATP expected a market return on investments of 6.1% for 2001.

---

[2] The change was formally passed in 2000 by the Danish parliament.

In 1999 ATP launched a multi-year development project for its asset management to meet the highest international standards. The project included defining a new investment framework, refocusing on core areas and outsourcing significant parts of the portfolio to external asset managers. This required ATP to develop a whole set of new skills, most notably the ability to pick and manage external investment managers and allocate funds among them to complement its direct investment programmes.

Investment returns and strategy for the future

In 2000, ATP earned DKr 15.7 billion pre-tax on its investments, a rate of return on assets of 7.6% pre-tax, 6.8% after tax. The return for the year was boosted by very favourable returns on Danish equities: ATP's portfolio of domestic equities produced a return of 22.1% for the year, clearly an exceptional vintage. But things changed drastically in 2001 with the overall correction on worldwide stock markets. The portfolio earnings turned to a negative DKr 4.6 billion, or a −2.6% return on assets. An asset/liability management exercise was conducted, pinpointing a very critical portfolio issue for ATP: it was relying too much on too few asset classes. This was particularly troublesome since these classes had been shown to have a certain degree of correlation in their returns; too many eggs in too few baskets in a sense. ATP used historical analyses of return and risk patterns of equities and bonds, combined with analyses of pension commitments, to determine its optimal asset/liability balance.

Based on the analyses, ATP drew a profile combining risk and return for the coming years. On the basis of these analyses, ATP's board decided to increase its allocations to alternative assets, especially real estate and private equity. Alternative assets often produced a higher return than bonds and, for certain asset types, a higher return than equities, with often lower correlations to these respective markets, thereby helping reduce the risk of the overall portfolio.

In the longer term, ATP established a target allocation of 10% to private equity. This was a very aggressive number compared to the standards used by other pension funds and institutions in Europe, more than the average US (public) pension fund typically committed, but lower than some of the most aggressive investor groups in the US—the university endowments.

Risk management

ATP's aim was to ensure that its members received the highest possible pensions at retirement. At the same time ATP had to protect the real value of pensions and pension commitments, as well as all fund assets against capital losses.

A prerequisite for achieving these aims was clearly for ATP to remain solvent at all times and be able to honour the pension commitments it had made. ATP's risk management strategy was determined by the legal framework set by the regulatory authorities, on the one hand, and by the investment strategy laid down by its management board, on the other. Safeguards were established at many different levels, including limits for interest rate, equity and foreign exchange risks and credit risk exposures, as well as transaction limits for individual portfolio managers.

ATP-PEP

ATP hired Jens Bisgaard Frantzen to set up and develop the private equity portion of the business. The private equity arm would be a separate, independent organization called ATP-PEP–ATP Private Equity Partners. It would be dedicated to private equity investment management, with a target of committing more than €4.5 billion in the period 2002–2005, with the mandate of obtaining superior returns and diversification of risk for ATP.

Jens had 10 years of experience in direct and indirect private equity investing and he had partnered with a number of management teams and fund managers to build their respective companies and funds. Jens had earned his MSc in Economics from Copenhagen Business School and served as a board member of the European Venture Capital Association (EVCA) and a director of Axcel, one of the leading Danish venture capital firms. Jens struggled with quite a few issues in mapping out the best strategy for ATP-PEP. Where within the private equity markets should he invest? Stages, size and number of investments, geography and technologies were all factors to be considered when balancing returns and risks. Furthermore, as managing director, Jens needed to recruit talent for the investments, strategies and building operational teams. He also had to consider other organizational issues, such as where and how many offices ATP-PEP should have. Even with the best team, implementing the investment strategies could prove a significant challenge: the private equity world was known as a small and exclusive club, where access was difficult—even when backed by a serious and wealthy source such as ATP.

The route ahead for ATP-PEP

Jens summarized his findings and major thoughts. First, European private equity markets were only about one-fourth the size of US markets, even after adjusting for the relative size of their economies. That could indicate a huge growth potential in Europe. Second, private equity had originated in the US and still represented a larger part of the assets/investments than in Europe.

This could possibly be linked to cultural dimensions, and the convergence of cultures could lead to greater flows toward private equity instruments. Third, within the private equity umbrella, seed investments had received by far the least attention in Europe. Considering how critical the early stage fundings were to technological developments, this was bound to change and could offer opportunities for investment. Moreover, to be able to outperform, an investor would have to develop superior screening capabilities and sufficient credibility to gain access to the most sought-after fund managers, while larger funds seemed to perform better overall (leaving aside the so-far untested megafunds), although they were also the most difficult to enter... And last, although private equity experienced wild economic cycles, and hence could only be considered as a long-term investment opportunity, sub-segments seemed to have their own individual cycles. In investment terms, that would seem to offer the opportunity to hedge some of the cyclic volatility by diversifying across the private equity spectrum.

Jens was faced with the challenge of deciding how much of the available resources should be allocated to the different private equity classes and segments. The returns looked most attractive in seed and early-stage markets, but uncertainty was at its highest, too, with huge performance gaps between top and bottom quartiles, gaps much deeper than for buyout funds.

Being allowed to "play" in the most exciting segments and with the most interesting funds was also a challenge. How could ATP-PEP gain credibility as a long-term equity investor? It was clearly new to this field and would have to "pay its dues". Should it bring in so-called gatekeepers or consultants such as Cambridge Associates with the experience and networks to facilitate the move into that new and exciting area? Many questions for one day, each one of which could prove decisive for the future of ATP Private Equity Partners...

Source: Case study written by the authors and included with permission from the ATP.

Choice of investment vehicle

Let us assume that an investor concludes that private equity should be part of his portfolio, and decides on a modest allocation of around 5% of his total portfolio to the asset class. Now, how should he go about investing in private equity? In particular, how should he go about investing to make sure that the future returns offset the time and energy needed to understand this whole new asset class?

The first question the new investor needs to answer is: should he manage the GP selection and investment process himself, or should these be outsourced to another organization? The question seems simple, yet a large part of the investment strategy depends on the answer.

Direct fund investments

Obtaining diversification across these broad categories and over vintages requires a relatively large investment effort, with commitment probably to 5–10 funds every year. At $10 million a pop, this effort quickly escalates to a $100 million a year effort, consistently applied year after year... and that is assuming no constraint on the actual access to funds. At this stage of the private equity industry's development, access to the very best managers is probably still the most important determinant of success.

Indirect fund investments

For smaller investors though, pooling vehicles such as funds-of-funds have emerged to provide diversification in economically interesting conditions. These vehicles are created to pool investors who lack size, manpower or sophistication to invest directly into funds. They are, of course, also of interest to fund managers, limiting interactions with small individual investors and yet giving access to potentially large pools of capital without the administrative and regulatory headache normally associated with smaller investors.

While manager selection and portfolio creation can be left in the hands of funds-of-funds and other forms of gatekeepers, the costs associated with those intermediaries often far outweigh the benefits for large investors, except in the total absence of in-house competence. With an allocation over €100 million to private equity, an investor should definitely start considering an in-house solution, even if it proves more expensive initially. Gatekeepers and funds-of-funds often claim privileged access to top funds, a definite attraction on paper. In practice though, most offer very limited benefits, in particular because the most sought-after fund managers often specifically exclude pooling vehicles from their investor basis. That said, funds-of-funds often remain the only entry channel for smaller investors without the experience or the capital base to envision direct fund investments.

Pooling turns into a very profitable business line for some fund-of-funds managers, gatekeepers and other asset managers such as banks and insurance companies. Significant economies of scale do exist in screening fund managers and managing portfolio reporting, with minimal marginal costs of adding additional investors to the pool. Pooling vehicles can take the form of funds-of-funds, which are normally private but also sometimes publicly listed, but also of feeder funds run by larger banks investing in single funds, of nominee structures used by the private banking industry for larger clients, of exclusive investor clubs for family offices and of the new kid on the block, the SPACs or Special Purpose Acquisition Companies.

The smaller the investor, the higher the fees for participating in a pool. Feeder funds and publicly listed funds-of-funds focus on the smallest investors and are the most expensive structures as a percentage of funds invested, followed by privately held funds-of-funds. Nominee structures are efficient but only for investors with several millions to invest in private equity. Investor clubs, by contrast, tend to have little or no structure and consequently little cost, but only large investors can play. Finally, the SPAC is very much a hybrid between a private equity and a hedge fund.

We will review the characteristics of these vehicles, pointing to the pros and cons of each one of them. **Exhibit 7.1** summarizes the main characteristics of various investment vehicles.

Exhibit 7.1 Comparison of characteristics of various investment vehicles

	Costs	Investment size	Diversification	Liquidity
Listed private equity	Very high	Small	High	Public
Feeder funds	Very high	Small	Low	None
Funds-of-funds	Medium	Medium	High	None
SPAC	High	Large	Low	Public soon
Nominee structures	Low	Medium large	Possible	None
Investor clubs	Very low	Large	Low	None

Source: Prequin

FUNDS-OF-FUNDS The most common structure to outsource the selection and management of private equity positions is the fund-of-funds, which is often a privately-held, finite life entity that replicates the approach taken by the underlying funds it invests in. An investor in a fund-of-funds makes a commitment to invest a certain amount of money, which is drawn in small increments over a certain period of time. The fund-of-funds manager, in turn, makes commitments to a range of private equity funds and generally acts as a single investor on behalf of its own investors, who consequently get a well-diversified portfolio of private equity funds and exposure to several hundred private equity transactions. As an investor category, funds-of-funds have become one of the largest contributors to private equity funds.

Fund-of-fund managers usually charge a management fee and a carried interest, but at lower levels than the fund managers themselves. For smaller funds-of-funds, a 1% management fee and 5% carried interest have for a long time been the benchmark. Larger ones charge less, although in more frothy markets funds-of-funds' fees approach those of direct fund managers, which, of course, render the notion of post-fee performance rather ludicrous and pure wishful thinking. The double-layering of fees very much guarantees mediocre performance overall, even though with a much reduced risk exposure.

Large funds-of-funds have become very much indices for the private equity industry overall. As indicated earlier, the average performance of the industry as a whole is just that, i.e. very average and not really exciting when considering the illiquidity associated with the investments. Because of their size, large funds-of-funds are bound to replicate that average performance unless they opt to "deviate" by also running co-investments, secondary transactions and even direct investments.

LISTED FUNDS-OF-FUNDS, OR LISTED PRIVATE EQUITY (LPE) LPEs are listed vehicles owning unlisted private equity fund positions. LPE funds-of-funds are thus traded on a stock exchange, offering small, retail investors access to a diversified private equity pool with the added benefit of (some) liquidity. The concept is to some extent a bit intriguing, in particular in the way liquidity can be built on positions that are fundamentally not liquid. And this is precisely where the rubber hits the road: liquidity is conditioned on a large number of buyers and sellers, which is often not present in the market for those securities. Large investors very much abstain from investing in LPEs and, therefore, pricing depends on the whims of the less sophisticated, smaller investors. As a result, market pricing may prove erratic.

Fee levels also need to be considered, since they can easily get out of control. Finally, an insidious problem is the upfront call of the investment, instead of the gradual calling of the money in direct fund investments. This upfront call means that a significant amount of money will not be put to work immediately, leading to lower returns than in direct investments in funds. Governance issues are also likely to be tricky, with the removal of bad management difficult in practice. Finally, conflicts of interest may arise between the LPs and the shareholders, with the former focused on the portfolio companies and the latter on the evolution of share price.[3]

LPE funds have in general not been very successful. They are often launched in bubble times, when investors' urge to invest in the asset class far outstrips their common sense, and end up suffering disproportionately in market downturns when they trade at large discounts to NAV.

The bottom line is that listed private equity only seems to make sense for very small investors who absolutely want exposure to private equity. The quality of managers, the fee levels, the general outlook for small cap stocks and the discount between the market value and the NAV should be carefully evaluated before making investment decisions. For large investors it makes, of course, a lot more sense to consider investing in the unlisted variety.

FEEDER FUNDS Feeder funds are structures created by banks to typically allow their (primarily) private clients to invest in a single fund. In practice, the banks

---

[3] OECD, "The Role of Private Equity and Activist Hedge Funds in Corporate Governance 1", *Related Policy Issues*, January 2008.

will make a single, often very significant commitment to a single private equity fund using the bank's balance sheet, but only when it is (nearly) certain to place the same amount very quickly with its clients. It is basically an underwriting of a private equity commitment.

Feeder funds, like LPEs, tend to appear in droves during bubble periods, i.e. periods when private equity is popular and in high demand, with private investors not usually involved or interested in private equity. Only banks with relatively large balance sheets would get involved, and, of course, only with a clear incentive motive. Feeder funds usually offer only limited or no diversification other than the investments in one fund or in a very limited number of funds. They are also expensive, although they allow small investors to get into the fund of their choice.

Often in feeder fund advertising, reference is made to the historical performance of prior vintages of the fund to be invested in. For example, a feeder fund prospectus would highlight the exceptional IRR net of fees realized by Private Equity Funds I, II and III of a particular fund manager, to peddle an investment in new Fund IV. What the prospectus often fails to mention altogether, or only in insanely small fonts, is that these performances were realized by direct investors in the fund, i.e. under the standard cash call and distribution mechanism in place for these. Feeder funds, contrary to direct commitments to funds, usually require that all commitment be deposited upfront into the vehicle, which will then respond over time to the cash calls by the fund managers. This disconnection between cash calls and cash deposits in the feeder fund practically reduces the expected performance by 50% compared to the expected performance in a direct fund investment...

There is also the risk of a conflict of interest. Since the banks creating these feeder funds put their own capital, albeit briefly, at risk and these feeder funds are very lucrative, the banks may at times see their own interest diverge from the one of their clients. In other words, the temptation may be great, when a fund does not place well, to oversell it to unsuspecting clients.

Feeder funds, like funds-of-funds, can make sense in certain cases; for instance, when access to a particular fund is deemed highly desirable. It is, in our view, rarely an optimal tool for creating a private equity portfolio.

NOMINEE STRUCTURES   To cater to the need of some clients to invest directly into private equity and even venture capital projects, private banks sometimes set up nominee structures, whereby the individuals remain directly responsible for their commitments to underlying funds as well as for the related tax liabilities. The private bank will only vouch for the quality of its clients, who will have accounts and sufficient money with the bank in question. Banks will not necessarily reveal the identity of their clients, but since this is becoming an increasingly sensitive issue, clients will probably have to accept more transparency. One nominee structure can act as the investor in several funds or direct investments. With these nominee structures, private banking clients can create tailor-made portfolios at relatively low cost. But to justify this more sophisticated approach, the amounts committed to a single fund by an investor will obviously have to be higher compared to fund-of-funds. Depending on the institution, the minimum commitment per fund per client would usually be in the $500,000 to $1 million range. The investment management and the selection can be delegated to the private bank if the investor prefers. In either case, the bank will usually take care of administration and reporting.

SEGREGATED ACCOUNTS   Investors may be too large for funds-of-funds, and still too small to organize their own private equity investment programme. This is where institutional mandates can come in handy. Through them, banks, asset managers or funds-of-funds will be given a mandate, discretionary or not, to manage the entire process. Compared to individual investors, institutions tend to be less involved once they have taken the decision to outsource private equity.

Institutional mandates combine the advantage of expertise and economies of scale with negotiable fee structures, which at times can be significantly lower than those faced in funds-of-funds. But the burden of the extra layer of fees remains present, while access to top funds is not guaranteed.

INVESTOR CLUBS   The least formal type of pooling is the "investor club". This loosely organized group of large, private investors, often family offices or high net worth individuals, usually know each other and are comfortable making joint investments. There is very little structure to the club: it is more of a gentleman's agreement between the participants. Each individual transaction is likely to have shareholders agreements and standard agreements appropriate for private investments, but there will be no obligation to invest and there will be no fund manager per se. Some private banks are known to organize such clubs as services to their clients, often meeting on desirable premises.

SPECIAL PURPOSE ACQUISITIONS COMPANIES (SPACS)   The use of SPACS is not widespread yet and is unlikely to make much of a dent in the volume of other, more traditional forms of pooling vehicles. It is a corporation formed specifically to facilitate a private investment, but it usually rapidly transforms into a public vehicle through an initial public offering. The proceeds are used to buy one or more existing companies. When money is raised for a SPAC, the funds are placed into a trust until the purchase is made or a predetermined period of time elapses. If the transaction and associated legal formalities are not completed by the deadline, the money is returned to the investors with allowances for bank and broker fees.

Diversification in a rich marketplace

The private equity market is extremely broad, encompassing a multitude of geographies and investment strategies. Fund diversity can only be compared to the choice at your local supermarket, with the important caveat that most products are only for sale for limited time periods… As private equity matured as an industry, the spectrum of specialized offerings increased, making the segmentation and selection ever trickier. This is a far cry from the historical "opportunistic" approach that prevailed not so long ago, when one of the world's largest buyout groups was able to write in its Private Placement Memorandum (PPM) that *"investments in oil exploration were excluded and that it would limit itself to investments in North America, Western Europe and possibly Asia"*. After a few months, investors were asked to approve an "exceptional investment" in an oil exploration company with an exclusive focus on some promising opportunities off the African coast. The investment was made and proved to be successful…

Portfolio diversification originally meant diversification across traditional asset classes. Today, that also involves diversification within asset classes, as with maturity comes more specific positioning. Private equity is a perfect example of this progressive maturing, offering today a breadth of strategies never seen before. In its Global Private Equity Report 2010 surveying LPs, the consulting firm Bain & Company put it quite clearly:

> *"Historically, many LPs' fund investments were concentrated in US and European buyout and venture capital funds. Our interviews confirmed that this definition has expanded to cover mezzanine, distressed debt, turnaround, infrastructure and real estate, among others. Even as most LPs maintain their PE target allocation overall, they will diversify their capital among fund types to maximize returns and manage risks."*[4]

According to that Bain report, LPs increasingly prefer to work with focused GPs, and construct their own portfolio across the industry, rather than work with GPs offering a one-stop shop. As more and more private equity firms compete to attract capital from investors, many leading firms elect to raise their game by specializing in just a handful of industry sectors. Sector specialization enables private equity firms to mobilize proprietary insights about sector trends and tap networks of industry insiders to give them an edge in sourcing and screening good deals and winning the best ones. Specialization covers sectors, but it can also extend to geographical markets and regions, stages of development, value-creation strategies and deal sizes.

---

[4] Global Private Equity Report 2010, Bain & Company.

For a broad-based portfolio, the typical segmentation variables would include the following:

Stages of investment

Opportunities differ by the purpose for which the investment is required. As we have seen in Chapter 1 with the definitions, and in Chapter 5 with the main characters, the private equity industry is divided up across stages: at the low end of the spectrum, one finds venture capital transactions, including seed, start-up and venture growth. Opportunities focused on a slightly later stage, and somewhat larger transaction size, fall under the expansion capital category. Next along the spectrum, one finds buyouts and turnarounds.

Geographic focus

Private equity firms also differentiate themselves by geographical focus, as we have seen in the preceding chapters. Some of the biggest private equity firms are becoming increasingly global, opening offices and launching new funds on different continents. Many more remain regionally or domestically focused, either out of choice, such as venture capital firms, or out of constraints, such as smaller buyout firms. Diversification generally includes US, Western Europe, Asia, emerging markets, and others like frontier markets.

Sector and size of investments

Deep sector knowledge, experience and networks allow firms to be more successful at creating value post-investment. As mentioned above, GPs interviewed by Bain for its Global Private Equity Report 2010 see value in specializing in just a handful of industry sectors.[5] Hot sectors have come and gone over the last decades, attracting large influxes of capital from LPs, as with the internet sector at the end of the 1990s. Technology-focused funds (information technology, life sciences, etc.) remain attractive, though, to many investors.

Firms also do differ by the range of capital they allocate to deals. Buyouts firms operate in very different markets if they fall in the "small", "mid-market", "large" or obviously "mega-" buyout categories. Whether the size difference in turn affects performance is—as we have seen in Chapter 3—still very much up for debate.

Strategic approach

Private equity funds also specialize in terms of strategic approach. Some might choose to focus on turnarounds, others on secondaries or special situations. Most, though, remain opportunistic.

---

[5] Ibid.

Types of private equity firms

The majority of private equity fund managers are independent, i.e. they raise their capital from external sources. A small minority, though, belong to the captive category: they are typically wholly-owned subsidiaries or divisions of a parent organization, usually a financial institution, and they manage or invest funds on behalf of that parent. That parent could also be a public entity, as is the case with many regional development funds. Captive firms are increasingly becoming semi-captives, investing funds on behalf of a parent company, or investing their own funds, in addition to investing funds raised from external sources.[6]

Timing

With hindsight there are good times and bad times to invest, but this is very difficult to predict. The market sentiment about private equity investments tends to swing widely between extremes. During good times, fund managers tend to come to the market regularly and with relatively large funds, and will be quite choosy at to their investors. In more difficult times, fundraisings will be less frequent and the funds will remain open for investment over longer periods of time, sometimes as much as two years.

The most sought-after funds rely extensively on their original investor base and may not be opened at all to new investors. Planning in such hectic times becomes critical to gain access: frequent contact with the fund managers helps. In general, managers will not be allowed to raise a new fund until a large share of their previous fund has been committed.

Contrary to most other asset classes, investment in private equity takes time and an investor cannot suddenly increase his private equity allocation, since commitments can only be made when funds are being raised. Vintage diversification is thus critical, as is a fairly even allocation to each vintage. To gain vintage diversification, considering that a single fund manager is unlikely to get back to the market more than once every other or third year, requires investments in a number of different fund managers.

Like wine, private equity has good and bad vintages. Unlike wine though, vintages are not easy to predict. A certain mix of sunshine, rain and temperature may give a wine expert a fairly good indication of what the wine is going to taste like. In private equity, by contrast, money is raised for investments that are unknown and will not be made for another 3–5 years. It is fair to say, though, that the best vintages tend to be associated with periods when investment opportunities exceed the amount of capital available and thus the best deals can be negotiated. Good economic times tend to lead quickly to over-priced assets under the pressure of too much money chasing too few deals. The timing effect was described earlier in Chapter 4.

---

[6] Arundale, K., *A Guide to Private Equity*, British Private Equity & Venture Capital Association, 2012.

An interesting example is the situation that prevailed in 2006. Despite the fact that most people agreed that prices paid in 2006 were high, the world's markets and economies carried on long enough for many investments made in 2006 to be sold or recapitalized at (even) high(er) prices. EVCA reported one-year returns from 2006 vintage buyout funds of 28.9%[7] as fund managers took advantage of widespread availability of debt finance on exceptional terms to refinance companies. With high prices paid and the onset of the "credit crunch", 2007 is unlikely to be a vintage that many will remember with fondness.

Private equity comes in and out of fashion with brutal regularity. Considering a typical economic cycle is about 7–8 years long, and the typical private equity fund will run for 8–10 years, a rational strategy—and one that will endear you to the fund managers to boot—is thus to commit quickly at the beginning of boom times when the private equity market is lower on everyone's wish list. In other words, under-commit quickly during hot private equity periods and over-commit consistently during colder periods…

The ATP investment programme detailed earlier in the chapter is the perfect example of a well-conceived strategy further helped by phenomenal timing. The Danish pension fund manager decided to increase its allocation to private equity mostly over the period 2002 to 2004, shifting about €4 billion into the asset class. As it continued to invest strongly over the next five years, ATP also delivered some of the strongest pension fund performance in Europe over the period that followed.

The pitch

The formal investment process will often start with an e-mail or phone call asking an investor to agree to a meeting. At this stage, what the investor only sees is a "teaser", a very short description of the new fund sent out to whet his or her appetite. If there is a positive response a conference call or a meeting will follow.

Managers raising money are invariably very nice to a potential investor: they will be ready to meet him—provided he has money at his disposal, they will flatter him and generally act as good salesmen. The reason is simple: there is a great deal of money at stake. We saw earlier that an investor committing $10 million to a fund will provide an average fund manager with a total of some $1.7 million in fees over the life of a fund[8], which can be broken down approximately into $1 million in management fees, $0.6 million in performance fees (much more for the best fund managers) and $0.1 million for various transaction and monitoring fees. So when a pension fund thinks about allocating $100 million to a new fund, $17 million in fees are at stake. It should, therefore, come as no surprise that fund managers work hard at being

---

[7] Pan-European Survey of Performance 2007, EVCA/Thomson Financial.

[8] Metrick, A. and Yasuda, A., "The Economics of Private Equity Funds", 2007.

liked by investors and race around the world to meet with as many potential investors as they can.

At the meeting, a senior partner and one or more senior professionals will be present, accompanied by the placement agent if one is used. A constructive first encounter will lead to more meetings, either in the investor's office or at the fund manager's. Small investors use these interactions to get a better understanding of the direction of the fund, and to start conducting due diligence. Larger ones will use their clout to negotiate better conditions. These large investors are courted by hundreds of fund managers every year and will end up only investing in a limited subset. For the investor, interacting with multiple fund managers every year is a relatively cheap and easy way to gather market intelligence.

When a fund manager starts raising a fund, rapid and sizeable commitments are very welcome and may be rewarded by better terms and a seat on the advisory board of the fund. Such early investors are referred to as cornerstone or anchor investors. Their reputation and visibility may help convince other investors to join the fray. Funds often have a first "closing" to allow the fund manager to start making investments and draw fees even if the target amount has not yet fully been raised. Several closings may follow until the agreed period of fundraising has come to an end or a maximum fund size has been reached. Investors who join the fund at later closings have to pay a modest premium, though,[9] to compensate for their later investment.

Fundraising will give rise to extensive documentation exchange. This typically includes the inevitable PowerPoint presentation, a more formal PPM, a (draft) legal agreement between investors and the fund together with other accessory agreements, an executive summary, a full due diligence package, subscription documents and a variety of disclaimers, which take up nearly as much space as the rest of the documentation...

Due diligence documents have become much better and also more voluminous with many (larger) groups using so-called electronic data rooms. There is also the dreaded "due diligence questionnaire", a long list of questions or a checklist to which fund managers must respond. The only lifesaver is that fund investors tend to produce similar questionnaires, so there is much overlap. The legal side of the investment has especially grown, without usually benefiting anyone but the lawyers. Excruciating negotiations often take place between the lawyers for the two sides, leading to protracted further communications. It is, therefore, extremely rare to see final legal agreements until a fund is well past its final closing.

For a new investor in the asset class, the best way to identify the best managers in a given sector is to search performance databases, such as the ones published by Preqin, Thomson Reuters and State Street. As indicated earlier, private equity exhibits a unique level of persistence in its performance. Whereas in most asset classes the usual prospectus disclaimer that "past performance is a poor predictor

---

[9] Interest based on LIBOR or other targets, plus a margin.

of future performance" is highly relevant; this is not the case so much for private equity. Historical performance data is highly relevant in private equity, and a fairly good predictor of performance in succeeding funds...

A number of US pension funds—particularly state-sponsored ones, such as industry giant CalPERS—have promoted the need for higher transparency in the sector, in particular towards their primary constituency, i.e. retirees from the state public sector. The results can be consulted on the internet at no cost (visit, for example, www.calpers.ca.gov and view the AIM Program Fund Performance) to get an indication of the performance of a wide range of funds.[10]

For newcomers to the asset class, it pays to meet other private equity investors at conferences and exchange notes on new and interesting groups. Private equity groups identified as being active in a particular sector are usually open to discussing their fund with prospective, bona fide investors. Access to the best funds remains, of course, a critical issue, especially in venture capital, where the difference between the best and the rest is the greatest.

Manager selection

For an investor, the most time-consuming step, which also happens to be the most crucial, is manager selection. The key to success is the rapid elimination of a large number of candidates, in order for the due diligence process to focus only on a handful of GPs. In no other asset class is manager selection so important. The difference in returns between good and bad managers is greatest in private equity: in fact, it is most pronounced in venture capital and somewhat less in buyouts. As indicated above, persistence means that good managers are likely to remain good managers and bad managers are likely to remain bad ones. So proper due diligence of a manager's track record should help indicate whether future returns are likely to be good or not. Private equity investment remains very opportunistic and, therefore, beautifully crafted strategies often do not work, no matter how clever they may look on paper.

A common mistake is for fund investors to wait for the fund managers to show up at their doorstep. This brings about a strong "local bias", i.e. a selection of funds that are mostly local or, worse, that are trying harder to raise money. It will not ensure that the investor meets with the best managers, who can only be met by being proactive. In order to identify the most sought-after candidates, an investor should talk to as many people as he can. Fellow fund investors tend to be happy to share (good) experiences. They will probably not get the investor into the best funds and introductions and other help are rare, but most are happy to share knowledge freely.

---

[10] http://www.calpers.ca.gov/index.jsp?bc=/investments/assets/equities/aim/private-equity-review/aim-perform-review/home.xml.

But picking the right managers is the easy part; getting access is critical. Top fund managers will very actively select their investors, on the basis of consistency (will they come back for the next funds raised, in good times and bad?), reliability (are they unlikely to default on the cash calls?), value added (can they bring deals in? Can they attract other interesting investors?) or expertise (can they enlighten the fund managers with respect to some interesting industrial developments or economic trends?). The best are choosers, as mentioned earlier.

Choosers tend to turn rather expensive, especially when the courting by investors is assiduous. Private equity funds in high demand have been able to impose conditions that would make other professionals blush. While compensation was meant to be primarily performance-driven, hence aligning fund managers' interests with their investors, the quest for growth and size in funds has progressively created a fee-based compensation model. There is a built-in mechanism to bring underperformers in line: without results, the next funds are unlikely to be as big, and hence management fees will drop. But that correction mechanism is very, very slow. Until then, the larger, best performing funds will continue to very much dictate their terms.

Surprisingly, it is actually quite difficult to establish empirically a list of criteria that strongly correlate with successful manager selection. A number of studies, including those by McKinsey and BCG/IESE presented earlier, seem to indicate that only private equity managers who focus on making companies better (with a little help from outside consultants) outperform in the long term. Making companies better means increasing their sales, improving the bottom line, or making a more efficient use of assets. It is also widely believed that managers who invest a larger proportion of their own money in the fund, say 2% or more instead of the usual 1%, perform better. This is a fair sign of commitment, but investors should not read too much into it. A brilliant investor starting out in private equity may simply not have this kind of money before being successful personally. It is, therefore, something of a chicken and egg situation. In the rare event of general partners actually owning more than 20% of the fund itself, the realignment of incentives usually works wonders, but again this is a relatively rare situation, especially in European private equity.

Another common saying is that first time managers are hungrier and are, therefore, more likely to deliver spectacular results. Unfortunately, the facts do not support that story: most first time managers are on average not successful and fail to raise a second fund. First time managers also tend to create much more work for the investor, as there is in general no smooth-running fund management operation in place and fund investors will be required to do much more work themselves on legal agreements, tax issues and general governance.

Investors should check carefully that managers that claim they are "sticking to their knitting" really are, as many claim to be doing so whilst doubling fund sizes. This means the same key people in the same geography, in the same kind of industries, in the same size companies, reapplying the same recipe that worked in the past. Unfortunately, many managers who were successful in a certain niche raise much more money for the next fund and rise to their level of incompetence. It may, therefore, be very rewarding to invest in a spin-off from a larger private equity team, but it is unlikely that great rewards will come from a few consultants or bankers who have never had to live with a deal as owners. Although some of the most successful private equity firms today have their origins in strategy consultancy, the failure rate remains exceedingly high. Despite the focus on improving the operations of companies, pure, industrial operators are not the answer either, as they will lack deal-making skills.

Finally, before deciding whether to proceed or not with full due diligence, the investor should look at the GP team. Good private equity investing is hard work and people intensive. One partner cannot possibly manage 10 investments. More good professionals per deal or per dollar invested usually leads to better investments...

Due diligence

Due diligence is the professional way of saying that an investor should do his homework before investing. Selecting a fund is a big responsibility for an investor since it will ultimately lead to disbursing millions of dollars of a client's money to a fund, without knowing exactly what it will be used for or when it will be invested. The investor will, therefore, have to have an awful lot of faith in the abilities of the fund managers. Due diligence is the extensive "check process".

Keeping in mind the stage at which the due diligence actually takes place, i.e. relatively late in the investment selection process, it should normally not generate many surprises, even though that certainly does not mean it should just be a box-ticking operation. It is after all the last opportunity for the investor to verify that what the information provided in terms of track records, past investments and the like is accurate. The process which unfolds looks very much like a funnel, with fewer and fewer funds making it to the next stage. Due diligence is time-consuming. It is not uncommon for the process to take up to three months, depending on the complexity of the fund and the number of external professionals brought in by the investor. It is expensive, since it ties up valuable human resources and should, therefore, only be undertaken once there is a high probability of investing in the fund.

Due diligence is a must and should never be skipped, whether the potential investment is in a new group or a successor fund from a group in which the investor has already invested. Private equity groups do change, partners leave or grow less hungry. Strategies and fund sizes change. The best and most consistent investors in private equity funds to date, the university endowments, have a greater tendency to drop fund managers than less successful investors, with endowments reinvesting in only 50% of successor funds, compared to around 60% for public pension funds and insurance companies, according to seminal research by Josh Lerner, Antoinette Schoar and Wan Wong, "Smart Institution, Foolish Choices?"[11] Don't let your guard down: every fund needs to stand on its own!

The paper trail created by due diligence may also save an investor's skin when an investment turns sour. It is very basic fiduciary responsibility of the investor vis-à-vis its clients and its own investors to perform the most comprehensive due diligence process possible. If that advice had been heeded by the hedge fund investors that ended up committing their clients' money to the infamous Madoff funds, the whole scheme would never have lasted so long. That said, many professional investors actually smelled something fishy long before the scheme was uncovered. Madoff's most extraordinary feat, not surprising for someone so accustomed to working with professional investors, was to carefully eschew the investment professionals and raise money mostly from naïve rich individuals not asking too many questions...

Compared to other asset classes, the due diligence analysis tends to be less quantitative and concentrate on the hardest skill of all—people judgement. There is no short cut to just spending time with the managers, not just over the beautifully-prepared presentation but also in informal settings and without a prepared agenda. The more one can talk to different people at the firm and with people who work with the firm, the better. The investor should also spend time with junior people, who tend to be less polished and give more honest answers to certain questions.

Most investments will be with experienced funds, which have accumulated track records. Three basic questions need to be asked:

Question 1: Have fund managers produced good profits for their investors in the past?
Question 2: If the answer is "Yes", are they likely to do so again?
Question 3: If the answer is "Yes", are the market conditions conducive to a success?

The first question requires a full examination of the track record to understand the role the GP has played in the success of a previous fund. This is particularly relevant because of the strong persistence in returns discussed earlier, a phenomenon unique to private equity.[12]

The second question requires a detailed examination of the success factors that generated the positive track record, such as team, investment strategy,

---

[11] Lerner, J., Schoar, A. and Wong, W., "Smart Institution, Foolish Choices?: The Limited Partner Performance Puzzle", Harvard University and National Bureau of Economic Research; Massachusetts Institute of Technology and NBER; January 2005.

[12] Kaplan, S. and Schoar, A., "Private Equity Performance: Returns, Persistence & Capital Flows", 2005.

industry, target size, geography, etc., and the confirmation that these drivers are still in place for a repeat performance.

Until recently, a positive answer to the first two questions was enough for an investor to feel rather comfortable. But a defining characteristic of the economic environments of the last few years is the accelerated speed with which macroeconomic factors change. It is thus critical nowadays to conduct a thorough examination of the global supply and demand for private equity to understand whether the industry as a whole, or a particular niche, is likely to remain attractive, and whether opportunities are in line with the amount of capital available.

If the answer is "Yes" to all three questions, things are on the right track for investment. Practically, this sounds relatively simple compared to other asset classes, where past performance has little predictive power. Past performance in private equity is a good predictor of future performance... if and only if internal and external factors remain stable.

So what factors should be stressed in a professional due diligence? Although some voices in the industry would like to see a standardized "due diligence questionnaire" being used by investors and managers alike, the truth is that most investors have their own due diligence "recipe". The coming section is not meant to be exhaustive, but offers a list of key issues that need to be addressed.

PEOPLE Depending on available manpower, it pays to physically visit offices of fund managers, where the prospective investor should speak to every member on the team, the juniors as well as the senior partners. There is a lot of truth in the saying that "the more junior you are, the less you lie". At this point in time, no one precisely knows what his money will be used for. In the case of (early-stage) venture capital, the companies in which the fund will invest may not even exist yet, and in the case of buyouts, nobody knows beforehand which companies or divisions will be on sale, nor the market conditions that will influence a fund manager's strategy.

The investor should find out whether the same team will be investing in the next fund or not. Private equity is a boutique industry and typically firms depend on a handful of senior professionals to make the critical investment decisions. The largest groups are slowly institutionalizing, but a limited number have more than 100 employees. Washington-based Carlyle Group, with more than $157 billion in assets under management across 101 funds and 64 fund-of-funds vehicles, has more than 1,300 professionals operating in 32 offices in North America, South America, Europe, the Middle East, North Africa, Sub-Saharan Africa, Japan, Asia and Australia.[13] The median venture capital fund has only 10 professionals and the median buyout fund has 13 professionals.[14]

---

[13] www.carlyle.com, September 2008.

[14] Metrick, A. and Yasuda, A., "The Economics of Private Equity Funds", 2007.

Group interviews are often carried out by investors to understand team dynamics and interactions between key decision makers. This is especially important for first time funds and for teams that have never worked together before. As mentioned in "The Guide to Private Equity Fund Investment Due Diligence", *"the best-performing teams are often those that have a long-established, stable working relationship and where the personal chemistry is strong"*.[15]

It is important to determine who were the greatest contributors to the past funds' performance and investigate whether they will still be present, with the same time dedication and motivation. Particularly important is to try to establish if these managers remain "hungry", especially if they have been successful before. In general, egos and ambitions are sufficiently strong to keep private equity professionals' eye on the ball. One should not lose sight of the fact that success is based on hard work, discipline and intelligence. With millions of dollars at stake in a fairly unstructured environment, laziness, sloppiness and stupidity are immediately taken advantage of. Performance is not measured on one lucky deal, but across more than one fund and scores of investments.

Good managers are good salesmen, so prospective investors should aggressively seek independent references. Reference checks are always provided by the fund managers, but the critical investor should always try to obtain information from people not on the list provided by the firm. The more revealing stories often come from disgruntled ex-partners or employees, though the investor should, of course, bear in mind that these people may have an axe to grind. In the current economic climate, investors increasingly invest time carrying out those reference checks, sometimes making up to 20 calls with former colleagues, portfolio company managers and bankers to learn as much as possible about the human aspect of the team.

INVESTMENT STRATEGY   Once the team has been carefully reviewed, attention needs to be paid to the fund investment strategy. The objective is clearly to evaluate the manager's ability to define and execute a winning strategy in the markets pursued. But it is also to assess his/her ability to remain focused and execute the stated strategy, in the face of a strong temptation to pursue attractive opportunities outside the predefined strategy. The investor, therefore, needs to watch out for any past "strategy drift and slippage", such as investments in markets that were not part of the initial strategy or explicitly excluded, or overly aggressive allocations to a particular industry, sub-sector or region despite clear diversification requirements.

PROCESS   A third area that requires true investigation is the process put in place by the private equity firm to carry out its work. Prospective investors need to sit down and carefully review all companies in the manager's portfolio to be able to fully

---

[15] "The Guide to Private Equity Fund Investment Due Diligence", PEI 2010.

understand how the investment manager sources deals, conducts the due diligence process and evaluates investment opportunities, and finally helps maximize post-investment value. It is not unheard of for investors to accompany the manager on visits to portfolio companies to understand how the work is carried out. Every step of the process needs to be examined, even the manager's approach to reporting and auditing. Investors may also want to test a manager's ability to reasonably assess investment opportunities by checking past records to compare how the manager estimated a portfolio company right before an exit, against the realized value.

TRACK RECORD The area where investors spend the most time is undoubtedly the review of the manager's track record. Track record is not about having spent a whole lifetime in private equity, or showcasing a team with combined experience of 150 years, even though that never stopped firms trotting out these figures. Track record is not about longevity: it is about performance, since past performance remains the best predictor of future performance. However, the task is more complicated than it sounds, and a track record may need to be ascertained. Whilst more and more track records are audited, there is still an enormous amount of room left for "undue creativity" in reporting. For example, teams will list past transactions as "representative" of the fund being raised, whilst conveniently leaving out "unrepresentative" ones that, completely coincidentally, did not perform so well. Or they will conveniently report "pre-fee" performances, i.e. leaving out taxes, transaction fees, management fees and carries…

During the dotcom bubble of the late 1990s, many buyout groups, no doubt attracted by the easy money and afraid they were missing out on the new, new thing, dabbled in internet and technology plays such as telecoms infrastructure. To remove the "stain" of the tech bubble that followed, the funds were conveniently split *ex post* between better performing buyouts and worse venture investments, with the potential investors strongly guided to look only at the buyout side of performance. This move was very similar in spirit to the "good bank–bad bank" recapitalizations implemented during the financial crisis to salvage financial institutions critically crippled by poor real estate loans.

Another trap to avoid are fund managers showing rather exciting returns but obtained out of a limited number of one-off spectacular deals, such as privatizations, when there is no chance of such deals being repeated. It pays to be thorough and have a very solid sense of cynicism when checking track records. After all, it is likely that the fund will be reacting to the market and making opportunistic investments going forward.

In order to get a picture of a track record that is as objective as possible, investors should ask to have access to all the deals, good and bad, that have been done by the firm, and conduct a full examination of performance by sector, year, region, fund, exit type, etc. This full examination also allows the investor to get a clear picture of the post-investment strategies (operational improvements, financial engineering or multiple arbitrage) the firm adopts to create value, and their relative success. Positive as well as negative trends need to be identified. It may be worth picking some deals at random and asking the manager to provide detailed data on acquisition and sale. If the track record has been properly audited, the full audit report should be available, and it would be worthwhile to speak to the auditors directly. Sensitivity analyses, also known as stress tests or outlier analyses, should be performed to see how performance would have been affected if the best and the worst investments had been removed. Overall performance can then be attributed intelligently and compared to one or more indicators, such as a targeted or required rate of return (nominal, real or risk-adjusted), public equity performance, the universe of private equity funds, the private equity portfolios of peer groups, the performance of the GP relative to its peer group (e.g. leveraged buyouts, venture capital, mezzanine debt, etc.) or the performance of underlying portfolio companies.[16]

Unrealized investments (those that are still part of the portfolio) are often thorny issues because their valuation is by definition extremely subjective. In March 2005, a number of private equity trade associations joined forces to produce the International Private Equity & Venture Capital Valuation Guidelines.[17] These were based on the principle of "fair value" to be consistent with IFRS and US GAAP, but managers were given considerable leeway into how to interpret them. Again sensitivity analyses should be conducted to see what impact different assumptions would have on the valuations. Many investors carry out their own valuation of unrealized investments and compare it with the number given by the manager, but most lack the necessary resources to analyze all the information required.

Private equity is highly cyclical, so track records should be evaluated against industry averages and, if possible, against the specific segment for a given vintage. A number of commercial organizations, notably Preqin, Thomson Reuters, State Street, Venture Economics and Cambridge Associates, produce relatively reliable benchmarks. Large institutional investors also have their own history of investments in private equity as resource, and some US state pension funds disclose real performance data at the individual fund level.

Private equity only makes sense if an investor can access the better funds. Only upper quartile performance can adequately compensate for the lack of liquidity.

Terms, conditions and fee structures

In Chapter 2, we covered a number of possible conflicts of interest that could arise between the LPs who bring the capital and the GPs who manage it. Because incentives are not always perfectly aligned between both parties, investors need to protect themselves by negotiating contractually binding terms before investing.

---

[16] "The Guide to Private Equity Fund Investment Due Diligence", PEI 2010.

[17] www.privateequityvaluation.com.

There is a lot of variation between fund offerings, but a large proportion of the key terms and conditions are fairly common. The principal fund document is the PPM, a document that generally covers hundreds of pages, to the disappointment of just about everyone in the industry (except, of course, the lawyers themselves).

Most PPMs are structured in the following way:

- Fund description
- Investment objectives
- Target fund size
- First and subsequent closings
- Minimum commitment
- Major investors
- Currency
- Investment

Most of the headings above are self-explanatory. Fund description and investment objectives are there to help explain what the fund is all about, but also to ensure that the manager stays focused and does not succumb to the so-called "strategy drift". A small forest's worth of paper will be devoted to defining just how far from the strategy the fund manager is allowed to drift, though potential investors should be wary of the fact that moving away from familiar territory has rarely laid the foundations for successful investment.

Unfamiliar territory can also pertain to the fund size. In boom periods, such as 2006–2007, many fund managers took advantage of the enormous demand for private equity and repeatedly increased their targets. Funds should have a maximum "cap" that cannot be exceeded because doing so would mean that investments would not be in line with the strategy and investment objectives outlined earlier.

A fund will typically also have a minimum amount of capital. After this amount has been raised, the fund can hold a "first close" and start investing. At this point, the fund can be said to "exist". If the minimum is not attained, investors are not bound by their commitments and the fund will not start its existence. Any number of subsequent "closings" can be held to allow investors that have come in after the first close to participate in the investments the fund is making. Once the fundraising process is complete, a "final close" is held, after which no new investors will be allowed into the fund.

Although the minimum commitment tends to range from $5 million to $15 million, depending on the size of the fund, managers typically reserve the right to waive the restriction, particularly for private investors, friends, managers of past investments and other people in their network. Major, or so-called "cornerstone", investors are large investors that come in at the start of a fund. These are often past investors who have committed to multiple funds or an organization that is "sponsoring" the fund, perhaps through a past relationship. For example, FTSE 100-listed private equity firm 3i is usually the first and largest investor in the third party funds it manages. Cornerstone investors are usually rewarded for their support with preferential fee and co-investment agreements. For start-up private equity firms raising a "maiden" fund, a cornerstone investor is usually regarded as essential to give other investors the confidence to invest.

RESTRICTIONS PPMs will usually contain a number of restrictions as to what and where the fund can invest, though, as previously mentioned, it is not unheard of for the manager to seek exemptions from these restrictions. The main areas of exclusion are:

- Geography;
- Maximum investment size;
- Investments in listed securities.

Investments are limited to certain geographies, although the largest buyout groups today are raising funds to invest on a global basis. Maximum investment size is defined in order to ensure sufficient diversification of investments in one fund and reduce risk. For buyout funds the maximum typically amounts to 15–20% of the total, while for venture funds, which have a wider portfolio of investments in each fund, it is typically less than 10%.

There has been a big increase in recent years in takeovers of public companies, known as public-to-privates, where the target company is listed on a stock market, but becomes a private company through the acquisition process, as well as in PIPEs (Private Investments in Public Equities). However, private equity will very rarely be involved in hostile transactions, as two key ingredients of their investment approach—the close collaboration with management and the ability to conduct detailed due diligence by cooperating with the target company—would not be possible in a hostile situation. Private equity funds also often invest in equity-like instruments such as subordinated debt or convertible debt, which may be more attractive while providing better protection.

DRAWDOWNS AND DISTRIBUTIONS Unlike mutual funds, the capital committed to private equity funds is only called upon when it is needed, rather than at the moment the investor signs on the dotted line, and funds are returned to investors as soon as the underlying assets are sold. This process, also known as "playing the clock", creates an unusually favourable environment when calculating the realized IRRs since only the time during which the cash was actually in the hands of the private equity fund is taken into consideration, not the time between initial commitment and final liquidation of the fund. There are three stages in this process:

- Drawdowns;
- Distributions;
- Liquidation.

Drawdowns are typically made during the period when the fund is making new investments, which is usually the first 3–4 years of its life. There will usually be some flexibility about when drawdowns can be made to allow for delays in investing, while a portion of the fund may be retained for follow-on investments in portfolio companies of the fund.

Distributions are made whenever the fund sells, or realizes, its investments. In some cases, proceeds may be reinvested, but the general rule is that investors receive a distribution the moment the fund receives a distribution. The investor may decide to re-invest these distributions in the next fund, but the discipline in private equity is that the moment investments are sold, the money is given back to investors.

The life of a fund is typically 8–10 years, after which it must be liquidated. There usually is the possibility for a manager to extend this for 2–3 years, flexibility many funds use to exit the last remaining investments. In some instances, shares in the unsold portfolio companies may be distributed to investors, though for most, holding a handful of shares in quoted and unquoted companies is not an ideal solution as we will see below. A number of "direct secondaries" investors have, however, emerged to buy unwanted portfolios from investors in funds, though these transactions are usually completed at a substantial discount to market value.

FEES AND INCENTIVES There are a variety of mechanisms through which a private equity fund manager generates fees and income. Some are straightforward and seen by all parties as being effective mechanisms to align the interests of GPs and LPs. Others are harder to justify from that perspective and have attracted considerable criticism. The usual fees are:

- Establishment costs;
- Management fees;
- Transaction and monitoring fees;
- Underwriting fees and broken deal costs.

Private equity fees are substantial, but good funds have also created excellent returns for their investors, who have not pushed hard for changes to the fee structures.

Management fees, as discussed earlier in the book, can range from 1% to 3% with most funds charging between 1.5% and 2.5%. Larger funds tend to rely on more external professionals of the more expensive variety, but clear economies of scale remain in favour of larger funds. In a 2006 study, SCM reported on average four professionals and three partners for funds under $50 million, that number going up to 25 professionals and 10 partners for funds managing more than $3 billion. Consequently, the percentage management fee tends to go down with increasing fund size. The same SCM study reported average management fees slightly above 2.0% per annum for funds under $50 million, with that number going down to an average of 1.56% for funds managing more than $3 billion in 2006.

Carried interest is nearly always 20%, with the exception of the most successful venture groups that have managed to increase this to 30%, a move partly justified by their keeping fund sizes at reasonable levels. They have been copied by a very select group of buyout firms, with a sprinkling of firms managing to get 25%. It is actually quite surprising that almost all successful buyout groups have increased their size rather than their carry, generating an ever-larger misalignment with their limited partners.

The exact origin of the 20% focal point is unknown, but previous authors, such as Gompers and Lerner (1999) and Kaplan (1999), have pointed to Venetian merchants in the Middle Ages, speculative sea voyages in the age of exploration and even the Book of Genesis as sources.

Many other fees crept in during good times, without must pushback from investors all too keen to get into the funds. These include establishment costs, transaction fees, monitoring fees, underwriting fees and broken deal costs.

Establishment costs are the costs associated with the setting up of a new fund, which is usually capped. **Transaction and monitoring fees** are charged to cover the costs of doing transactions and monitoring investments afterwards. Many investors are of the belief that this is very much the day-to-day business of a private equity firm and should, therefore, be covered by the management fee.

Underwriting fees are charged when a fund underwrites and then places part of the investment with other investors. **Broken deal costs** are the costs involved in working a deal, including the costs of outside advisors, which need to be covered when the transaction does not happen.

Some investors have balked at these additional fees and asked that all actual transaction fees received by the private equity firm be fully disclosed and some formula put in place to offset at least part of the additional costs against management fees. However, the offsetting process still lacks transparency in many instances.

INVESTOR REMEDIES   Private equity funds often provide investors with a variety of protections and possible remedies in case things don't proceed as planned in the relationship. These include but are not limited to:

- Termination for cause;
- No-fault divorce;
- Key-man clause.

Once the commitment has been made, investors in private equity funds have very limited influence. This is the direct consequence of the "limited partner" status of investors, which precludes any form of active involvement in the vehicles and shields them from financial responsibility in the normal course of business. Active involvement could also negatively impact their preferential tax treatment. In other words, their "limited liability" status is premised on an "arm's length" relationship.

A major weakness of many private equity structures remains the near impossibility to fire an underperforming manager. Criminal behaviour such as fraud is normally a cause for termination, and the departure of key professionals should also give the investor the opportunity to suspend further investments ("key-man" clause). If the fund managers are simply not good at their job and perform poorly, leading to massive loss of confidence from fund investors, the "no-fault divorce" clause can be triggered by investors if a super-majority of them wants to stop further injections of capital, but it is still too rare as a contractual clause.

OTHER TERMS   A number of other interesting clauses are worth a quick look, such as:

- Co-investment rights;
- Investments prior to final closing;
- Reporting (see section below);
- Successor funds.

Co-investments rights are generally quite popular with investors. Managers offer co-investments opportunities when the investment they plan to make is too large for the fund alone, which is often precluded from committing more than 10–20% of its funds to any single deal. If an investment would force it outside that range, it can syndicate it with other private equity funds and/or with fund investors who will be offered an opportunity to invest an additional amount alongside the fund. The manager will charge significantly lower fees on the co-investment portion or sometimes remove the fees altogether. Co-investments are often said to be more profitable than fund investments, although statistics are limited on the subject.

The other reason investors like co-investments is the additional benefit of a closer involvement in the investment process alongside an experienced buyout investor. As part of the investment process, a buyout investor will devote many man-months (even man-years) understanding the business, developing a strategy, conducting due diligence and negotiations and so on. By contrast, fund investors are typically only allowed a few weeks to conduct due diligence, generally with not enough qualified staff to even do a small part of the work required.

Co-investment rights are usually reserved for the bigger investors and there is a fair amount of discretion for the fund manager on how to allocate these rights.

Investments prior to final closing are common, as fundraising usually takes more than a year. There are often several closings, but after the first one the fund is in existence and investments can be made. Investors coming in after the first closing will have to pay a modest premium or interest and allocations will be adjusted to reflect the commitments of new investors.

Successor funds are also an interesting part of the landscape. To a large extent, players, as in most professional activities, like to stay active to continuously hone their skills and stay "ahead of the curve". By the time a fund is nearly fully invested, the fund manager will start raising the successor fund, usually when the current fund is 60–70% invested.

FUND STRUCTURE The **legal structure** used in most cases is some form of Limited Partnership in a lenient tax jurisdiction, if not a complete tax flow-through vehicle. The fund investors act as limited partners in the structure, with no say on the management of the fund or in any investment decision. Quite a lot of variations on that scheme exist as countries develop new formats to facilitate private equity investments, so it is crucial to involve legal and tax experts.

In our view it would be much simpler and better for virtually all parties involved to bring the whole structure "on-shore" and allow similar tax treatment in the geographical markets where players are really active. Governments and politicians take note. However, until governments and politicians see the light, taxation will probably be the determining factor for how funds are structured and in what jurisdiction they are based. Popular jurisdictions are Delaware for US funds and the (European) Channel Islands, Jersey and Guernsey, for European funds as well as Luxembourg. Caribbean islands and many other islands have also jumped on the bandwagon. Usually these are jurisdictions which are relatively stable and are at least part of a larger, reputable system.

The main rules of a fund are rather simple. There is an amount an investor commits, there is a fee for the manager and there is an extra payment for the manager if he does a good job. There is a period during which the committed amount can be invested and there are some rules imposing a certain discipline on the manager on how and where he can invest. After a given period the manager can no longer invest and has to start selling investments and give the money and most of the gains back to the investors. That's it.

Once this is given to lawyers and regulators it is converted into several hundred pages of documents. Limited partners will also involve their own lawyers to split hairs before finally committing to invest in a fund. Several millions of dollars are typically spent on the (very standard) legal documents of a fair-sized private equity fund. In an industry driven by a ferocious focus on returns and cost efficiency at the level of investments, it is hard to understand how savvy investors can still justify this expense.

The **GP** carries out the actual management of the fund. The general partner will often be advised by an **investment advisor**.

The **advisory committee** is a grouping of the largest and most important investors in the fund with limited powers to intervene. As mentioned above, investors cannot intervene in the affairs of the fund, lest they are willing to lose their limited liability status. They can only vote with their feet and forego investments in successive funds. The advisory committee's major function is to enable more direct contacts with the fund manager. Possible conflicts of interest of the fund manager will usually be discussed with the advisory committee and the fund manager will in most cases follow the committee's recommendation.

Subscription to a fund

The subscription process itself is not very sophisticated. It requires form-filling, though unfortunately all groups seem to have different forms. Disclosure, anti-money laundering and other measures must also be taken into account when investing in private equity. These regulatory hurdles have increased in recent years but are seen as necessary evils. The subscription usually is an agreement to send money as and when requested by the fund manager, with the investor rarely parting with any money immediately.

At the top of a cycle the best houses will be so sought after that they may close a fund in a single close rather than having consecutive chunks of commitments. Existing investors will get preferential treatment; newcomers may have trouble getting an allocation.

Capital calls

Private equity managers rarely know precisely when or how much capital they are going to need. Investors are asked to commit to making the money available as and when asked to do so. It takes time to find opportunities, to analyze them and then negotiate and structure the deals. It is not at all unusual for deals to take six months to complete and some transactions may take years to materialize. Given the uncertainty about when and where investments will be made, the system of commitments followed by capital calls does seem to make sense for all parties involved.

When an investment is ready, the fund manager will formally call the money from its investors, giving them a reasonable amount of time to transfer the funds, usually a few weeks. Other calls will be made for management fees, or in some cases, management fees are called at the same time as the capital calls. In venture capital, one call may cover several (small) investments, as venture capital will make more investments per fund and capital calls would otherwise be very frequent and small. ILPA recently released its "Capital Call and Distribution Notice Best Practices" template, a set of standardized reporting templates to help regulate reporting to LPs, and improve transparency and efficiency when GPs make their capital calls.[18]

---

[18] ILPA, Capital Call and Distribution Notice Best Practices, October 2011.

Calculations for the IRR and other performance measures start the moment money is transferred by the investor. This "cash-on-cash" IRR calculation approach has always been controversial since it makes the numbers not easily comparable to other asset classes where all the money committed is usually handed over immediately. In effect, private equity managers, as indicated above, free themselves from the duty of managing the unused liquidity in the fund by simply passing the duty on to the investors...

Monitoring

Private equity is often seen as a risky asset class because of the various combinations of high leverage, long and illiquid commitment periods, and for venture capital the early-stage nature of portfolio companies, etc... Furthermore, contrary to public equities that are monitored on a daily basis by the market, private equity-held portfolio companies remain private and as such do not benefit from the market discipline a listing provides.[19]

Investors need to remain vigilant throughout the duration of the fund. Even if the GP is paid to closely monitor the investments in the portfolio, investors can also participate in active monitoring themselves. They have an opportunity once a year to learn about the fund's portfolio at the Annual General Meeting, where the GP reviews his strategy and the portfolio companies in the fund. However, a seat at the Advisory Board of the fund is what investors often try to get when negotiating an investment in a new fund. During those close interactions with the management team, investors can better understand the investment strategy, as well as provide advice and suggestions to the GP. It is also the right forum to discuss possible conflicts of interest and address them early on. Informal discussions also allow investors to get a better idea about upcoming capital calls, drawdowns, distributions and liquidation, making cash flow management somewhat easier.[20]

The goal of monitoring is, however, more about reducing the potential for losses than about actually improving the performance of the fund. Some risks can be detected early on. Has a portfolio company underperformed recently, without warnings from the GP? Have members of the management team suddenly left the private equity firm? Is the GP actually adhering to the pre-defined investment strategy or is it drifting away when attractive opportunities occur?[21] Is enough information disclosed about the investments made?

[19] See Bassi, I. and Grant, J., "Structuring European Private Equity", Euromoney Institutional Investor, 2006 for a comparison.

[20] Ibid.

[21] See Mueller, K., "Investing in Private Equity Partnerships: The Role of Monitoring and Reporting", Gabler, 2008 for a discussion.

Distributions

Good investments will pay an investor his investment back and then some. But in private equity this takes time. On average, it takes 6-7 years before the money an investor puts in is distributed back. After that, arguably, everything will be pure gain. The combination of early distributions and a typical investment period of 5 years results in a net cash flow to a private equity investor that is relatively hard to predict. Investors new to the asset class are often frustrated by the slow pace at which money is put to work and, when on top of that distributions come in, their private equity exposure tends to be well below the levels they had anticipated.

Distributions are made when investments are sold or refinanced. Return and performance calculations are measured from the moment the money is returned to investors. Normally, fund managers do not have the right to re-invest such proceeds, a vital element of the private equity discipline.

As detailed in Chapter 3, measuring performance in private equity funds is a tricky exercise, especially during the life of the fund. At the end of the fund, on the other hand, once all cash contributions and distributions have been completed, it is relatively easy to compute the fund's lifetime IRR and its Total Value to Paid In (TVPI) capital ratio with precision. It is hard to argue with cash, so the discipline of having to distribute proceeds and having to liquidate a fund at the end of its life make for excellent, albeit *ex post*, governance.

One pressing issue in private equity is the medium through which these distributions can take place. In particular, are cash-only distributions required? The issue is not an important one for most liquid instruments, and would be even perceived as an incongruous one. Unfortunately, the very nature of private equity investments, in particular their lack of liquidity, makes the question highly relevant. Does it always make sense to force the fund manager to turn the exits into cash, or would it possibly make more sense for both parties to consider distributing shares? We discussed in Chapter 2 the reasons behind the distribution of shares. Let's briefly review a number of situations where shares are actually distributed instead of cash.

The first situation is the private-equity owned company that gets exited through a listing on a major stock market. The company shares acquire immediate liquidity and as such become valuable currencies. Should the fund manager sell its (usually quite large) stake to the market to return cash to its investors, or should the manager simply distribute the shares to the investors and let them decide if they prefer to keep on holding to the stake? In the first case, the fund manager runs the risk of depressing the stock price by putting a large stake on the market at once. Furthermore, as a large insider, the fund manager will in most cases be subject to stringent requirements on the sale of the stake, possibly involving prolonged lock-in periods. On the other hand, when shares are distributed to the investors, each and every one of them will usually not be large enough and will not be treated as an insider, and hence may face fewer restrictions in selling the shares immediately.

A second situation is where a buyout business is sold through a trade sale and payment is made in the form of shares of another private business. In this case, the "exit" essentially substitutes one private set of shares for another. Distributing unlisted securities to investors is a more serious problem since they are in no better position to dispose of them than the fund itself. This imposes a heavy cost on the investors. In this case, it is clearly the fund manager's responsibility to find a way to convert the shares received in cash, and the recognition of the sale should only occur upon that conversion.

Finally, there might still be portfolio companies in the fund that have not been exited at the termination of the fund, despite repeated efforts by the fund managers. At that point, the options are indeed limited and distributing the shares to investors may be the last resort. The only question remaining is at what valuation these share distributions should be accounted for. It should be obvious that any valuation in excess of zero should be heavily substantiated...

The description above very much covers the situation of a single fund investor. In reality, most investors hold investments in many funds at the same time, including successive generations of funds by the same fund manager. In the portfolio of funds, distributions are made when other funds in the portfolio make capital calls. This allows the investor, say a large fund-of-funds manager, to make larger total commitments than the total funds made available by its investors. This over-commitment obviously alleviates the single fund cash flow problem outlined above, in particular the cash call and reinvestment issues. Many funds-of-funds managers claim to have developed highly sophisticated models that can predict the interaction between distributions and capital calls. Clearly, the smaller the private equity allocation of a portfolio, the less critical such strategies are. However, in the most extreme cases where the private equity allocation is indeed 100%, like funds-of-funds, badly executed over-commitment strategies can lead to disaster. To provide liquidity in periods, some managers negotiate standby credit lines in case capital calls exceed the total of their commitments and distributions. Unfortunately these models mostly fail to account for systemic shocks to the economic system, such as the credit crunch that hit in 2007–2008. The crisis saw distributions dry up, valuations drop while some capital calls still came in, mostly to recapitalize portfolio companies that were sinking into problems of their own. Many private equity investors were wrong-footed during the financial crisis and were forced to sell stakes and commitments at major discounts on the secondaries market when the drawdown to distribution ratio significantly increased in 2008 to around 65:35, well up from the approximate parity of 2007.[22] This evolution is described in **Exhibit 7.2**.

[22] SCM Industry Research, June 2009.

Exhibit 7.2 Ratio of capital calls to distributions for global buyout funds

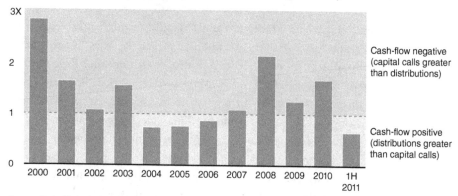

Source: Bain Global Private Equity Report 2012 based on data from Preqin.

Reporting

Good reporting is absolutely critical, allowing investors to follow on a regular basis the evolution of a fund. The quality varies enormously between fund managers and it is surely an area where a more standardized approach would benefit investors and the industry in general. Typically there will be an annual, audited report together with three quarterly, unaudited reports. Organizations like ILPA have called for quarterly reports to be audited as well, but it is difficult to see anyone, bar the accountants, being particularly keen on the suggestion.

Before agreeing to invest in a new fund, investors will have accepted how reporting will be conducted. That includes the **frequency** of reports, the **information** to be contained in these reports, the **manner** in which the reports are to be made (e.g., in writing, by e-mail, on a secure website) and the **basis of valuation** that will be used for such reports.[23] Typically, those reports contain an overview of the performance of each company in the portfolio, information about new investments and divestments, and a breakdown of the fund's financial situation.

Investors will normally receive a report that identifies their investment and performance. The validity of those numbers is, of course, constrained by the very nature of the private equity investments, by definition companies that are (usually) not quoted on a stock exchange. Frequency of reporting is relatively low, as more frequent reporting would not add much value and still be subject to the same caveats. All reports are, therefore, by nature somewhat out of date. Nearly all fund managers hold annual investor meetings and informal meetings are often organized throughout the year. Fund investors should not hesitate to proactively contact and visit fund managers.

Private equity reporting is a tremendously challenging task due to a number of interacting factors. First, it is always difficult and somewhat arbitrary to value a portfolio

---

[23] *EVCA Handbook*, June 2011.

position, let alone the portfolio as a whole, before that position is actually sold. Second, accounting for initial commitments, drawdowns, distributions, management fees and carries is quite complex. Third, the actual mix between cash flows and unrealized capital gains and losses can also create challenges. Finally, data entry is usually done manually in sophisticated electronic spreadsheet entries, which sometimes require judgement calls as to how and when to record specific events and data.

Small investors in private equity have a fairly good understanding of the performance of the individual funds in their portfolio because this is the level at which reporting is conducted. What is often lacking is a consolidated report of several funds and of consolidated performance. Larger investors have in-house teams or rely on outside specialists to create comprehensive performance reports for their investors. Specialized boutiques have emerged that focus entirely on providing private equity reporting services. An example would be WealthTouch[24], which, according to its website, offers to:

> "... transform the complex, multi-faceted financial data in ultra-high net worth portfolios into clear, concise portfolio reporting. Our comprehensive solutions consolidate, reconcile and report across all asset classes, custodians and currencies to create an unbiased and independent view of the client's complete wealth picture."

The industry, under the guidance of organizations such as EVCA and ILPA, is moving towards greater standardization of its reporting under a set of industry guidelines intended to facilitate easier comparisons across funds.

Fund liquidation

The finite life of most private equity funds is a key ingredient of their governance system. The forced conversion to cash and the obligation to go back to investors to obtain their capital for another fund are effective disciplining devices, forcing a final "correction" to the incorrect valuations that may have been put on individual positions during the life of the fund.

The end-of-life stage of a fund is one that is paved with difficulties, even for the most experienced operators. For the less experienced ones, the fund liquidation is sometimes lived as a rather traumatic event not unlike realizing that one is a mere mortal. The realization that the flow of management fees would not be going on forever can be painful. Interesting situations can emerge with the handful of investments left in the portfolio, collectively known as the "living dead", on which a management fee continues to be paid, usually calculated on a cost basis, which by that point in time may be much higher than the positions'

---

[24] http://www.wealthtouch.com/.

current values. These investments are often going nowhere, but are not so weak as to mercifully die a natural death. They take up very little of the fund manager's time, and still generate some decent fee income. Quite often it is clear these last remaining positions will make little or no returns to the fund investors, and hence should be disposed of expeditiously. A number of specialist secondary funds have been set up specifically for the purpose of "liquidating" funds' leftovers, a task most primary fund managers often dread and resent.

When the fund managers have not been able to complete the sale of the positions, an actual liquidation will be implemented. A liquidator will be appointed to effect the orderly sale or disbanding of the assets, as well as to ascertain that no unexpected claims will emerge after the closing of the fund, i.e. that all bills have been paid and all possible issues settled.

In theory investors can be called upon after the liquidation of a fund to dip into their pockets for missed or unexpected claims. Such events are rare, but they are likely to increase with the number of funds in the market. At the end of liquidation, after all advisors and experts have taken their cut, whatever is left is distributed amongst investors.

8

The future of private equity

Executive summary

Private equity always found ways to reinvent itself in the face of adversity. This resilience can be traced back not only to the acumen and skills of its professionals but also to the very definition of the industry's activities. Private equity is intrinsically opportunistic and evolves its business model to respond to short- or long-term value creation possibilities. It is highly competitive, internally and externally, permanently adjusting to the new requirements of capital and expertise providers. Finally, it operates under the highly flexible framework of private capital, i.e. whatever rules can be negotiated with its institutional investors. As long as it remains "free to roam", private equity will find new ways to create value in markets that are inherently imperfect.

Private equity is here to stay, despite difficult market conditions that continue to affect the industry and force adjustments to its business model. The premises on which it operates, such as the positive impact of strong performance-based incentives, the discipline of finite-duration investment vehicles and the astute use of leverage, bring focus and alignment of interest to the industry.

After decades of high growth, private equity has reached a certain level of maturity in most developed countries. Inefficiencies and arbitrage opportunities are less prevalent and investors will have to work their companies harder to get reasonable returns. Large groups will diversify and become increasingly focused on asset gathering with sophisticated sales operations. We expect to see small groups who will identify niches in which they will become specialized. GPs will have to look broader and deeper to identify targets, and work harder to squeeze value out of them. The market will likely polarize into a limited number (10–20) of larger generalist firms and a plethora of specialized smaller players focusing on niche markets. This specialization also implies a move away from the simpler buyout game plans to more sophisticated value creation scenarios. Private equity is bound to continue shedding its "arbitrage" foundations for a more sustainable "partner for growth" image, in which earning its money will require more active and more collaborative ownership strategies. These models are already visible today, providing for a form of convergence with family businesses investment strategies, with longer investment horizons, more operational hands-on interventions and the willingness to work with instead of against the prior owners.

Limited partners, for their part, are also growing more professional. Pension funds and endowments have become more assertive, questioning the performance disparities among fund managers and showing a willingness to engage in more thorough and lengthy due diligence before investing in new funds or even reinvesting in their current GPs. Some have gone even further and have become increasingly active as direct investors, or direct players such as Carlyle acquiring LPs like AlpInvest. The picture will become larger and even more complex with GPs and LPs from emerging markets entering the fray.

Doomsday prophets saw in the financial crisis of 2007 the last nail in the coffin of private equity as an industry, not to mention those who were all too happy to lay the very root of that crisis at its feet. Of course, what is partly to blame for that scapegoating feast was partly the general public's incapacity to separate the private equity sector from the financial industry in general. While the two clearly roam the same territory, their overlap was actually small. Private equity always used leverage when it was available, and probably as much as it could get. So it goes with most "good things" that bring outsized rewards. But putting the blame on the borrower, as in the real estate crisis of 2007, does not make much sense: it was lenders and governments that failed the system for the most part. By forcing mortgage lenders to facilitate access to capital for sub-prime customers, governments seeded the demise of the credit boom. Private equity investors similarly indulged in the largesse of banks for as long as it would last. But leverage is a nice-to-have element in the buyout game plan, not a must-have. Weaning private equity from its dependence on leverage would be painful but ultimately beneficial, putting the onus back on its true value creation potential, away from the financial engineering prowess of deals.

Private equity always found ways to reinvent itself in the face of adversity. This resilience can be traced back, not only to the acumen and skills of its professionals but also to the very definition of the industry's activities. Private equity is intrinsically opportunistic and evolves its business model to respond to short- or long-term value creation possibilities. It is highly competitive, internally and externally, permanently adjusting to the new requirements of capital and expertise providers. Finally, it operates under the highly flexible framework of private capital, i.e. whatever rules can be negotiated with its institutional investors. As long as it remains "free to roam", private equity will find new ways to create value in markets that are inherently imperfect.

After decades of high growth, private equity has probably reached maturity in most developed markets. Inefficiencies and arbitrage opportunities are less prevalent and investors have to work their companies harder to get reasonable returns. Simple game plans are becoming more difficult to execute. Players now have to identify niches in which to specialize, looking broader and deeper to identify targets, and working harder to create value. This specialization also implies the use of more sophisticated value creation tools requiring specific knowledge and skills. Private equity is progressively shedding its "arbitrage" foundations for a more sustainable "partner for growth" image, in which earning its money requires more active and collaborative ownership strategies. These models are already visible today, providing for a form of convergence with family businesses investment strategies, with longer investment horizons, more operational hands-on interventions and the willingness to work with owners.

In parallel, limited partners are also developing in size and professionalism. Family offices are hiring specialized teams to conduct in-depth due diligence prior to investing in private equity funds. Sovereign wealth funds are starting to flex their muscle and impose overdue changes to the standard arrangements. Nothing, in essence, is really standard anymore in the world of private equity, and this new-found flexibility is an opportunity to reshape the industry into the value engine of the next 50 years.

So, what will be the key drivers and trends for the future of the industry? We venture a number of propositions.

First, the days of low hanging fruit, arbitrage- and financial-engineering based, are numbered. Money is becoming more and more a commodity, i.e. access to it does not in itself provide the basis for consistent value creation. Similarly, financial engineering skills are not in short supply anymore, and can't serve as the prime base to generate value. Today's and tomorrow's deals will require more and more operational involvement, i.e. private equity will have to earn its money the hard way. Active ownership strategies, which were in effect often limited to board interventions, are not going to generate the returns expected. Active ownership will now mean what it says: operational intervention. This implies the development of distinct expertise at the funds level, expertise that will help differentiate but will also force more refined definitions of the target deals.

Secondly, as in all maturing industries, increased specialization will complement the large players seeking scale. Specialists will know earlier when good assets are for sale and how to make them better. They may buy and build, creating synergies

between investments made in the same sector. This may be part of the necessary consolidation in a sector or it may help companies to become ready for the next step in their evolution. Private equity has grown enormously but it still owns only a fraction of small to medium–sized companies and merely a small part of merger and acquisition activity is related to private equity. There is definitely still room for growth but penetration will be slower and the industry will have to bring real benefits, not just the re-shuffling of assets amongst peers.

Thirdly, private equity itself, as an industry, is going to come increasingly under scrutiny. Not because of its inherent potential for creating havoc in economies but because of the impact it can have on their growth dynamics. Governments nowadays are in desperate search for growth engines, and private equity can be a key enabler of that movement. Governments need to understand the industry better and respect its contributions. Opening up might provide an acceptable substitute to regulation.

This opening up will be facilitated by a new generation of very professional limited partners with deep pockets and a willingness to invest in riskier asset classes but also higher expectations in terms of transparency. The balance of power between limited and general partners has been incredibly slow to shift: underperforming funds have been allowed to continue operating way beyond their useful lives, abusive fee structures have lived on, etc... But that shift is happening and will continue for a while, forcing the hygienic changes required in a well-functioning industry. To some extent, this is nothing more than the healthy expression of a maturing industry finally earning its stripes as a valuable contributor to society.

Private equity in a changing world

A MATURING INDUSTRY   The rapid growth of the industry over recent decades is probably over in mature markets like North America and Western Europe; it will continue for a good while in Asia, South America, Africa and Eastern Europe.

Professionalization is also increasing across the industry. Companies are increasingly well managed in developed countries, where general management skills are available on the market. Publicly listed companies are under constant pressure from financial markets to become more efficient and grow faster, while private companies—family-owned companies in particular—are increasingly benchmarking with the best practices of listed ones, hiring quality outside managers and industry veterans. By the time buyouts are considered, many of the easy fixes have already been implemented by the existing management teams; the low hanging fruit, from a value creation standpoint, has for the most part already been plucked. The result of (too) much money chasing (too) few deals is clearly seen in the rise of secondary buyouts. The challenge for the industry going forward is to find more "real" (primary) opportunities, which will have to display characteristics other than those previously looked for. It has always been hard to cope with a sudden inflow of funds into the industry. This in part also justifies the increase of minority participations and growth equity helping companies to grow bigger and better. That trend is likely to reinforce itself, leading to the creation of a new positioning of private equity funds: from equity providers to partners for growth.

However, private equity only touches a fraction of private companies. In countries like Germany, only a small percentage of the famous "Mittelstand" companies have private equity involved. In that country, and a few others in Europe, banks have historically provided funds for growth and hence have been major competitors of private equity. With continuously evolving banking regulation, in particular with respect to capital adequacy requirements, banks will have to use their equity much more sparingly, in particular when it comes to deposits from customers. A cynical observer would probably surmise that one should never discount the ability of markets and governments to generate new, large inefficiencies in the most unexpected sectors, and of private equity to identify them quickly and take advantage of them.

Arbitrage will still happen but more as a matter of happenstance, not strategy; private equity cannot count on a sustainable supply of such opportunities. The time when a naïve seller could be convinced to sell at a ridiculously low price to a savvy buyout shop is over. In reality, such deals have been very rare. Even the smallest transactions now involve professional advisors on both sides.

In order to survive in this new context, private equity firms have to adapt, and adapt they have. The traditional "easy wins" based on standard financial engineering have become a commodity, hence generating commodity-like returns. Clearly, leverage in itself does not create value: at best it only amplifies increases and decreases in value. Quick flips will become increasingly rare. Instead, value creation will result from real, time-consuming operational improvements, with a likely impact on the duration of investments and the types of skills private equity investors will have to be able to offer to target firms.

How does this affect investors? Actually, extracting returns from operational value instead of leverage and price arbitrage might provide better diversification to investors' portfolio, especially in an increasingly globalized economy where correlation between financial markets is high and increasing. A more mature industry might mean a better use of LP's capital: as market inefficiencies become rarer, the generous fees GPs pocket during the life of the fund will tend to reward real effort to improve and transform the operations of companies, rather than luck or special access to information or to proprietary deals.

To be able to create operational value, private equity firms increasingly hire people with significant consulting or industrial experience and who have shown the ability to effect operational change. Competition for these talents is already fierce, as profits will be increasingly driven by the ability to develop and implement the right strategies for each industry. Smaller teams may find this harder to do for economic reasons and will, therefore, have to specialize. Niche players are likely to increase, focusing on less courted segments where plain vanilla players will struggle to generate returns. This change will require focus on a specific know-how, a geographic zone, a particular industry like energy or a particular discipline like turnaround management.

THE RELATIONSHIP BETWEEN LIMITED PARTNERS AND GENERAL PARTNERS

When money is tight, LPs with money to invest are very much in demand and can impose their own agendas more easily than when capital is abundant. The question that remains to be tested is whether the current trend of LPs gaining more influence is cyclical or a more structural one.

Returns remain the ultimate factor for survival in the industry. Managers not delivering on the return front will not survive; the litmus test of the market efficiency is, of course, how long it takes for an underperforming fund manager to disappear. Also, some funds able to deliver average returns but wrapped in superior investor relations seem to have been able to continue operating way longer than expected. There has been a clear flight to safety—read size. Large groups, despite warning potential investors that future returns may be lower than historical ones, have still to be able to increase assets under management.

Increased transparency and accountability should enable investors to more actively supervise their fund managers and the industry would clearly benefit from easier ways to remove poorly performing managers. The so-called **no-fault divorce clause**, which enables a supermajority of limited partners to remove fund managers without having to justify the move, is gaining acceptance, but it is still mostly limited to managers with less clout. It is highly doubtful that groups like Blackstone will accept such a clause any time soon...

The abundance of information—access to industry reports, performance rankings and deal data—makes LPs better informed than they have ever been. In theory this makes for more sophisticated decision making, but it also creates a herd instinct, as LPs all work with the same data and follow similar analysis processes. An association of LPs such as ILPA, with a mission to defend the interests of LPs, encourages the adoption by GPs of best practices for reporting and governance. Interestingly enough, the "sophistication gap" does not seem to have significantly shrunk: GPs remain on average smarter and better educated than LPs, which one usually attributes to the fact that they are significantly better paid. Many institutional investors are public entities that are simply not allowed to offer investment banking and private equity level compensations, even if they are fully aware of the competitive disadvantage this puts them at. The move towards more operational, hands-on models of investment will bring back to the forefront the importance of good CEOs and entrepreneurs as the true unsung heroes of value creation. This may well lead them to capture a bigger slice of the pie, a phenomenon already clearly visible in the growth capital segment of the market.

Because compensation structures currently reward size over performance, most GPs often raise the biggest fund possible regardless of whether it can be invested well. Again, because of a dearth of LP funding today, all fund managers large and small are under pressure on fees. Aberrations such as transaction fees and monitoring fees, which only larger funds got away with, have been strongly reduced and this evolution is likely to be permanent.

Banks and insurance companies have been significant LPs but now face increasing pressure to reduce their exposure to private equity significantly. Heavy-handed regulation may also increase the cost for pension funds to dedicate significant portions of their allocations to private equity, leaving sovereign wealth funds and family offices to fill the gap. It will be interesting to see how banks cope with the new regulation era. Clearly, they will not be able to use their balance sheets as freely as before.

With the maturing of the industry, "branding" and successful marketing are likely to become important, to attract deals and high-calibre professionals, and also to facilitate exits. Many groups are already strengthening their investor relations teams to reduce some of the inefficiencies that plague the lengthy and time-intensive fundraising process. Public listing is viewed by many as another way to improve access to capital and benefit from permanent funding. The very large US-based groups—Blackstone, KKR, Apollo and Carlyle—have already shown a liking for this option, diversifying into other asset classes and becoming more and more like "merchant banks". Many also favour public listings for succession reasons, as many of the more established groups' founders are now in their 60s or 70s and in the process of stepping back. Succession for small groups of bright and ambitious people will never be easy. The key players usually have strong personal networks of investors and deal sources, which are difficult if not impossible to transfer. It seems likely that many (smaller) managers will disappear and new generations of ambitious and well-trained managers spinning off from older groups will create their own firms.

LIQUIDITY Liquidity is a non-issue if an investor only has a small proportion of its assets tied up in private equity. The average allocations to private equity are well under 10%, with admittedly a few more active investors allocating in excess of that. This level of commitment is very manageable even in the worst of times. Shortly after the Lehman collapse, when the secondary market bought commitments at huge discounts, volumes remained very low, i.e. most private equity investors managed to cope with the lack of liquidity. The notable exceptions were funds-of-funds, which are by definition 100% allocated to the asset class. To boost returns many had even over-committed based on very sophisticated cash flow simulations, which turned out to be completely wrong in times of hardship. Thanks to these fair-weather computer models, investors, and in particular the listed funds-of-funds, teetered on the verge of bankruptcy, requiring rescue financing in various forms. The secondary market for commitments has attracted large amounts of money over the last few years. This has reduced significantly the discounts offered, producing a workable liquidity management tool.

Another option for investors concerned by the lack of liquidity is to focus on listed private equity funds. These include funds-of-funds, direct funds and special listed vehicles created by the likes of KKR, Carlyle and Blackstone. The liquidity of some of those instruments can actually be questioned considering the shallowness of their market. On the other hand, it is clear they offer access to private equity for small investors who normally would not be able to enter it, but with high corresponding costs.

LACK OF TRANSPARENCY IS EXAGGERATED AND THINGS WILL GET BETTER STILL   For those willing to do their homework, private equity is quite transparent. There is no daily share price, but GPs provide ever better information and are usually very available for LPs taking the trouble to meet, telephone and ask questions. Remarkably there is still no commonly used electronic platform to report mundane information like net asset values, or returns net of fees. Each GP uses its own system, which creates more work for everybody, with no obvious beneficiary other than perhaps the professionals slaving away to create a comprehensible report out of a hodgepodge of differently reported data. Several good electronic platforms for data rooms and reporting have sprung up in recent years and one will eventually emerge as a quasi-standard. ILPA, or one of the large associations like EVCA, BVCA or NVCA, could take the lead and encourage its members to converge on a single provider, a move that would be more than supported by institutional investors.

Regulators demand more information and LPs ask for increasingly detailed data, which they are getting. In fact, we recently overheard an exasperated GP wonder what LPs were doing with all this data. More and more detailed information may all be very well, if LPs do something with it. But LPs have neither the right nor the desire to act on this data, as their status and risk exposure would dramatically change if they did.

GLOBALIZATION OF THE INDUSTRY   Emerging markets will play an increasing role in the private equity industry, as illustrated by the success stories out of India, China and Brazil discussed in Chapter 3. The *McKinsey Quarterly* singled out emerging market-based family-owned companies as entities that would particularly benefit from private equity's managerial and sectorial know-how to excel internationally.[1] Although often mediocre today, legal and fiscal systems are likely to improve, which will help private equity tremendously.

---

[1] Kehoe, C., and Palter, R., "The future of private equity", *McKinsey Quarterly*, April 2009.

The role of emerging markets will, however, not be confined to the "destination" of capital, but also to its "origin". Increasingly, private equity players from emerging markets are investing in companies in more established markets. Chinese cross-border investments, initially only targeting natural resources, now focus on know-how, technology, brands and distribution channels. Similarly, emerging markets LPs will become major investors in the industry.

A globalizing industry where cross-border investments become more common will call for global players. Private equity firms able to this will be well positioned for large transactions.

Conclusion

Private equity has the potential to be a powerful engine for value creation and growth at times when economies are desperate to find such catalysts. By the nature of its investment vehicles and interventions, it has taken an unusually long period of time to sort out the good from the bad, the sustainable investment strategies from the opportunistic ones. But with the insight provided by a few decades of practice, a number of clear messages have emerged. First and foremost, the pure arbitrage plays based on crass market inefficiencies and financial engineering pyrotechnics are very much behind us. While it is impossible to rule out governments' ability to recreate new market failings, they certainly don't constitute sustainable opportunities for a growing private equity industry. The future will still include buyouts as a standard fare but with a higher proportion of capital moving towards longer-term, more operational deals with stronger management or family business involvement. These growth capital deals already represent significantly higher percentages of all investments in the industry, especially in emerging and developing markets, where they often represent a majority of the deals. This renewed focus on operational value creation is a welcome development, one that will also provide ample public relation benefits.

Interestingly, as the industry became more professional, it also became a lot more standardized, i.e. somewhat boring. The difference between the best and the worst managers has shrunk, as most have come to follow the same models, using the same intermediaries and advisors. In other ways, best practices are more easily shared, which makes big mistakes less likely but homeruns also rarer. The convergence of models and performances is a sign of maturity, and a call for innovation and renewal.

LPs are a constantly evolving mix. Banks and insurance companies have been large providers of capital for years but are facing a period of significant uncertainties following a wave of new regulation. The final impact of such regulatory measures is still unknown but it is fair to assume that their age of dominance is over. Pension funds have been and will continue to be large investors, whereas the importance of funds-of-funds has shrunk. Sovereign wealth funds have enormous amounts of money to invest in pursuit of returns and are likely to channel some of that wealth to private equity. Some of the largest pension funds (especially in Canada), sovereign wealth funds and funds-of-funds have started to experiment with the DIY model, creating their own private equity funds instead of investing in others. The jury is still out as to whether this approach will bear fruit.

The industry was able to raise huge amounts of money in the boom times of 2007–2008 and quickly adopted this as the "new normal". Much work went into investor relations and the sales process when less money became available. As a result the industry may have created a capacity to raise more money than it can really invest. The trillion-dollar question is whether the industry will be able to generate new deal flow to match its newly found capacity to attract capital. To a large extent, this will hinge on its ability to adapt to new market needs. Historically, this meant simply going for bigger transactions and, by paying higher prices, edging out trade buyers and public markets. This approach is generating decreasing returns which are likely to continue to get even lower in the future. The new approach involves finding new pockets for superior returns, such as more operational deals with more flexible capital structures, for example partnering for growth with promising family firms. Emerging markets also have the potential to provide superior returns but with deal formats that have to be adapted to individual circumstances.

Private equity deserves its place in the sun. Despite what the press would like to convey in general, it is made up mostly of boutiques with 10–100 bright, well-educated professionals with an entrepreneurial streak. Such teams are naturally resilient and creative—open to change. They have proven time and again that they can reinvent themselves in pursuit of great economic opportunities. As such, private equity is a great "invisible hand" of capitalism, channelling money from pension funds and insurance companies towards the most dynamic segments of the economy. The great "wealth recycling machine" is not broken; it is just undergoing its next revolution, ushering in a new era of more assertive, more operationally driven operators. With business models slowly converging with those of other longer-term investors, private equity should be on solid ground for decades to come and play its magic on economies that desperately need new inspiration for the benefit of future generations.

Index

CPSIA information can be obtained
at www.ICGtesting.com
Printed in the USA
LVHW061808030422
715181LV00008B/427